SIR HUGE

Also by Paul Ferris

SIR HUGE

The Life of Huw Wheldon

PAUL FERRIS

MICHAEL JOSEPH
London

MICHAEL JOSEPH

Published by the Penguin Group
27 Wrights Lane, London w8 5tz, England
Viking Penguin Inc., 40 West 23rd Street, New York, New York 10010, USA
Penguin Books Australia Ltd, Ringwood, Victoria, Australia
Penguin Books Canada Ltd, 2801 John Street, Markham, Ontario, Canada l3r 1b4
Penguin Books (NZ) Ltd, 182–190 Wairau Road, Auckland 10, New Zealand

Penguin Books Ltd, Registered Offices: Harmondsworth, Middlesex, England

First published 1990

Typeset in 12 on 14pt Ehrhardt
Printed and bound in Great Britain by
Richard Clay Ltd, Bungay, Suffolk

A CIP catalogue record for this book is available
from the British Library

ISBN 0 7181 3464 8

CONTENTS

LIST OF ILLUSTRATIONS

Copyright owners are indicated in italics.

ACKNOWLEDGEMENTS

My principal debt is to Lady Wheldon, who made the papers available, met and talked as often as I asked her to, and then left me to get on with it. Huw Wheldon's life could not have been written without her help and understanding. But the account is mine alone.

Family members I must thank for interviews and correspondence include the Wheldons' three children, Wynn, Sian and Megan; Mair Rees, the elder of Wheldon's sisters, who also translated many letters written in Welsh, together with her husband Dai; Nans Wheldon, his younger sister; Nerys Vaughan, whose first husband was Huw's brother Tomos; Rod Waldo Lewis, the family historian, who, I have to say, disagrees with some of my interpretations; and Wynn Rees.

It would be invidious to distinguish between Wheldon's friends, acquaintances and occasional enemies, except in the case of a handful – all friends – who were especially valuable. The Rev. Huw Wynne Griffith, who knew Wheldon from boyhood, let me see the many letters he has kept (and where necessary he translated them as well); he and his wife Mair had memories of early days in Wales. Desmond and Ben Leeper similarly had memories and letters. Joan Murphy, second wife of the late Brian Murphy, Wheldon's closest friend, was an important link. Three more-or-less anonymous women, 'H.', 'Celia' and 'Ruth', were more forthcoming than I could reasonably have hoped, about the Huw Wheldon they knew long ago.

I am no less grateful for the help of Kingsley Amis, Sir David Attenborough, Michael Bakewell, Roy Battersby, Donald Baverstock, Roy Behenna, Peter Black, John Bowen, Melvyn Bragg, Malcolm Brown, Hugh Burnett, Humphrey Burton, John Cain, George Campey, Sir Roger Cary, Alan Champion, Michael Charlton, Michael Checkland, Sir Ralf Dahrendorf, Lorraine Davies, Prof. Mansel Davies, John Drummond, Brigadier John Drummond, Martin Eckley, Prof. James Griffith Edwards, Matthew Evans, Paul Fox, Catherine Freeman, Tony Garnett, Norma Gilbert, Michael Gill, Joseph A. Gómez, Doris Greening, Prof. John Griffith, John Grigg, Harman Grisewood, Ida Groves, Joe Harper, Stephen Hearst, Stuart Hood, Anthony Howard, Paul Hughes, Sir Ian Jacob, Ann James, Sir Antony Jay, David Jones, Geraint Stanley Jones, Jonah Jones, Richard Lewis, Anne Macartney, Tom Main, Judith Maro, Towyn Mason, Leonard Miall, Jonathan Miller, Charles Monteith, Dr Ian Munro, Peter Newington, Sydney Newman, Lady Enid Parry, Dr I. G. Patel, Michael Peacock, Gilbert Phelps, John Pike, Tony Pilgrim, Jennifer Pinney, Sir John Plumb,

ACKNOWLEDGEMENTS

Hugh and Mary Purcell, John Read, Alwyn Roberts, Diana Rose, Gunnar Rugheimer, Ken Russell, Colin Shaw, Bob Sheridan, John Silverlight, Aubrey Singer, Shirley Sleigh, Sue Slipman, Sandy Smith, Pat Spencer, Joanna Spicer, Meic Stephens, Dr Anthony Storr, Aneirin Morgan Thomas, Nancy Thomas, Michael Tracey, Cliff Tucker, Ann Turner, Allan Tyrer, Marjorie Walker, Dr Doris Wallace, Prof. Glanmor Williams, Maggie Winkworth, Sir Paul and Lady Wright. Three of those I saw have since died: T. Mervyn Jones, Freda Lingstrom and Aled Vaughan.

A few names are deliberately omitted, by request; I am sorry for any left out by mistake.

For help with archive material I must thank Rhoda Cousins, records manager, BBC Data; Jacqueline Kavanagh and others at the BBC written archives centre, Caversham, and in particular Gwynyfer Jones; Mark Jones, manager, BBC sound archives; Anne Goddard, supervisor, BBC Wales record centre. BBC copyright material is quoted by permission. Tomos Roberts, archivist at the University College of North Wales, Bangor, made the Wynn Wheldon archive available, and Prof. J. Gwynn Williams threw light on Huw Wheldon's education and background. Lieut.-Col. Robin Charley at the RUR Regimental Museum, Belfast, supplied written and video material about Wheldon and the regiment.

Author and publisher acknowledge permission from Faber & Faber Ltd and the estate of Philip Larkin to quote three lines from the poem 'Church Going'.

Finally, a large amount of written material and all Wheldon's correspondence had to be organized and kept in order. I would have had difficulty coping with this – and other things – without Mary, whose help at all stages of the book I gratefully record here.

CHAPTER ONE

Welshman

MORE HAS BEEN written about the BBC than about any other broadcasting body in the world. This is the story of one man who worked for it and helped to shape it. As television history it is geared to Huw Wheldon and not the organization, seeing events reflected in his eye. Half his life was bound up with broadcasting, so his story is frequently the BBC's as well. But it is a story with other dimensions.

People plan their lives without meaning to. Huw Wheldon – born 1916, died 1986 – was brought up in Wales by God-fearing parents. He should have felt obliged to become a lawyer, a clergyman or a university teacher. He was no rebel, and his father's sober expectations weighed on him. His eloquence would have ensured a career in a profession. It was what he assumed would happen. But he was frightened of failure, and drifted into less rigorous alternatives: a glorified clerk, a wartime soldier, an Arts Council official.

At thirty-five he still hadn't found what he was looking for. Then he stumbled on television and the BBC, which fitted him perfectly. Until he retired, twenty-four years later, he behaved increasingly as if the BBC's kind of television constituted a noble profession, not a branch of the entertainment business. In the end he ran it. He came to believe that 'the Service' fulfilled some moral purpose beyond the making of programmes. This was not an original idea, being part of the BBC's character from the start. But Wheldon worked on it and became a brilliant

1

exponent of the doctrine – the last, as it turned out. He was funnier and more fallible than all this makes him sound; and knew how fallible he was.

A Celt by nature, Wheldon adored England and kept his Welshness up his sleeve, like a conjuring trick. The private doubts he had about himself when young were concealed. His conversation was brilliant, with hints of an obsession to keep talking at all costs. This mesmeric repertoire of stories and patter was part of an act, or the satisfying of a need, that he maintained all his life. He loved performance, and is one of the few people to have made a popular name for himself in front of BBC television cameras, and then risen to high office in the same place.

His first appearance made him famous in an odd sort of way, inasmuch as British television could make anyone famous in 1952, when there were no more than a million sets in the country. At the beginning of the year Wheldon had joined the BBC as its television publicity officer. This was too lowly a job for his liking (years later he said he refused to do it for more than eighteen months; in fact he did it for over two and a half years).

In September that year he met Freda Lingstrom, who ran children's programmes, on her way to a meeting, and heard from her that items were needed to fill a gap. Without thinking he suggested a conker competition. Would he run it? asked Miss Lingstrom. Of course he would. The idea was referred upwards for approval. 'A brilliant idea,' wrote Cecil McGivern, controller of programmes. 'This excites me. It is not conkers. It is childhood.'

When the competition was announced, tens of thousands of children wrote in, some enclosing their battle-scarred conkers, with boasts about how many rival conkers they had smashed. 'All these damned conkers had to be sent back,' said Wheldon in his BBC archive history.[1] He recalled a boy of twelve from

---

[1] The BBC Oral History archive contains interviews with selected staff, specially recorded. Wheldon was interviewed by Frank Gillard in 1978. The transcript covers 150 pages. It is quoted often in this book.

Surrey who wrote, 'Dear sir or miss I have a conker it is 254 it has a crak in it but it will not brack . . .' Wheldon thought it read like Chaucer. The letter, from a boy called Billy Williams, was still in his papers at his death.

'Anyway, this conker competition was set up, and although I became a public man or whatever you call it, a man of some notoriety over the next thirty years, I have never met before and will never again achieve the actual front-page-news notoriety I had during the conker competition.' There were arguments about rules. 'Was it in order for conkers which were nine years old, hideous little black, hard balls, was it appropriate for these little stones to be used against fresh conkers?' A clergyman wrote to *The Times* to complain that the opening blow was being awarded on the toss of a coin. 'He was perfectly clear, the first blow in a conker competition always went to the boy who first said, "Oblionka, my first conker". There were other people who said it was incorrect to treat conkers, and was this being gone into properly? Was it in order? It was perfectly in order, of course, to have conkers kept in linen chests during the winter, but was it in order to put turpentine on them? Other people said that everybody knew the best place to keep a conker was in a cowpat.'

Only the finalists appeared on television, a half-serious contest, egged on by Wheldon, with his 'rules for clean conker fighting' and his wild enthusiasm. 'As you remember, conkers cannibalize in their scoring. If you've got a fifty-er and you beat another fifty-er you become a hundred and one-er. So by the time we came to the semi-finals we were running into thousands.' The final blow was struck by a boy with a 3,521-er, bursting a 3,827-er.

Whimsical, in the English fashion, the episode was also a harbinger of televised pastimes to come, like darts and snooker; and for Wheldon, 'a fantastic piece of luck'.

The Wheldons of North Wales are thought to have come from Cornwall in the eighteenth century. A John Wheldon or Weldyn worked as a miner and married Lowri Pyrs (in English, Laura Pierce), whose family were early Methodists. Their son, Pyrs John, married Elinor Ffowc. Pyrs and Elinor kept an inn at Dolbadarn, in the Pass of Llanberis. Snowdon rises to the southeast, the peak hidden by foothills: tourist country now, savagely remote two centuries ago.

The son of Pyrs and Elinor was Sion or John, born about 1815, the earliest Wheldon to have left a ghost of a personality behind him. He was a quarry worker, later a farmer at Llwyncelyn, with a 'wild temper', who married a Mary Jones in 1840, and was rescued from sin – what sin? – by illness and the prayers of his children. John went nervously to the deacons of the chapel, asking, 'Is there a place for an old sinner like me?'

This much is known about John because one of his two sons, Thomas Jones, became moderately famous in Wales and had his biography written, in Welsh. T. J. Wheldon, born 1841, and Huw Wheldon's grandfather, was a preacher, a Calvinistic Methodist with a finger in various Welsh pies of the day – denying the Church of England its special status (the forgotten battle for 'disestablishment'), giving Wales its own system of education. The *Manchester Guardian* wrote that for fifty years he was 'a leading figure in Welsh Nonconformist and political life'. According to his grandson, he was also useful with his fists, and broke the jaws of two men when he was a minister at Blaenau Ffestiniog, to the south of Snowdon. Slate was mined and quarried there for world markets by workers who wore bowler hats and were fierce defenders of their faith and their mining methods.

There is a hint of excess about the Wheldons. A family tale, possibly about John Wheldon, Llwyncelyn, says that in the quarries once he determined to frighten a suspected pilferer into confessing. He wrote the man's name in candlegrease on the slate, and announced that if the culprit didn't come forward, he would reveal his identity in the stone. Then he flung a handful of dust, so that it stuck to the grease. For unknown wrongdoing the Wheldons are even supposed to have been cursed 'unto the seventh generation' by a parish priest, the curse expiring conveniently in the generation before Huw Wheldon's.

The Rev. T. J. Wheldon married a Mary Elinor Powell. They had one son who survived childhood, born 1879, christened Wynn Powell, Huw Wheldon's father. Wynn Wheldon occupies another niche in the Welsh pantheon, where the heroes are rarely admirals or even politicians but rather poets, preachers and schoolmasters. He was a man of the world who would write matter-of-factly about 'the hand of God' in everyday matters. His life was structured around ideals of service and belief, and his moral certainties, his air of cheerful austerity, may have instilled permanent doubts in the son about his ability to live up to them. 'My father,' said Huw Wheldon, 'mortgaged *his* father's will to go to university. He looked like a soldier among academics, and an academic among soldiers. He also dressed a bit like a farmer, but when you saw him among farmers, you could see that he was really a man of affairs – he was impossible to classify. Extraordinarily patrician, that Victorian generation. I'm not a bit like him.'

Wynn was born at Blaenau Ffestiniog, but while he was still at school, his father was 'called' to a chapel at Bangor, a more salubrious town on the Menai Strait, looking across to Anglesey. There the boy spent three years at a grammar school, a little Welshman growing up in Victorian Britain, where it was wise to begin sounding like a little Englishman. Pupils were expected to buy a booklet written by the headmaster, *A Dozen Hints to Welsh Boys on the Pronunciation of English*.[1] Wynn read law at Cambridge, an achievement then for someone of his background, and before the First World War was a solicitor in practice with Lloyd George's firm in the City of London, Lloyd George, Roberts & Co. The Wheldons all knew Lloyd George, who, like

---

[1] For their tuppence, pupils got fifteen tiny pages with such injunctions as, 'When Eng. initial *w* is followed by an *oo* sound, do not merge the former in the latter, and say, eg, "*a 'oolf 'oonded a 'ooman in a 'ood*," but keep the two sounds distinct, tightening the lips . . .'

them, belonged to the heartland of Wales, its mountainous north-west. In his early years, when he was a 'Welsh' politician rather than a 'British' one, Lloyd George drew his strength from the network of Dissent, both religious and political, of which T. J. Wheldon was a part. Personal connections were always crucial in Welsh public life. Society is (or was) on a small, comparatively intimate scale. Nepotism is taken for granted. Wynn Wheldon became a master of inner circles, to the incidental benefit of Huw.

From the end of 1914 he was an officer of the Royal Welch Fusiliers, marrying, in the middle of the war, a London Welsh girl, Megan Edwards, whom he had met at the Calvinistic Methodist church in Wilton Square, where Welsh gentlefolk in exile went to be among their own. Captain Wheldon was thirty-five; she was thirteen years younger. Megan was as Welsh as he. She spoke the language and played the harp. Married on July 31 1915, their honeymoon was at Leamington Spa, where their first child, a son, must have been conceived. He was born in North Wales, at Prestatyn, where Megan's mother, a widow, now lived, on May 7 1916. His father came back for three days' leave immediately afterwards, registering the birth on May 11. He called his son Hugh Pyrs, presumably a compromise between two cultures.[1]

Wheldon was in the thick of the war for years, fighting at the Somme and in Flanders. In the summer of 1917, by then a major, and acting commander of his battalion, he won the DSO during an action in the Ypres Salient, on the first day of the offensive that ended in the swamps of Passchendaele that winter. He said that for years after the war he had a horror of rainy days.

Megan and Wynn brought up their family in Bangor, adding a second son, Tomos, and two daughters, Mair and Nans. Huw's childhood was secure and conventional enough. The greying

---

[1] 'Hugh' soon became 'Huw'. But at least one school document uses the English form.

hero and his musical wife presided over a comfortable villa at the posh end of town, with sea breezes in the back garden. They had a couple of maids, Welsh-speaking of course, and entertained visiting preachers and Liberal politicians; among them Lloyd George, radiant, attended by secretaries. Huw said that up to the age of fifteen, the people who impressed him most were clergymen, storytellers with the Old Testament on their lips, figures of 'immense dignity and verve'. His was the post-1918 generation that broke its connections with the past, or had them broken regardless. He regretted that it was so. The child may have envied the man.

His father knew what was right. On the other hand, he was not self-righteous. Mair, his elder daughter, born 1923, suggests that the word for him was 'long-suffering'. His uprightness didn't make him narrow. Women's company appealed to him. As a student at Bangor he was even accused of 'misbehaviour' on a picnic; he had lingered in the company of a girl, and a puritanical regime disbarred him from office in student bodies. In later life he had no liking for men-only occasions. Drawn into the Freemasons once, says Mair, he kept 'a little apron on a shelf' for about a week, before his interest waned.

Megan is harder to picture. There are hints that she feared she was shallower than her husband, that he overshadowed her at times. Her talents were jollier than his; a good ear for speech as well as music made her a capable mimic, and her wit, though ladylike, was sharp. There may have been more of her in Huw than he admitted.

For years after the war, Huw's father had the makings of a disappointed man. In 1920 the University College of North Wales, where he had been an undergraduate before going to Cambridge, appointed him registrar. His office was five minutes' walk from the house. But a comfortable life became by degrees a dead-end. In 1926 a new principal had to be found. Wynn Wheldon put his name forward. The selection committee reported on all the candidates except Wheldon, who took this as a slight, which it was. They saw him as lacking in scholarship;

he should be satisfied with what he had. He wasn't in their mould. The strong language of an old soldier didn't go down well in Bangor. In a college photograph, taken when the Duke of Windsor was paying a visit, Wheldon is the odd man out among his fellow dignitaries – gown held back to show his medals, hair short and spiky at the front, like a rugby player.

Outside the college he had powerful friends, helping cautiously. Lord Davies of Llandinam,[1] his commanding officer in the war, wrote persuading him to swallow his pride and shut up. Otherwise there might be 'unpleasantness', and his future could be jeopardized. Bide your time, said Davies, and I might be able to help you become principal somewhere else. Wheldon took his advice and withdrew his name. Tom Jones,[2] a ubiquitous Welsh figure, who was on the university council, wrote smoothly to say how much they appreciated his 'admirable reticence'. Wheldon went back to being registrar; his acquiescence wasn't forgotten, although it was another seven years before he had his reward.

Huw was another source of aggravation. The boy was not a scholar. At his father's old school he sank to the bottom of the class and stayed there – except once, he said rhetorically in 1961, when 'I had the pleasure of having a chap from Llanfairfechan who was even duller than I.' Dull is the last thing he was. He may have been rebellious, congenitally idle, or – more likely – an insecure child, made to feel inadequate by his father; Wynn Wheldon wanted his first-born to be top of the class and achieve what had eluded him. Whatever the reason, Huw managed to fail his school certificate, the forerunner of 'O' levels, in 1930 and again in 1931. His boyhood, he recalled thirty years later, was 'one long waking idle day-dream'. Saturday nights were devoted to parading up and down Bangor High Street with a

---

[1] David Davies, first Lord Davies of Llandinam, 1880–1944, was a grandson of the David Davies who made a fortune from South Wales coal and railways. He was a Liberal MP, and an associate of Lloyd George.

[2] Dr Thomas Jones, CH, 1870–1955, civil servant and diarist, was deputy secretary to the Cabinet, and another associate of Lloyd George.

gang, 'in a world totally unknown to my mother'. They were looking in vain, he said, for 'young women, we never quite knew how many, between the ages of fifteen and nineteen, whose one overwhelming desire and passion was to be ravished on the side of Bangor Mountain, by us.' The point of the story was that the teenage Wheldon was 'buttressed by values and standards', which stopped him being a proper delinquent. But his poor showing at school, as ambition rusted away for the registrar, would have been bad enough.

Mair suspects 'some kind of arrogance' in him. His father persevered. When the family spent summer holidays at Pwllheli, along the coast, Huw and his younger brother Tomos had Latin lessons in the boarding house after breakfast. In 1932 Huw passed his school certificate at last, but failed to reach the level needed for matriculation, which would admit him to a university. So his father sent him to the National Institute of Industrial Psychology in London, to be assessed by its vocational guidance department. This gave him an above-average intelligence rating, found he had 'imaginative ability and a facile pen', and suggested law, or possibly journalism or business, as a career. That was all very well, except that in January 1933, he failed his matric again. He began trying harder. In July he finally qualified for Welsh, though not English, matriculation; an English university was still beyond him.

That year his father's affairs suddenly prospered. He was fifty-three, seemingly stuck as the number two at Bangor for ever. Ways of escape had come to nothing, among them someone's scheme to set up 'a kind of GHQ' for Welshmen in London, with Wheldon as superintendent. Then, in February 1933, he was asked *very confidentially* if he was interested in becoming permanent secretary to the Welsh department of education.[1] At last a real prize came his way. He was formally offered

---

[1] In 1907, after years of a 'Welsh Revolt' over education, a Welsh department of the board (later ministry) of education was set up to cater for local needs, an early gesture towards devolution for Wales.

the job a month later, and by June he was in Whitehall, effectively in charge of Welsh education. His salary was £1,633 a year (worth more than £40,000 today), a sum that has stuck in family memories, remembered down to the last pound.

They lived at Woodville Gardens, Ealing, in a house called Argoed, meaning 'of the forest'; the name suggests the mythical period in Welsh literature and history that Wynn respected, and his son would have no time for. A Welsh chapel was nearby; Huw wrote scathingly to friends in Bangor about the singing. Everyone still spoke Welsh at home, maidservants included. A visitor who was invited to stay for supper remembers that 'as Mr Wheldon put his knife in the meat, he started to sing *Calon Lan*,[1] and everyone joined in'.

For Huw, the move to London was a severance with the past, not so much because he forgot about Wales, but because he found he liked the other place so much. Almost the first of his letters to survive was written soon after they moved to Ealing. It hints at a side of his nature that disturbed him for years. He was seventeen. His correspondent was a close friend in Bangor, Huw Wynne Griffith, a minister's son who would become a minister himself. Huw wrote that he was 'gradually sinking into the life of London. It certainly is opening my eyes to some things.' He describes walking home late at night along the Embankment, the wind blowing clouds that were reddened with light:

> As I approached Cleopatra's Needle I saw a woman literally staggering along. When she remarked my curious glances, she twisted her features into a grotesque facsimile of a grin. Horrible. But something about her tickled my curiosity. She was obviously a prostitute, and a sick one, at that, but nevertheless, I went up and spoke to her, and, you know the daft kind of brain I've got, like a complete ass, I took her into a Lyons Cafe conveniently near. I had my week's wages in my pocket, altogether amounting to 8/6 [about 40 new pence]. I bought a coffee for myself, and

---

[1] *A Pure Heart*, a famous hymn.

ordered a meal for her. She was so obviously starving I couldn't help myself. Boy, you should have seen her eat; she fell upon that food like a hungry dog with a bone.

Then I began to question her, by now I felt so damned sorry for the poor thing. Underneath the paint of the prostitute, and her obvious sickness, I thought I could see rather a decent girl. She had lovely eyes. (I always was incurably romantic!) By degrees, I got her story out of her. And do you know what she thought I was doing? She thought I was sort of feeding her up, so as to get a good time with her afterwards. Hell! Anyway I pacified her on that point, and got out of her a most amazing story. Her Father, still alive, was a foul man, who was actually contemplating, nay more, had already determined to *give* her to a friend of his for the White Slave Trade! I was almost sick; honestly, nausea almost overcame me in the damned cafe. Apparently she was of no more use to him since she could do no more 'business' as she was suffering from V.D. She had managed to creep out of her house, and was trying to 'do business' with any scoundrel to get some money. It turned out that she wanted money to get to a place named Midhurst in Sussex somewhere, I think. She *thought* she had some relations or something there. (I never knew people like that had relations.) By now, I knew I couldn't let her just go home to her damned Father, so I took her along to Euston, bought her a ticket for Midhurst, and saw her off. No luggage, no nothing! I asked her to let me know whether she'd succeeded in finding her relations, and gave her the address of the Central YM in Tottenham Court Road. I gave my name as Richard Stanley! But so far I've heard nothing. The Y.M.C.A. office has received no letters written to R. Stanley Esq.

You'll probably say 'what a fool!' when you read this, but what else was I to do? Anyway the only thing I got out of it was no lunches for a week!

But isn't it hellish to think of a Father like this. Do you know that five thousand women disappeared from London last year? Hellish, you know.

I shudder to think what would have happened if a friend of

the family had walked into the cafe, & seen me deep in conversation with the woman.

It was that first attempt at a grin that did it. God, I felt sorry for her!

If you don't mind, I'd prefer you to keep this episode to yourself . . .

It sounds like the encounter a genteel young man from a small town might improvise. So could Huw have invented the whole thing? 'Euston' sounds odd: trains for Midhurst go from Waterloo and Victoria. He had a taste for sexual fantasy, which whispers behind the walls of his life, difficult for him to reconcile with the moral, heroic side of his nature. The Prostitute's Tale was probably fiction.

Wynn Wheldon had chosen Ealing with an eye on St Paul's, a public school not too far away with day-boys as well as boarders. This was in summer 1933, when it was known that Huw had passed his Welsh matric. 'I may go to St Paul's,' he wrote to Wynne Griffith, 'since Father says it is part of diwylliant cyffredin [common culture] to have been to one of the great Public Schools.' Then the plan changed. He would go to a crammer's in Holborn and get his London matric. There was talk of law or the pulpit. Either way, more scholastic grind lay ahead.

London itself was endlessly fascinating, from the day his father showed him the city of his own young manhood – the Temple, the Law Courts, an eating house where 'you pick your own chop & state how you want it done. Best chops in the world, says Father.' The trouble was in living up to his father's expectations. It must have been demoralizing to do so badly when your parent was the man whose facsimile signature appeared on the fake parchment of every Central Welsh Board school certificate.

To help him with languages he was packed off to Germany the following year and spent three months living with a family at

Soest, a cobbled town in Westphalia, paying a visit to Berlin where a 'great Nazi exhibition' was in progress. 'Yr wyf wedi gweld HITLER yn Berlin!!' he wrote to his sister Mair, 'I have seen Hitler in Berlin.' Soon after, on June 30 1934, Ernst Roehm and his stormtroopers were purged in mass murders. 'Hitler having acted with such promptitude and bravery', Huw wrote to Wynne Griffith, no doubt taking his cue from his hosts, 'is up sky-high in popularity.' He was bemused to find Britain 'famed above all' for 'that great spirit of honesty & ultimate morality which for want of a better word has been called the Public School Code.' His correspondent also heard about girls. In Welsh Huw wrote, 'Here, my friend, I'm once again in love. The real thing now. Jet black hair, dark dark eyes, dark skin, beautiful – and the body . . .' In English he boasted that he had now 'tasted the lips' of eight nationalities, nine 'if the Swedish woman turns up next Sunday.'

The plans changed again. That autumn, 1934, now aged eighteen, the day-dreaming son returned to Bangor to lodge with a clergyman's family and enrol at the university college. There he made his usual hash of things. His father sent stern letters from Ealing. A generation earlier it had been Wynn's father, the clergyman, writing to *his* son in ringing tones of authority. 'In regard to the rowing,' said one letter, 'I do not object to your taking an exercise in that way or in any other. A little "tubbing" is no harm. What I do object to is that anything be taken up [by] you – anything whatsoever – that distracts the mind and weakens the sense of duty. Every man must learn to face his duty or fail in his higher life.'

Huw, in his turn, was told to plan his work, identify his weaknesses and limit his social life. There is no evidence that he did any of them. Three enjoyable terms at Bangor drifted by. He was in Soest again in 1935, having a holiday with his German friends, when he heard he had failed his first-year exams in Latin and German. He was nineteen now. Heads were being shaken. 'I feel I've let my Father down pretty badly so far,' he wrote to Wynne Griffith. Back in London, he made one last effort, worked for most of the summer, passed his London matric, and arrived at the London School of Economics to read sociology ('as good a background as any, especially from the point of view of the modern world') in October. Things were arranged hastily. As late as September 22, when he was helping at a boys' camp in South Wales, his father was writing, in Welsh, 'I don't want you to feel you *have* to go to College . . . If you have different ideas it would be easy to discuss them.' There had been talk of joining an insurance company. But in the end, more of the same was the only real option. Huw's LSE application was dated October 1, the references two days later.

Ten years afterwards, following a war and other disturbances, Huw Wheldon wrote to his father, 'I must say Sociology is really the most unspeakable nonsense, by & large.' But in 1935 he had found a place that agreed with him. Unlike radical students who went to LSE because they wanted to understand how society worked, the better to change it, Wheldon was not interested in the revolution. The nearest he came to that was in the army, in the first years of the war, when he encountered young English officers with airs and graces, and didn't like what he saw. But he had no stomach for social reform. What LSE offered were technical skills. 'If I ultimately decide on the ministry,' he wrote to Wynne Griffith, 'this course will have certainly done me no harm, while should my choice be pure social service, [it] is definitely the best on the market.'

There were famous names among the staff. The director was the economist William Beveridge, already scratching away at the theory of a Welfare State. The socialist Harold Laski, who made old ladies in Cheltenham tremble when Labour came to power after the war, was professor of politics – 'witty, malevolent and malicious, a most engaging chap,' said Wheldon, who recalled a 'wonderful time' at LSE, sitting around in pubs with 'anarchists and communists and fascists . . . when everything was in the melting pot'.

Nothing melted as far as Wheldon was concerned. He and his group kept clear of active politics. In his first year he was elected treasurer of the Students' Union. A dispute about union matters

14

arose while the president was away. Wheldon enjoyed the row – 'just four of us, leaderless, to hold the fort against an army of socialists', he wrote to Wynne Griffith. One of his friends at LSE was Desmond Leeper, whose father sent him there for a business-school education. Leeper was amused to see Wheldon the treasurer 'walking around with a briefcase, taking short, sharp steps', unconsciously official. He was a bit of a chameleon. When it suited him he was good at playing the fool, charming people at the same time. On St David's Day he marched through the library handing out daffodils, waving to the librarians. When Beveridge invited some students to his flat in Temple, the guests were suitably in awe, except for Wheldon, who warmed things up by declaiming speeches from *Hamlet* in broken German. He was rarely if ever drunk, though. All his life he smoked heavily and enjoyed food and drink. But sobriety, the being in control, was essential.

The correspondence with Wynne Griffith helped keep him in touch with Welsh Wales and old certainties. Griffith was talented but made in the Nonconformist minister's mould. When they disagreed in their letters, it was Griffith who had the role of dissenter. He favoured anti-war protests on Armistice Day. 'You pacifists always infuriate me,' wrote Wheldon, 'with your bally cheek in trying to enforce your opinions on anyone within range.' How dare 'raw youths' who 'remember nothing about the War' go 'breaking in on the sanctity of the Armistice Service'. When the Welsh nationalist Saunders Lewis and his mild-mannered confederates did token damage to Government property in 1936, and were gaoled for arson, Wheldon admired their bravery – he liked bravery – but couldn't resist adding that 'anarchy & destruction is not the best way of overcoming anarchy & destruction'.[1] The paradox nagged its way through the correspondence. The protestors were admirable: their protest was illegal. 'Although you think the whole affair is worthy of transcription

---

[1] The writer Saunders Lewis (1893–1985) and two others objected to an RAF bombing school that was being built in a Welsh-speaking part of the country. After setting fire to sheds, they phoned the police and gave themselves up.

15

into an immemorial epic poem, yet, as a sensible being, you cannot possibly blind yourself to their absolute guilt in law.'

Wheldon's charm and high spirits sweetened attitudes that might otherwise have appeared priggish. He was argumentative and boisterous, a keen if undistinguished rugby player, thin, with dark good looks. In 1936 and again the following summer he went alone to the Continent, walking on mountains and across frontiers, making friends among the international rucksack brigade. Everything made him enthusiastic: fast rivers, deep valleys, bed and breakfast for ninepence, Alpine views, Venice (a 'shell of beauty . . . made of air and clouds'); and homecoming. 'Came over the highest of these this morning,' he wrote from Werfen, near the Austro-German border. The picture postcard shows snowy peaks. 'Nine hours to get here & it rained the whole time. Writing wrapped up in a blanket. Everything else drying. No time tables etc here, but I'll be home for dinner, *I think*, on Saturday. Anyway, I'll be home for certain sometime on Sat evening. Can there [be] lots of bacon, & two (or so) eggs when I come home please? Gosh, it's good to be dry again. Love to all, Huw.' The card is addressed to his mother at Ealing, date-stamped July 28 1937.

His third and last year at LSE got under way, with gloomy thoughts about how he was going to perform. He wrote to Wynne Griffith (November 1937) to say that after attending a finals seminar in social philosophy, he had concluded that 'my brain is only third class'. He had always thought, 'in my heart of hearts', that it was 'well up to standard'. But 'goodbye to all that'. Taking the chair at a union meeting when the speaker was Bertrand Russell hadn't helped. The guest's 'icy concentration' left him 'staggered'.

As usual Wheldon laid on the effects. Perhaps he meant what he said. He always judged himself harshly. His file at the school includes a patronizing comment from a teacher who saw him as 'capable of developing an interest in any subject not too remote from everyday life'. His style was 'anecdotal'; he had 'shown no evidence of an ability to reason on paper'.

Wheldon's degree in July 1938 was a respectable upper second. His father was soon having chats with Sir Alexander Carr-Saunders, who had succeeded Beveridge as director. But nothing much happened. In the summer he had an interview with Unilever, who might or might not offer him a job as a graduate trainee. Killing time, he was in North Wales, working as a porter at an hotel in Conway. 'I hope you don't mind?' he wrote to his parents. 'Experientia docet. It seems to me as good as anything else.'

September found him in Paris during the Munich crisis, when Hitler nearly invaded Czechoslovakia. The city was in a panic, he wrote to his friend Leeper. 'It's them newspapers . . . Thank God for the *Daily Mirror* and its Other News on Page 3. Nice, homely, flippertygibberty obscenities.' When Hitler made a speech at Nuremberg on September 12, he heard it on the radio in the company of 'two highbrow young Germans' who 'threw off their intellectual pretensions like snakes shedding their skins and settled down to an hour's passionate listening'. German attitudes fascinated him. Soon after, he listened to another young Nazi defending Germany, and hinted to Leeper of his admiration for any point of view, as long as it was held with passion – an oblique comment on his own manner in later years, where his style sometimes counted for more than the argument. He wrote:

> The boy didn't stop, he went on with his drivel about instinct and race-superiority & other regurgitated muck like a gramophone. And although he was surrounded by hostility he still went on, dead loyal to his creed. All of which brings up once more the old question of does it matter what you do so long as you do it with enthusiasm & genuineness. A question which our Mr Murphy [1] is fond of putting from time to time. I don't know. It's

---

[1] Brian Cullinan Ouseley Murphy, another fellow student at LSE, who became Wheldon's closest friend. His father was a Colonel Murphy, late of the Royal Irish Constabulary. People saw the friends as two of a kind. Murphy had a career in electricity management. He died in 1980.

heresy to say yes, of course. And any sort of systematic philosophy kicks it up the backside without hesitation. Yet it was with mixed feelings that I heard the German boy plough on, adding further absurdity to absurdity; I liked his tight constricted little smile & above all his determination to go on with it ... He did at all events have a creed to which he clung. While I, and you for that matter, I suppose, are without any such focus of emotional attention.

His friends were finding jobs in research or the Civil Service. Leeper travelled on a scholarship. Murphy went into advertising. 'There remains Mr Wheldon, as yet unsuited,' he wrote to Wynne Griffith (October 9 1938), admitting to 'a mad desire to quit civilized society in its middle-class manifestations and do a simple job somewhere in the country'. The fact that his brother Tomos hoped to be a farmer filled him with 'black envy'. 'How I loathe myself, sometimes,' he wrote. '. . . Outside the gripping interest of my own personality there is nothing I love more than music, nothing that interests me more than religion and friends, nothing that takes up more of my time than time-frittering, and nothing I would rather be able to do than write with skill and direction. What a jumble!'

In the same letter he enjoyed himself trying to shock Wynne Griffith with a memory of Paris. 'Lechery ... took me to its bosom, and one evening I visited a night club where the forty or fifty dancing girls on the premises were dressed simply and solely in shoes and wrist bangles. (You want the address, eh? 32 Rue de Blondell.)'

When the Unilever job failed to materialize, the National Institute of Industrial Psychology (where his father had had him 'assessed') offered him temporary research work in Glasgow at four pounds a week. He went to factories and asked questions about working practices: 'money for dirt', he told Wynne Griffith, and emphasized that his real occupation now was reading for the Bar. But in January 1939 he was offered a job of dispiriting sobriety in Kent as an 'assistant vocational guidance officer'. 'This without nepotism, believe me,' he assured Griffith. A woman who helped appoint him says they had no idea his father was in the business. His starting salary was £150 a year.

A week later he was in a district office in a London suburb, in a converted house with coal-fires and a garden, learning about the dead-end jobs that awaited children who left school at fourteen. His own career promised £200 a year after two years. The office was in Beckenham. The woman he was there to assist found him lodgings. He used to listen to the landlady's wireless, feeling lonely, trying to tell himself he was lucky.

CHAPTER TWO

Soldier

ACCORDING TO THE WOMAN Wheldon worked with in Kent, he was 'the most God-awful vocational guidance officer that ever breathed. Absolutely frightful. We had a wonderful form that had to be filled in, when young people were put into a job. Every night the forms had to go to the Ministry of Labour without fail. Huw kept them in his drawer for days. I'd say, "God almighty, what are these?"'

Her name was Celia, and she was immediately attracted to Wheldon. A fair, pretty woman with blue eyes and long lashes, she was five years his senior, making her twenty-eight in 1939. She was unmarried and lived with her parents. Her father was a senior civil servant; her background was Tory, smart and Home Countyish. Wheldon was unlike anyone she had met before. For years, he was to be important to her, and she to him. It was a strange love affair. As Celia says, most of it happened during a war, when things are different. But some of its strangeness arose from an irresolute streak in Wheldon.

Girls crop up frequently in his early letters, more than they would be likely to if he had been a serious womanizer. 'The women are luvvely. All Queens,' he announced on arriving at LSE. In reality he was keen but wary. Jo, his first-year girl-friend, was dropped because, he told her, she was 'too master-ful'. He added that if he married anybody, it would be a Welsh girl. There was a Stella he fancied for a while. Years afterwards, in 1945, Wheldon's friend Brian Murphy was writ-

20

ing to him about the Celia affair, and reminded him of his awkward high-mindedness over Stella. Murphy wrote:

> Returned from the Alps you'd off-saddled Stella and with a tortured groan sent her loose to other paddocks. Poor velvet-eyed, velvet-nosed Stella, loath and bewildered! And that, you said, was because at Victoria you found yourself as glad to see Desmond and I as to meet her 'and that wasn't *good enough*'. My dear man, what the hell. Why not?

Celia was a new category of friend. They visited London for plays and concerts; they went walking in the countryside, a pair of innocents, says Celia. 'I was utterly and completely an innocent young woman. I didn't even know what you did. I had been kept that way. Therefore sex didn't enter my head.' The friendship was 'very amusing, very joyous, great fun'. The way Wheldon set about vocational guidance left her speechless. He would get carried away discussing a school-leaver's prospects with the parents. Ridiculous suggestions would be made – 'There's no reason why the boy shouldn't be prime minister one day.' She would 'have him in afterwards and say, "Don't be potty. I've never heard such balderdash". And then we'd laugh.'

In her memory, half a century later, Huw was 'utterly confused about what he would do with his life', unhappy with education as a career, lacking in confidence. Celia believes, too, that whatever his views about democratic principles, he didn't care much for the poor and downtrodden. They 'activated some feeling in him'.

None of his surviving letters mentions Celia in 1939; few mention her ever. He kept his life in compartments, and both were secretive about the relationship. How long it lasted that year isn't clear. Kent education authority began to move Wheldon about the county – Sidcup, then Chatham, then Deal. He joked about the 'refainment' of his landladies, who never said 'Goodbye', always 'Gudbay'.

The work bored him in Deal, as it had done everywhere else, but he liked the town and the Channel coast. Trips to London kept him in touch with the LSE gang and Celia. In between he sent school-leavers to the canning factory down the road, corresponded with friends, and listened to wireless concerts or his gramophone. Bach, Elgar, Beethoven, Handel, are invoked in letters like talismans against the seediness of life in lodgings, the gaslight, the smoky fire, the fried-fish suppers. In 1970 a man who had known Wheldon in Deal wrote to him from Australia:

> 'How do I know what I think till I see what I say?'
> You quoted the above to me in 1939 in Deal. You lived in a basement room and played Beethoven on a little gramophone . . . There was quite an attractive blonde in the first floor back. Sometimes we went out and got drunk. One night we had a midnight swim, and should all have been drowned. You were quite a Red when you were in Deal. What colour now?

Wheldon was managing director of television. The letter is in a private file. Unusually for Wheldon, he didn't reply; or if he did, kept no copy.

Sex bothered him enough to write to Desmond Leeper about it, in a letter dated June 15 1939. At first he claims to be sexually experienced, although his 1961 account of looking in vain for young women to ravish on Bangor Mountain is probably the true one. 'As a boy of 15', says the letter, 'I enjoyed a good deal more sexual licence than most . . . I lived in the country, and had my fill. And never a moment of conscience-smitten shame.' The 'dreadful discomfiture' has come later:

> I told Ben [Desmond Leeper's fiancée] that the fruit of promiscuity was misery; which it is and has been in my case. I can't, in a word, take a women to bed with me and like it. Not, that is, unless I like the woman too, which I don't, and won't, if things go on as they are at present.

It was about this time that H., a woman he had known at LSE, and was fond of, went down to Deal. H. was clever and attractive and probably in love with Wheldon. He said to her (she recalls),

22

'Shall I tell you why I don't make love to you?' H. has forgotten the explanation, if there was one. They undressed and got into bed. Nothing much happened. After five minutes he jumped out, grabbed his clothes and vanished. They continued to see one another, but the incident was never referred to, nor was it repeated as far as H. was concerned.

Friends and his parents thought of Huw and H. as a good match. His difficulty lay in committing himself to a woman. His Welsh-chapel background may have encouraged guilt feelings although most of those with a similar upbringing seem to survive it well enough. Wheldon's uncertainties were deep-seated. In his late thirties he is said to have had treatment for an unresolved 'Oedipus complex'. In Freudian theory, he was unable to reconcile an ideal image of women, based on his mother, with the kind of woman who excited him sexually. Whatever the explanation, he was awkward and evasive with women for years, retreating from encounters. The BBC's Wheldon in his prime was different in all respects; no one could appear more assertive and sure of television's destiny and his own. Uncertainties led to certainties.

The relationship with H. lasted well into the war. 'I am not in any sense in love with [her] although most people think I am,' he complained to Wynne Griffith in June 1940. 'There is a complicated & private situation, but marriage is not its resolution.' In 1942 the affair still lingered. Wheldon was stationed on Salisbury Plain. They met in Salisbury (she says) and she told him that 'someone else is interested in me. For God's sake say something, black or white.' He waited till he was back at camp before writing to end the affair, telling her he was 'bloody sorry, but there's no future in it for us'. She burned his letters and married someone else.

Wheldon told his father about it:

> I am deeply moved about the whole business – but for some incomprehensible reason I could never see my way to marrying [her], although she wanted that to happen. Goodness knows I

23

think she is a wonderful person & I haven't the faintest doubt in my own mind that if & when I do get married I shan't get hold of a woman to touch her in generosity & intelligence & whatnot. But there it is. Meanwhile ... should anything, as they say, happen to me, I would like you to let her know as soon as possible [an address follows].

Heigh ho.

In the summer of 1939, Wynn Wheldon was knighted in the Birthday Honours. According to Celia, Huw bitterly regretted not having taken her to the family celebrations that followed. In any case, the war separated them soon afterwards. Wheldon was suddenly busy, arranging for the reception of evacuee children from London. Two days before war was declared his father wrote to him, in English, 'Well, we are for it, or rather you and your generation are for it, and I am dumb with grief & disappointment'; and in Welsh, 'We are always in God's hand.' Huw was hoping for a commission, and had an interview at the War Office on October 17.

Celia's parents moved further from London, and she went to live at an hotel on Chislehurst Common. Army officers working at a secret radar establishment were billeted there. In the first week of the war she met a lieutenant-colonel in Signals, and married him three months later, in December. She says Huw went on writing to her. Other friends were moving into married life. Desmond Leeper was married in October 1939, Brian Murphy the following April. Wynne Griffith, who had vowed to be a conscientious objector, was in love ('the story of love given, received & given back is always good news,' wrote Wheldon, in pulpit mood). Deal was a place for brooding and reading. He discovered *Finnegans Wake* ('A perfect bedside book, Lear on a huge scale') and *Party Going* by Henry Green, whom he calls Herbert Green.

Like thousands of others, Wheldon needed time to come to terms with a war that began slowly, being fought for reasons that were less evident then than they soon would be. The present war, he thought aloud in letters, was surely irrelevant.

Totalitarianism was evil, but the issue was not our system versus theirs, it was 'Present versus Future'. Our liberalism was dying, their Naziism was ephemeral by definition. 'Other forces' were at work, though 'God knows what they are'.

Meanwhile he was short of money, and the winter of 1940 was freezing cold:

> Deal dead under snow, the country overwhelmed; the sea snaps at the coast a bit, but otherwise there is no movement save Mr Wheldon, administrator, hurrying to the office.

Returning by train from London after seeing H., he shared the carriage with a party of army officers, 'salt of the earth, I have no doubt . . . They gave me a pain.'

By the spring, with the German army on the move in western Europe, outlooks changed. Wheldon came up with simpler truths in his letters: 'One must fight for what one holds valuable' and 'I am filled with a sense of shame [because I] shrank within myself from dubbing Hitlerism evil, really evil.'

The war came nearer. Ships hit mines and sank off the coast. German planes appeared, only to vanish unscathed ('Deal sighs with disappointment. What we want is Blood'). Wheldon waited to hear from the War Office. At first it was to be the Royal Artillery. 'I can't get into the Army for love or money,' he wrote to Leeper. '. . . I tried to transfer, in desperation, Deal is such a God-forsakenly boring hole, into the infantry, but nothing doing . . . Now trying to get pushed by my Father's military mates into the Royal Welch Fusiliers, but I understand that there is a long waiting list.' At last he was told to report to an infantry training centre with the East Kent Regiment, The Buffs, in June, and became a soldier – as he was to see it, the crucial experience of his life.

Marching up and down barrack squares softened by the sun, working up appetites for cake and cheese, the raw intake were wryly aware of their role as front-line troops if the Germans invaded. Overhead they saw the Battle of Britain being fought, far off, by 'flying insects', 'incredibly beautiful'. Wheldon found himself content to be alongside men who were merely 'faces over tea & beer with cigarettes stuck into them. A species, like monkeys or sparrows.' But soon he was feeling bloody-minded about an army that wasted time needed for training or sleep on 'unbelievably stupid' kit inspections: 'this absurd laying out of toothbrush & socks in certain order – the windows are to be cleaned, the brass polished up. Hitler would laugh with delight could he see us.'

Wheldon's objections were never those of the barrack-room lawyer. They sprang from a sense of outrage that the admirable military could be, at times, so crass and hidebound. In a few years his nickname would precede him wherever he went, 'Bash-on Wheldon'. He flung himself into war with a savage delight. In the process he found a talent in himself for taking things to extremes, of making them, and him, seem larger than life. That became the essential Wheldon.

In October 1940, just before he was posted to an officer cadet training unit at Barmouth, in North Wales, he wrote to the Leepers in steelier tones than before:

> The air-raid warning is a white snake that lurks while we work, and when we finish, creeps out into the evening: a tape-worm that smears the air. It battens on my gloom, I find. When Wheldon is jolly, how you say? very jolly jolly, the snake is buggered, and can't move. Perhaps I could hire myself out as a siren-neutralizer . . . The wisdom of days, biblical phrase, has quietened the liberal arguments I extended on the arid Leeper air on the Ramsgate beach, and left me a revolutionary and an uncommitting Mandarin by turns . . .

He began telling people that Communism was damned attractive. Army snobberies got on his nerves, especially when they were seen in the context of a little town like Barmouth where 'the inhabitants are Welsh to a chicken, praise be to God'. Like many Welshmen, Wheldon saw his nation as less class-ridden than the English, lacking an aristocracy and thus the consequent levels of imitation from below. No doubt he exaggerated: as a child he lived in 'upper Bangor', which regarded itself as a cut above the old town a quarter of a mile away, and still does. But 'these sparrow-gents ... these English semi-people', as he called his fellow cadets, infuriated him. He wrote to his father:

> As far as I can see the so-called democratization of the army is merely an extension of the old-type classifications to include Secondary School boys as well as Public School boys. They, the new intake, have to fit into the old style. They want a new sort of material, but an old sort of officer: & I am certain that they are not getting what they want ... they are not combing the ranks for men who can lead & command irrespective of antecedent & accent (& there are plenty about – ex miners & ex carpenters in Canterbury, for example, who were tough capable men) but for men who may conceivably be able to write nice lecture notes and understand the King's English ... With the result that they pick very largely on Clerk types who say 'endeavour' instead of 'try' and 'require' instead of 'want', passing over the incomparably superior type who despises these clerical pansies & who speaks straightforward cockney without a declasse affect[at]ion of any sort.

To Ben Leeper he wrote in December 1940 – stressing his socialist inclinations, as he was inclined to, with the Leepers – that his political bias was 'towards roaring red revolution with hearty kicks in the teeth for all Tories from Winston Church[ill] to my platoon Commander'.

> If we are to fight a war at all, I am in favour of doing it thoroughly, & not in a gentlemanly way. These people know nothing of riot and hunger ... I only wish the working-class really was a bristling dragon that would provide substance for their footling narrow little anxieties.
>
> They'll go, of course, inevitably. I think the whole western bag of tricks is doomed, finished: and so be it ... Let the whole thing blow up, as it will; I am for it ...

One of his last exercises before he left Barmouth as a subaltern was to act as platoon commander, withdrawing his men across the hills. His map-reading was not as good as it might have been, until the unit came across a shepherd. Wheldon spoke to him in Welsh, and the shepherd, enjoying the joke, pretended to complain about his sheep being worried, while explaining the routes to take. This became another of Wheldon's stories, and he was still telling it years later. 'The officers,' he told his father at the time, 'who naturally regarded shepherds as being one with Private Soldiers & all the other unspeakables, suspected nothing, listening to our conversation with amusement as if they were being entertained by two clever little budgerigars in a Cheltenham drawing room.'

His father had gone on trying to wangle Huw into the Royal Welch Fusiliers. He wrote to the colonel of the regiment, calling his son a good lad with his share of brains, a rugger player, a swimmer and a horseman. Sure enough, in February 1941 Huw was posted to the RWF barracks at Wrexham, and had his first taste of a formal officers' mess, before, to his relief, joining the 12th Battalion. This was on coastal defence duty at Whitby, then a derelict seaside resort with sodden moorland at its back. 'If Hitler takes Yorkshire,' he remarked, 'it will bloody well serve him right.'

He had charge of a pioneer platoon, constructing defence-works. They were carpenters and builders, proud and crafty Welshmen whom he took to. Once again it was the officers he disliked, more 'bloody little pipsqueaks'. The mess he likened to a dentist's waiting room in Islington, filled with stuffed owls. Reacting against what he saw as loutishness and Tory dogmatism, he found himself sounding more radical than he felt. He called Churchill a mountebank, and enjoyed shocking the other subalterns with his 'Bolshie tendencies'. Sometimes his fellow officers were nice; always they were dull. Lieutenant Wheldon had mild attacks of intellectual arrogance, though not when writing to his father, where his strictures were guarded. He liked showing off to Ben Leeper, Desmond's wife:

In the mess I mutter . . .
Sancho Panza . . .
Orwell . . .
those Thurber drawings . . .
the fine Italians . . .
Palestrina . . .
and the words get no further than the gravy jug. Second Lieutenant Lever tells me about his second car, 'my second TROUT: I always call my cars my trout, ha! ha! ha!'

Over the next year, Wheldon came to terms with the army. He found himself on field-training courses, manoeuvring on northern moors. Stationed at Bellerby Camp, 'a smear of concrete huts', he was made an instructor with the acting unpaid rank of captain, the result, he said, of being 'plausible and bullshitty'. In February 1942 he nearly drowned in a vain attempt to save an officer who slipped on ice and fell into a whirlpool during an exercise. Wheldon went in twice, and the second time was taken out unconscious. His 'more than ordinary courage' was commended. Nearly forty years later he told the story in a film interview. Before he passed out, he remembered 'extremely meretricious, second-rate headlines going through my mind – Promising young man drowned in Yorkshire whirlpool – Mourners turn up full of grief – Lady Wheldon in tears – Young Bangorian's life cut short.' But 'I lived again'.

By 1942 there were 'battle schools', with live bombs and ammunition, and Wheldon became a senior instructor at one of them. Looking back, he saw the battle school as a turning point, presumably what battle schools were meant to be. In the 1960s he wrote to his brother-in-law (by marriage to Mair Wheldon), a surgeon called Richard Rees, to tell him about a psychiatrist he had met at the television studios:

It suddenly struck me that by God he was the chap who, dressed at that time in khaki, had made an enormous impression on me at the first Battle Drill Course at Barnard Castle by saying all our uniforms were womanly – mammalian helmets, blouses, forage-caps (unmentionably named you will remember) [1] while German uniforms fairly shouted potency & the manly qualities. It was he who made me take that place seriously; & had it not been for him I would not have got stuck into all that battle drill stuff, all of which led directly to the Airborne Brigade etc etc. He changed my life. And hence, yours.

The psychiatrist was Dr Tom Main, who lectured on morale, explaining war in terms of the individual's psychological response. He tried to make officers aware of hidden realities: the loneliness of men advancing ten yards apart; the fear of being bayoneted or run over by a tank, unlikely events but potent as fantasies; the 'terrible truth' about an army, that if a hundred soldiers are sent to take a hill under fire, about thirty will get there – the rest find ways of lagging behind.

Exactly what impressed Wheldon about the course is hard to tell, unless it was plain speaking about subjects that were usually taboo. All Main recalls of Wheldon from 1942 is 'a mad-keen chap, dark-faced, with a blue chin and a beaked nose'. They became friendly after they met at the studios, and Main, looking with a professional eye at his former pupil in middle-aged maturity, noted his 'manic capacity – got to keep things happy, got to keep things moving. Huw liked laughing and joking. The laughter was always a bit louder than it needed to be. Under the mania was – must have been – the depression.'

The idea of joining the airborne forces had occurred to Wheldon in 1941, when volunteers were asked for, but he decided against it. In May 1942 he talked to his father and changed his mind. He was interviewed by the commander of the 1st Air-landing Brigade, and was accepted. 'A plunge for the airborne divisions now, prompted by God knows what complex of motives,' he wrote to Desmond Leeper. 'For promotion read glory! Try all things.'

*

[1] Soldiers called them 'cunt caps'.

Wheldon's war was enjoyable and satisfying, or so he made it sound afterwards. Glory and honour were on the cards. 'You could even die in a manly way,' he said, 'and men would mourn you with a little cross and a trumpet call.' Aspects of his private life troubled him. The problem of women nibbled at his self-esteem. Being a soldier, however elite, was no remedy for such things. But it showed him how to draw a curtain over his difficulties, and one day become the someone else that the famous need to be.

Amateur film shot with a cine-camera in 1943 shows Wheldon appear at the downstairs window of a country house in Berkshire where his unit was in temporary quarters. Thin and mischievous, his hair like crinkled coal, he sways for a second, book in hand, before leaping out and falling full-length on the grass, on purpose. A touch of the showman is what people remember. By this time he was in the Royal Ulster Rifles, having transferred to a new regiment because it had vacancies in a battalion, the 1st, that was earmarked for airborne forces. They were training to be glider troops, and in May 1943 became part of the new 6th Airborne Division,[1] to be used in the invasion of Europe, the 'second front' that was already being called for.

Their permanent base was at Bulford Camp, on Salisbury Plain, a collection of ancient hutments. The second in command of the battalion, Major (later Brigadier) John Drummond, was in charge of training NCOs. He says he cheated to have Wheldon attached to his team. When he watched him in *All Your Own* after the war, dealing briskly with children in front of the cameras, he saw the same mannerisms. Wheldon thought the Ulstermen good soldiers, but 'thieves and scoundrels' compared with the chapel-going Welch Fusiliers. The officers he took to,

---

[1] There was only one other airborne division at the time, the 1st. '6th' was meant to mislead the Germans. The division had about ten thousand men, divided into three brigades. Two brigades consisted of paratroops. The third, the 6th Air-landing Brigade, was the glider force. It was made up of three battalions: one from the 2nd Oxford and Buckinghamshire Light Infantry, one from the Devonshire Regiment and one from the Royal Ulster Rifles.

finding 'a wider humanity' in them. It was at Bulford that he met his future brother-in-law, Richard Rees, christened 'Dai' by the Ulstermen, who was the MO.

1 RUR had a reputation as a hard-drinking battalion, fond of horse-play in the mess. Bulford was an unpopular camp, primitive and isolated, with no nearby town to walk to; entertainment was in demand. An officer from another battalion, Sandy Smith of the posher Ox and Bucks, was summoned to the Ulster mess and found himself the bride at a mock wedding. Wheldon was in charge. Bouquets of shredded paper were handed out. There was a chamber-pot and some charade with non-existent bedsprings. Condoms hung from lamps.

For a while Wheldon had acting command of a company; he told people he was surprised to find he liked the power. Training was intensive and continuous, some of it on the coast at Ilfracombe. 'God knows what will become of us,' he wrote to Desmond Leeper – 'a battlefield one day I suppose.' They crash-landed in gliders, marched around southern England by the stars ('an imbecility called Intensive Night Training') and watched, from a distance, as the war started to be won on the far edges of Europe.

'I envy the English their dwellings,' he wrote home, seeing old houses in pretty villages, rarely found in Wales, a poorer country. 'When I grow up I shall have to go into Holy Orders, live in a Berkshire vicarage, burn peat on summer's evenings and read Macaulay.' During the war he wrote hundreds of letters to his family, most of them to his father whose office was sometimes in London, sometimes Bournemouth. On leaves he was often with his mother, who for safety was in Prestatyn, along the coast from Bangor, where she now lived with her mother, the widowed Mrs Edwards; the house was called Canonbury, to remind Mrs Edwards of the London suburb she had lived in before the First World War.

Family tales would catch his interest. Writing to Desmond Leeper while on leave in Prestatyn, he passed on a reminiscence of an aged great-aunt, Jane, who had recently told him that seventy years ago when she was fourteen years old, the great terror of the Fenians was in full swing. She lived in a place called Oswestry in Shropshire, and when the Fenian stories got around, all the good people of Oswestry saw that they would have to defend themselves. They calculated that if the Fenians came to Oswestry they would come by train, so they dug an enormous hole outside the station, and covered it over with cunningly painted sacking ... Every day my great aunt Jane, on her way home from school, would stand gloating on the camouflaged lip of this lovely hole. But the Fenians never came.

In the early months of 1944, Wheldon was one among hundreds of thousands of men, ready and yet never quite ready for the assault they had been so long anticipating. He wrote to his father about the downs near Hungerford – 'expansive, rich, idle' – and the streams teeming with trout, feeling the unreality of what was happening, 'as if the evasive colours and moving distances of early spring were making the very lorries insubstantial'. To Ben Leeper he wrote about an England 'indescribably lovely with her parklands & beech trees & little hills':

although no doubt we should be naughty, you & I, altogether to disregard the dog beneath the skin, the forgotten wars, the mysterious wealth. But there it is, a bit shyly possibly, fearing comparison with Rupert Brooke (why?) – I can only say that my heart & head is full of the beauty of it all: happily full, no aches.

On May 13 he wrote to his father about a vast church parade, where the army chaplains entered like a flock of geese, 'after which we were gravely dedicated to the 2nd Front. I am tired of being dedicated to the 2nd Front, especially by a chap who speaks in a Noel Coward way.' Nor were they 'crusaders', as the chaplains liked to think. It was a necessary war, that was all, 'simply one of Those Bloody Things.'

Before D-Day the invasion troops were incarcerated and individuals could make no contact with the outside world. The 6th Airborne was to secure bridges and high ground at the eastern extremity of the Allied landings by sea. Their zone was a few miles inland from 'Sword' Beach. At about nine in the evening on June 5, paratroops and a small glider-borne force began moving to airfields. These would be the first British soldiers to land, in the small hours of D-Day. It was the noise of their transports, about two hundred and fifty Halifax bombers, passing over southern England and the coast, that people in their track still remember as 'the start of the invasion'.

Wheldon's battalion was to land on the evening of D-Day, with the main glider force. The day before, he was writing letters, along with all the others who felt a need to put things on paper, tentative lines drawn under lives, just in case. He had already written to his brother Tomos, an agricultural officer in Sierra Leone, improving the occasion with a dash of theatre, 'Nothing is wasted if death comes – but on the contrary, a positive thing is done, something rendered for all the anonymous cockneys & men of Kent and chaps from Wigan. And lads from Sir Fon & Carnarvon & Penygroes. Not their flaming sons (unromantic posterity) but they themselves, as they fight into France.'

There was a letter ready for H., too, his former girl-friend: 'I am not worth grief, so don't grieve if they get me – & in any case remember that I am myself all for the job, not a reluctant starter but a prancer . . .'

To his father he wrote on June 5:

> I have just finished packing. I wonder whether any major crisis will ever find me ready? The soap I meant to get, the bootlaces I put off buying, the holster which should have been repaired [. . .] Yesterday's procrastinations are at last bearing fruit! Wheldon goes to war pitifully ragged.
>
> My recent letters have been very colourless I fear – I could not help it, hated doing it, the partial deception. We have been in a closed camp for some time, sealed off entirely from everybody, & the tentacles of Security have reached into everything. Free at last, at least to tell you that the last few weeks have been very

very happy ones, working away at our operation orders (the whole thing has been very like working for an exam) – sunbathing and taking things easily.

We are off very shortly, & the sounds of whistling & shouting, odd songs, the gang round the goal posts, reach into this tent. Everyone is amazingly happy . . . I personally would not like to miss it, & I am going much more firmly based – spiritual values apart – than I ever hoped.

There is nothing else I can say. You know what my feelings are about most things – & you will realize that nothing is being thrown away in this venture: no matter what happens I personally feel that a service (again, on the purely tactical, not to mention any higher plane) will have been rendered. This makes everything worthwhile.

So please don't worry – this, like the note I scribbled to Mother is ludicrously inadequate: but the depths can't be plumbed in a phrase or a letter.

All my love & affection. Huw.

[Clothing] Coupons herewith! These will buy socks etc. I don't fancy they will be much good in France!

The letter to his mother was lame: 'I am honestly at a loss to know what to write to you,' he said. '. . . somehow I shrink from showing too much emotion.'

Next day, June 6, the Halifax bombers were back at the airfields for the gliders. Wheldon flew from Broadwell, in Oxfordshire; it is farmland now. The fleet of planes crossed to Normandy before it was dark, the 6th Air-landing Brigade 'streaming in from the coast in the evening light'. Wheldon's stories about the war avoided heroics. When it came to the landing, with gliders scattered across the fields like dead moths, and units drawing together, he spoke of a strange sound, a rustling in the twilight, rising over the countryside. It was the 6th Air-landing Brigade, communally relieving itself.

Wheldon was second in command of 'C' company. This was moved a mile or so to the south during the night, to occupy a small hill, 'Ring Contour 30' on the maps. In the morning, the battalion hoped to attack villages beyond, where the Germans were dug in. For the moment, this was the front line. The general idea (says John Drummond) was to 'keep the Germans busy and stop them shelling the beaches' to the north, where the British Second Army was still coming ashore.

In the event, 'C' company was seen to be dangerously exposed when dawn came on June 7. As one of the brigade commanders had told his officers before D-Day, 'Do not be daunted if chaos reigns. It undoubtedly will.' The Germans were a thousand yards away, in the village of St Honorine. They shelled, mortared and machine-gunned for hours. 'Almost without exception,' says Drummond, 'the company were new to this sort of thing. I had experience of Dunkirk in 1940, such as it was. Bob Hynds [the company commander] and Huw Wheldon between them kept the morale up, moving from trench to trench.' Wounded men had to be evacuated. Machine guns ran short of ammunition, and Wheldon took a truck to get some. Finally, when an attack on St Honorine by the rest of the battalion failed, 'C' company was ordered back.

Both Hynds and Wheldon won the Military Cross for bravery under fire. When brigade headquarters asked for recommendations, Drummond had the job of supplying them. He proposed the two officers, hoping that one of them would be decorated. Instead, that August they both were.

Wheldon received his MC from Field Marshal Montgomery 'in the field', describing the award (probably to his father)[1] as a 'rather shameful thing'. He is oddly vehement about it, as though unable to accept the role of a brave man, which Drummond had, and has, no doubt that he was ('He always seemed to be everywhere. There is no shadow of doubt that he merited the award'). 'Honestly and sincerely, and all modesty apart,' wrote

---

[1] Like many of Wheldon's letters, this one has no salutation.

Wheldon to his father in August, 'what I deserve is reprimanding for failure, & not this decoration. I have been very cowardly. The MC action was apparently a brave one to the onlooker – to me, most certainly not. When bravery has been required I have in most cases shirked it, being miserably frail. Still, there it is.'

In the last days of the war, Wheldon and Desmond Leeper met by accident at a military hospital in Brussels, and Leeper heard a longer version of the same self-deprecation. No doubt bravery is easily picked to pieces and made to seem something else. The issue isn't a pedantic analysis (even if one were feasible) of Wheldon's state of mind during the course of a long day on Hill 30, but rather his own apparently genuine sense of uneasiness, a pessimism about himself, when he looked back on the episode.

Leeper reported the conversation to his wife in a letter written from the hospital, April 1945:

> It seems that during the first days in Normandy, while under heavy shellfire, he rushed about in a truck picking up not only his own casualties but everyone else's too. This, he says, looked pretty heroic but was basically nothing but cowardice. His platoon was very exposed and not dug in. As a good officer, he should have stayed with them but he didn't, he shamefully leapt at the opportunity to go back out of danger and get a truck. Once he had got it he rushed around in it because he preferred doing that to squatting down inactive among the shells with his platoon. All this is much too convincing to be merely false modesty. He doesn't claim that he didn't deserve a medal, but not, he insists, for that affair of all things. Meanwhile he has recommended and secured decorations for several of his men by the simple expedient of writing up purely fictitious citations. His subalterns regard this as rather questionable, but, as he says, it is much fairer to pick a man who has done consistently better than the rest, and invent some bogus heroics for him (even set in a bogus battle, which gives greater freedom for inventiveness) rather than having to rely on some flashy action by a chap who deserved it less.

Following D-Day and the subsequent engagements, the 6th

Airborne stayed where it was for the next two months, holding the easternmost corner of the front; the battles were to the west, where the breakout by the Americans would come. Wheldon wrote to Ben Leeper, 'Living too soiled a life to read the New Testament – or too irrelevant possibly – one can only thrive hopefully on the dignified paganism of the 91st Psalm ['Thou shalt not be afraid for the terror by night; nor for the arrow that flieth by day'] and its like.' Much of the time he lived in a damaged house, with pistols, Penguin books and a bottle of cider on the dresser. 'Weapons are grown into ornaments,' he wrote home. Hares, kept in cages for their skins, had escaped, 'and now they are everywhere, silent and soft, nibbling at the wanton remains, passing noiselessly through the ruins, somehow hateful'.

Minor engagements took place and killed people. Wheldon went on a night patrol, 'storming out like a tiger, as vindictive as the very devil', because H. had written to say Ben Leeper was dead. But it turned out to be a false rumour. Cherry orchards made him think of Eden and the 'childlike state' in which they lived. Stories of the D-Day fighting grew more apocryphal every day. In August he set craftsmen to work converting a barn into a rest room, exulting over the result. 'That odd chemical reaction which confers both unity and domesticity on the most unusual foundations & which is part & parcel of an Army's nature is already at work,' he wrote home. 'I feel like Beethoven.' The army had moved a long way in his affections in five years.

In the middle of August, as the Americans swung towards Paris and the German armies in France began to collapse, the 6th Airborne was on the move again. This time its task was modest, to follow up the Germans as they withdrew along the Channel coast. A stray shell killed Wheldon's company commander, and he found himself in charge, an acting major. His letter home, on August 29, spoke bitterly of the 'dead man's shoes' he had inherited. It was in this letter that Wheldon gave the news of his Military Cross ('another rather shameful thing'), which had just been notified.

By now they were out of the line, on their way back to England, to retrain for the final stages of the war in Europe. Seven officers (of the battalion's forty-seven on D-Day) had been killed or were missing, and seventy-eight other ranks (of eight hundred and seventeen). The survivors arrived at Southampton to a band and thoughts of home.

CHAPTER THREE

Suitor

SINCE 1942, SOON after Wheldon volunteered for airborne service, he had been involved with Celia again. This time they became lovers: another drop in the ocean of wartime affairs.

The relationship caused both of them much pain, mixed up with happiness and a significance, in Celia's account, that transcended any flaws. She calls it 'a life-forming relationship', but she presents it – though with what degree of accuracy one can't be sure – as an affair that she was better equipped to handle than he. 'It gave him something to hold on to in the war,' she says. 'I didn't need it in quite the same way because my feet were on the earth very firmly, and Huw's never were.' She adds that looking back, 'I can't believe any of it ever happened, now I'm so old'; in 1990 she is seventy-nine, five years older than Huw Wheldon would have been.

Her memory is of letters from him that followed her around England in the first year or two of the war. Her husband, the lieutenant-colonel in Signals, moved about the country, and she went with him. He was twelve years older. They were in Scotland for a while; then he was sent overseas, and she went to work for the Ministry of Home Security.

One letter survives [1] from this period, written in July 1942, a chatty, old-friends' letter, in reply to one that she has written

---

[1] Celia says much of the correspondence vanished when household effects were stolen overseas after the war.

him. 'Very very good hearing from you,' he says, and regrets the 'tantalizing circumstances' of their both having been in places where they could have met, had they only known. For her benefit, and adopting the jocular tone that ran through his letters to her, he summarizes his army career so far, beginning with his 'rum job' teaching tactics on the moors: 'We lived in stone cabins, solitary. The dark figure of Wheldon, Capt, graced this blasted heath, grinning with the pains of ignorance, talking running ejaculating remonstrating dismissing lecturing with enormous speed and power in an effort to blind his stupefied pupils to his unfortunate failings.' Then the battle school (where 'I took up the technique of maintaining complete silence on everything'), and now the initial training in gliders and parachute jumping. He described his new regiment in harsher terms than he would soon be using:

> I command a company of Irishmen in this airborne racket & life is pleasantly eventful. I am hideously incompetent. I mean this very seriously – with a pack of commanders who haven't the sense of a flock of grade B sheep, & a gang of politicians who cannot can NOT be regarded by any possible stretch of imagination as being worth more than tuppence a bunch, the whole unity of the army depends on unit discipline; & discipline defeats me. I prefer the men to the officers, much prefer them: with the result that cheeribee & matiness are the order of the day in B Coy. I can't help roaring with laughter most of the time I am with the men (this is an accurate statement) & although everyday existence is pleasant enough, I am frightened for the future. When the laughter has been smashed out of us I don't see what there is to sustain us in further action.

Later that year, says Celia, they met by accident at an hotel in Salisbury. Wheldon was with other officers from Bulford. She was based in Bristol, and spent most of her time in trains, travelling around south-west England. The Salisbury visit was to give a talk about the importance of keeping towns blacked-out against air raids.

Wheldon was now twenty-six; she was thirty-one, newly

attached to the office of the Regional Commissioner [1] for the West Country. Her husband had been abroad for some time, but the abandoned wife is not a category she admits to. 'Men,' she says, 'made a lot of passes at me as a young woman. I had enormous blue eyes that I batted. Did you ever hear a song called *Jeepers creepers, where'd you get those peepers?* A Texas general at the American HQ in Bath used to take me to dances, and the band was always made to play it. I've never been short of men. But I was never that interested in them except to say, "Hello, isn't it fun, let's go to the dance, goodnight." They didn't mean anything to me. I was a bit frightened of them, in actual fact, as Huw was frightened of women.' She names two other men for whom she felt a physical attraction that might have led her to sleep with them. In neither case did she do so. Apart from this, 'the urge to get into bed, so to speak' arose only with her husband and Huw.

They had no sooner met in Salisbury – accidentally or on purpose – than they embarked on an intensified version of their old relationship. She resented her husband having chosen overseas service, when he could have stayed in Britain. Besides, he was 'a broad-minded man who led his own life'. As for Wheldon, he must have felt encouraged to take her seriously. He was hardly a philanderer; the affair might have caused fewer tears if he had been.

Their first outing, which Celia believes came soon after Salisbury, was a concert at the Colston Hall in Bristol given by the tenor, Richard Tauber. She bought tickets and Huw travelled to Bristol, either by car or motor bike. Afterwards they went back to her hotel. At one stage he was not capable of making love to her, and, despite her assurances that it was of no consequence, was distraught when he left. The letter [2] she says that he wrote

---

[1] Regional commissioners were originally appointed to run the country in the event of invasion. Their offices evolved into centres of local administration.

[2] Celia showed me this letter only when I told her that I already knew of Huw Wheldon's problems at the time.

immediately afterwards is dated only 'Monday night'. It seems to describe two separate occasions, perhaps two episodes during the same weekend. Some demon in Wheldon conflicted with his appetite for pleasure and self-fulfilment.

> Last night [he wrote] I left within an hour of you and drove like a maniac through fog and rain, and got in by 9 o'clock. Since then it seems I have not ceased to think about you. I went to bed and slept badly and woke up out of a surface sleep five or six times, and all night long I dreamt of you. I only remember one dream. You were walking about a room in a blue costume. Once I woke up harsh with desire, and I bit my fingers until the blood came. I cannot in decency come to you. Before, when I mattered nothing to her and she nothing to me, I have made love and we have both had our grain of pleasure . . . Only then has the desire drained out of me, leaving me hating her and myself and everyone. It hasn't lasted beyond the day and the woman. There was a woman who I admired more, and after that I was impotent for six weeks . . .

Wheldon says elsewhere in the letter that he was 'wrong and unforgivably wicked in Bristol', as if referring to some other occasion:

> As soon as it started I knew that being what we are, you and I, we could do nothing in small measure. This made me worry and not know what to do. But when you took me into your bed I knew then that it was all right and what had been wrong before was all right now. Because you had my heart as well as my flesh. That night it was, you remember, a long night. It was full of joy to me, a double and indescribable delight because it gave me, so to speak, not only you, but also returned me my own proper self.

Celia insists that all the references are to their first love-making, in Bristol. Wheldon's mood swings violently during the course of the letter. Calmness and balance, he suggests, can no more heal 'the mind's disease' than Christian Science can heal rheumatism:

Lust is horrible because one uses another person (reading the last couple of paragraphs I am I must say dismayed to see I have been writing like the Old Testament) . . . Love improperly based is worse because it would become maudlin. I feel your generosity and warmth might well fix everything but I can't foist my boy's body gone wrong and my distracted man's mind into your keeping. One can go on at such length. My darling, you must see what I mean. I suppose I ought to go to a psychiatrist. Possibly I will, I don't know, or await a miracle. And if a miracle happens, I would humbly pay court. By that time you will have forgotten. I don't know.

There is a companion letter, headed 'Wednesday', written, says Celia, after she had replied to the letter of 'Monday night'. In it, Wheldon says that 'Fear is such a diabolical thing . . . every action seems suspect.' He apologizes for 'these swathes of dull-ness, the petifogging scratchings of a third-rate man'. But he shows signs of recovery: 'I'll come down to tea when the sands have settled and this welter of humbug dies down and bring you your staybone.' ('He must have had a staybone from my sus-pender belt,' Celia says vaguely.)

For the moment, the crisis was over. Huw eventually told her of two previous women with whom problems of potency had arisen. The first may have been H. Celia describes her as 'a girl at the university that he was mortified and horrified over. It was because of some form of worry, some deep-seated horror.' What Huw didn't tell Celia was that he had already consulted an army doctor, to whom he complained of 'awful feelings of sexual inadequacy' in connection with a married woman. She came from Oxford and was in one of the Services, where she drove a truck. The doctor shrugged his shoulders and told him not to worry.

Celia's story is of difficulties overcome. They were lovers; she never forgot him. Nearly half a century later, what she concen-trates on is a rich, sparkling affair in which both were caught up and transformed. They met whenever they could – in Bristol, in

Salisbury, in London. They shared a sense of humour. She liked his jokes and fantasies at the expense of the pompous and self-important. She enjoyed his story-telling: 'I've never met a man who could relate so many anecdotes so beautifully, could tell a story with every little detail, every character.' According to Celia, he 'wanted to write from his earliest days', and often spoke to her about a book on Sir Walter Raleigh he wished he had begun. When she asked what had stopped him, he said he was afraid to attempt it because he doubted his ability to write well enough.

Of Wheldon's more sombre aspect, a 'burden of gloom' that she detected in the background, she took a brisk Anglo-Saxon view, and thought, 'Well, you're Welsh, I suppose it's part of the Welsh character.' She decided, too, that although he was a man with a civilized amount of kindness in his nature, he lacked compassion. But his genial mood was in good supply, what he liked to call his 'cheeribee', and she delighted in it. Once she was staying at the White Hart in Salisbury, on Government business. Huw had been away on a course. 'I was sitting in the lounge one morning, writing up some notes, and a voice outside was calling, "Seal-ya! Seal-ya!" which is exactly how he used to say it, and in he came holding an egg, which was a great prize in those days. Very quietly he said, "Celia. For you." Pure flamboyance. I took the egg and said, "How marvellous," and he went. That evening two old biddies who'd been sitting in the lounge came to me and said, "What a delightful man, dear, the one who brought your egg. He's your husband, of course. Is he an actor?" I said, "Well, no, he isn't an actor and he isn't my husband."'

Their relationship had a bleaker side; Celia half admits it, but prudently hesitates to disturb the past. They both thought of marriage. She stresses now how difficult it would have been to leave her husband, and how fond she was of both men. But her own account, together with the surviving letters, has an echo of painful times. Huw was not a very constant lover. He seemed to want to marry her. Among his presents was a silver snuff box inscribed 'C.W.' There was a plan for her to live with his parents in Prestatyn while he read for the Bar. But he blew hot and cold. 'Part of the time he was so anxious to be with me. Another part of the time he was so certain he oughtn't to be. Having said that, within a few weeks, back he'd come.'

Occasionally, says Celia, she may have said, 'Why don't you make your mind up? If you want to come, come. If you don't, don't.' She is sure it wasn't more than occasionally. As supporting evidence for her nonchalance she describes 'one classic occasion when I saw him off at Euston. He was going somewhere in the north, and we had an argument on the railway station. I can't remember now what it was about, but all the troops were there. I stalked out, saying something like, "Good God, to hell with it!"'

'Within two minutes, Huw came dashing after me saying he was sorry, he didn't know what he was thinking of. I turned round and said, "How dare you! Go back to the railway station. Your job is in the army. Go away!" and he ran back wildly. That was the sort of personal thunderbolt I used to give him sometimes.'

There were disconcerting episodes, more involved than lovers' tiffs. They went to an officer's wedding, followed by a reception in a Knightsbridge hotel, where a brigadier in the 6th Airborne came up to them and said, 'Ah, Wheldon my boy, so this is where you hide this girl I hear about. Are we coming to a wedding for you shortly?'

Wheldon said, 'No, I'm afraid somebody got her first. Her name's ———. In fact, I think you know her husband.'

The brigadier said, 'You're not ———'s wife? I'd heard he married a pretty girl. Oh well, bad luck, old son.'

When the brigadier had gone, Wheldon swore violently and said, 'Of all the places to meet him! Come on, let's get out.'

Telling the story, Celia says, 'Stupid things like that used to happen to us.' But why had Huw gone out of his way to tell the brigadier? 'Exactly,' she says. 'It was his own fault. He wanted me to be his wife at the time. But I was a married woman. That coloured his outlook.'

With his family, deviousness was called for. He told them nothing outright, though his mother knew enough to ask him once what he was going to do about the woman she had never met. Celia says this annoyed him. In general his relationship with his mother seems curiously empty, beside the vigorous manliness that flowed between father and son. Celia thinks he was never at ease with her, and found it hard to communicate; he said he was always telling little untruths to keep her happy. Celia's successor, a woman called Ruth, says she heard him talking on the phone to someone 'in the voice you would use to a nice little girl', before realizing it was Lady Wheldon.

All he put in letters home was a misleading reference here and there. Just before Christmas 1943 he mentioned a course he had been attending at Harlech, where one of his colleagues was a servicewoman called S——, 'a singularly delightful girl, engaged of course blast and hell . . . [She] and I travelled to Bristol together & there met Celia —— (my old K[ent] E[ducation] C[ommittee] colleague), as a result of which meeting we are all collecting again, Celia, me, S—— & boy friend . . . in a farm near Salisbury on Christmas Eve.'

The following year, back in Britain after the Normandy campaign, they were seen together in Cambridge, where the London School of Economics had moved temporarily, and Mair was a student. Someone told her of the sighting. The informant had seen Celia's wedding ring and misunderstood it. Huw wrote briefly to Celia after being on leave and seeing his family:

> I follow my slow intricacies. At lunchtime my sister Mair in a jolly hearty laughter way said 'I hear you were in Cambridge with someone wearing an engagement ring.' Fury in my throat, choked back. I conclude some skinny bitch from LSE lay on Kings College Chapel Roof with a telescope stuck to her pig-eyes, spying. How else. My forced-laugh reply a betrayal of you my darling. I could have killed her, and maimed everyone else. When I woke up yesterday morning my Mother was standing by my bed (she woke me, no doubt) and I said 'Celia, good morning

Celia: how are you darling?' & mother said 'Celia', very articulate, and asked no questions.

The note is postmarked December 14 1944. It has an ominous tone, as though betrayal is on the agenda. Not long before, he had been writing easy, affectionate letters, saying how much he adored 'the Provincial Lady', wishing she was with him to share jokes about army mashed potatoes, or the paintings of goggle-eyed monarchs in an officers' mess he visited. 'Forgive me for being so pedestrian,' he wrote on October 29, 'and imagine, if you like, the fugitive thoughts that hover over the commas.' Now, seizing an unexpected chance, he tried to extricate himself.

That Christmas they had arranged to spend a few days at the Mill Race, an hotel in Salisbury. It was common knowledge that nothing would happen to the battalion until the spring. A plane had already gone to Belfast to pick up turkeys. But on the evening of December 20, a signal got the adjutant out of his bath to report to brigade headquarters. Four days earlier, German tanks had broken through in the Plateau of the Ardennes, in south-east Belgium, initiating the 'Battle of the Bulge': Hitler's last strategic throw, as it turned out. The 6th Air-landing Brigade was moving to the coast within thirty-six hours, and thence by sea to the Ardennes.

According to Celia, she was already at the hotel when Huw arrived with the bad news, which can't have been later than December 21. Had their Christmas begun four days early? She was there, anyway, when he brought the ill tidings. He was a major now, in command of a company. He would be gone soon, to a destination he couldn't reveal.

At some point he implied that it would be better for her if this was the end of the affair. 'What it did to him I don't know. But he came giving me the impression that he never wanted to come again. Which was so extraordinary. He gave me the impression *afterwards* that they were going into a terrible business, and he was trying to save me from being a miserable woman.' Celia is unable or unwilling to say more. She was left at the Mill Race while he returned to Bulford.[1]

Two days after Christmas he was writing to her from an undisclosed address. They were to the east of Dinant, a Belgian town on the River Meuse with a violent history, finding what cover they could in the open, waiting for a possible attack. The Germans were close. They had advanced forty or fifty miles towards Antwerp. By Christmas Day they had been contained by the Americans, and the offensive had failed. But that was not certain at the time.

It was 3.30 a.m., the battalion's first night in the front line. 'The night shifts as usual provide the opportunity to write,' he began. 'The positions visited, sentries checked, rustle of mouse in bracken apprehensively investigated, routine attended to. I have now an hour, I hope, of freedom in my frozen lodging. A box for a table, the melodrama of a guttering candle . . .'

It must have taken the full hour to complete the letter in his brisk, well-organized hand. Most of it is about Europe, winter, war. He hints broadly at the region where they are, between the French border and Rotterdam, a land of 'hallowed places, the inescapable presence of the past linking up with the present. Waterloo, Namur, Ghent, Mons, the Menin Gate, the Ypres Salient, Cockpit of Europe atmosphere all around'.[2] He describes the journey from England. On the boat train 'I read all your letters, put the Thunderbolt in my wallet and tore the rest up into tiny pieces and scattered them into the darkness.'

What was this Thunderbolt? Celia thinks it was a letter that

---

[1] A garbled but unmistakable version of the story came from a businessman friend of Wheldon, T. Mervyn Jones ('Jones the Gas'), now dead. His version confused the Ardennes crisis with D-Day. Wheldon told him after the war that he had been having 'a torrid affair' with a brigadier's wife – which she was, by that time. Deciding to break it off, he waited till they were in the bedroom of the hotel, said, 'I'm going to France tomorrow, I may be killed, we must finish this,' and left.

[2] Namur, another town with a violent history, was about fifteen miles to the north; Waterloo, another twenty-five miles.

she managed to get to him in Bulford before he left. Wheldon's response, inasmuch as he makes one, is sanguine. 'Ought I to write to you?' he asks:

> What was our parting? [. . .] What particle of spirit God in His minginess gave me and what atom of feeling is left after its adulteration by circumstances and duty, lies at your feet. Horrid conditions, limitations, so far from a 'generous utterance' – I have been faithful to thee Cynara in my fashion [1] came too near the bone for me to like it.
>
> A parting it was of course, the inevitable clash – leaving me changed, fitter, a better person; leaving you a rash, my darling, and little else except sorrow. And if it comes easier, then I'll post your letters into the fire –
> MEANWHILE: can you, the spirit apart and the flesh triumphant, victory of selfishness,
> MEANWHILE while I vacillate & evade responsibility (which I won't do for long my sweet, for no doubt we will drift, drift into the right actions, & things as they say will sort themselves out)
> MEANWHILE: O Conquest, can you get me a pair of really warm gloves? Otherwise my hands will fall off onto the ground one day with a clatter like falling plates . . .

One page survives of another letter that was probably written early in January, where Wheldon talks about Celia's knack for quoting verse:

> Item. I am devastated by the poetry you can pick on, with what seems such uncanny skill. All the poetry I know is
> Innisfree
> Knight at Arms
> Nightingale
> Thing about a monkey
> King's Soliloquy in Hamlet

---

[1] Presumably Celia had quoted this line by Ernest Dowson in her Thunderbolt.

Three sonnets in Welsh
O Western wind when wilt thou blow? (four lines)
and about five pairs of miscellaneous couplets. Poems I have read carefully extend over about four times that much, and there I finish. Yet I love everything you quote, learnt when thou art with me from one of your letters, and, as I say, am continuously amazed, delighted and jealous.

And T S Eliot, I've read him pretty carefully.

Item, when I met you at the Mill Race I thought I'd just say 'going away' but [the page ends].

On January 5 Wheldon was writing the Leepers a letter they didn't understand, about

> a business which took me lock stock and barrel: and, treacherously, I forsook what I didn't want to ruin . . . I am swamped, having lit up fires I did not know existed (and which in my jejeune soul don't exist) and touched the most appalling depths of feeling – this incoherence does no good: but I can't allow an enormous storm of incredible complication to howl me into its vortex without making mention of it however inscrutable. A thing to be entered up on the history sheet as Vague Event, first importance . . . Life is unexpected, and there are hateful powers everywhere.

(When Desmond Leeper wrote to ask what it all meant, Wheldon replied that he couldn't remember his own letter but 'it was presumably about the Wheldon Heart. I wish I hadn't mentioned it. In fact I wish I wasn't such a bloody fool as to get myself into endless troubles over silly trifles.')

Meanwhile the soldiers were far away from domestic worries. No German attack came. On New Year's Day 1945 the battalion had begun to edge forward, sending out patrols to keep contact with the enemy, who were beginning to withdraw back into the Ardennes, fifty miles from the German frontier. The front line settled down to winter and stalemate.

Wheldon wrote often to Celia, mainly keeping his mind fixed

on safe subjects like the weather, the daily round of finding blankets and drinking-water, the always inaccurate accounts of the war that they read in newspapers. 'We are an army in winter quarters,' he wrote on January 14, relishing the historic parallels with armies back to Julius Caesar's, sensing 'the presence of the Duke of Marlborough & his riff-raff, Wellington and his scum, pressing us from the long avenues of history into this necessary existence'.

Towards the end of the same letter, amid a series of chatty replies to points raised in a letter of hers, he said:

> Regrets. All & any regrets my darling which I have ever stated are because pain came to you. In that sense I regret everything from Beckenham to the Mill Race, everything – because they added up to a grief which I cannot bear to think of as being lodged inside you, and because they darken the future, your future.

Then the letter went on, 'Hurray for *The Economist*. Yes indeed.'

The gloves he had asked her for arrived, enormous gauntlets with a cord between them; also a waistcoat:

> [The mail came and] Celia O my Celia your magnificent your glory be to God on highest gloves came into my life. This was high delight, and I laughed until I could laugh no more, laughed and loved & wished you with me. Sweetheart they are wonderful, and I have worn them all evening on my rounds: utterly impracticable, I can't flash a torch, read a map, turn over a notebook, write a message – already carrying nearly everything I have, there is no room for them in my haversacks, darling I *love* them. They form my one entirely unwarlike, utterly beautiful, quite unthinkable item of equipment. Beyond all expectation they are golden glory! When Montgomery saw us before Normandy he wore a pair just similar, except white. My habit of wearing my oiled sweater in the sunshine with no jacket has been carefully observed by the boys (thinks he's bloody General Montgomery). The gloves, adding to this drama, have the Company utterly disgusted. Wise heads are shaken on the trodden snow, up and down

looks follow the poor creature in his general's skin. All this I adore.

Now I would never in all my life *ever* buy a pair of gloves like that. I wouldn't think of thinking of having the courage & brilliance. Done for me, it increases my stature: fills my thoughts of you with laughter, and is a terrific gesture. My darling I can't describe to you my gorgeous feelings of happiness when I wear your undreamable gloves.

The waistcoat is fine, of course. Practical. Fits. Useful. Grateful, naturally. Just the thing. Needed, too. But the GLOVES sweet, the GLOVES are the trumpet & cornet, the gloves outshout the proper & lovely. Darling, thank you so very much, not for sending them, but for getting them. Thank you for your lovely gloves. Off now, gloves & waistcoat, to cheer the boys.

Goodnight my sweet. Huw.

About a month later Celia sent him a second, more dextrous pair:

The gloves GLOVES II arrived in glory Sweetheart superb gloves and ideal. I have a gun, ektually, but never use the silly thing, never never. I have fired machine guns at where I thought there might be Germans, in idle moments. Purely jolly. And I have aimed a rifle at

(a) a pig

(b) a tree trunk at night

(c) a German in the flesh – Normandy it was. Missed him . . .

At times there are unexpected flashes of anger, as in a letter where he complains that when the battalion commander organized a concert, 'the bastards' couldn't be bothered to attend, and the few riflemen who did, sat giggling at 'a Scotch boy with a sweet and true voice'.

Nothing gets done without a PARADE. The men are bone stone idle, that is the truth. Damn the lot, I say. If there is one thing I cannot abide in what we call in our genteel way the lower orders it is their utter and ugly irresponsibility about anything except their own families & things like pay. One wants to be an

Athenian, and yet one is surrounded by chaps who starve or are spoonfed, starve sullenly, but bloody well starve.

One of the most hateful experiences which comes the way of all officers is to spend all morning, say, thinking and working sincerely for the wellbeing & comfort of his men, and then at lunchtime to learn that one of those very men has stolen his watch or done something equally heinous. It feels like a treachery and is honestly heartbreaking. Loyalty is a meaningless word except among the educated as a class: and among, I dare say, certain sections, even of the poor – but the army depraves them. Discipline we understand. There is no loyalty [. . .]

Why am I so angry? I know all this long since, and am accustomed to humanity which I recognize as bad and smelly as well as good and radiant – I think because of that Scotch boy and the revelation of the deep and sincere gracelessness of the young man of today [. . .] Man is born with his quota of instincts which are always moving and admirable when at work [. . .] What has merit is the addition of sweetness, a matter not to be defined but easily recognized, and pretty well absent in the factory worker of today, pretty well absent. This is my testimony. I am a poorer thing than my own father in the same way, but not to the same extent as the worker is shabbier than his peasant ancestor [. . .] Sweet, I am so angry with this bloody awful world [. . .] I am stopping now to read Howards End. I shall go to bed eventually, by then in a flux of thought positively electrical I should think. My looted pillow will no doubt be singed by the morning.

Have you any ideas about Battalion concerts? What could I do? My God, I need a manager. What is the young genius to do? I must find myself a sketch. If I do one, perhaps other chaps will quit their stupefied cells, and lend, as we say, lend a hand. I don't want to be funny much. I wish I could

Sing like Tauber

Play like Heifetz

Alas, I can only sing like me and play like the cat gone for a stroll on the piano during dusting time.

After breakfast, & the Runner, a square little man called

Waterton is waiting for this – the post is due out. Lots to do: you would be tremendously at home in this world. I imagine your effect on this room, & on these men. A rich thought.

Seeing one's Aunt is a knobbly business. Campaigns always constipate me: embarrassment & the loathing of public motion (my God!) providing the brake, not health.

Keep lovely

Huw.

Whatever Wheldon was telling Celia, his tone to friends about the relationship was not optimistic. He must have written explicitly to Brian Murphy, now an army captain serving in the Middle East.[1] Murphy wrote back on February 23 to say:

I searched my brain for recollection of meeting your love. Haunch of Venison?[2] Tall, fox fur, Kensington, dark: do I remember you stumbling to your feet and a quick introduction. Or is that cock. My poor old memory. Yes, I suppose you do tend to be gethogh (trans: left-handed) with women, though I've only your word for it. But there appears to be no norm in that matter . . . If you are to be a paradoxical Lovelace, a scrupulous rake, well there it is.

By March the 6th Airborne was back in England for a few weeks, preparing its last operation in Europe, the Rhine crossing. On the morning of March 24 the gliders landed in enemy territory again, this time inside Germany. Wheldon, commanding 'C' company of his battalion, was in a glider that cast off too early and put them down in the wrong place, where a machine gun in a farmhouse raked the aircraft.

On the way to find his battalion he came across three Germans on the edge of a wood. The magazine had dropped out of his pistol when he landed. In his hand he held his ration pack. He pointed it at the Germans, who dropped on their knees, begging him not to shoot. The story sounded apocryphal after the war, but a letter to his father dated April 3 tells it matter-of-factly.

[1] None of Wheldon's letters to Murphy has come to light.
[2] Salisbury has a pub called The Haunch of Venison.

Four days later he was wounded during an attack on a small town, Coesfeld, thirty miles from the Rhine, when a bullet went through his thigh: the happy flesh wound of heroes in Westerns. He recovered in a military hospital in Brussels. 'I share a ward with a Dentist,' he wrote to Ben Leeper. 'He loathes me for my frantic cheeribee.' Then he found that Desmond Leeper was also at the hospital. For the first time Leeper heard some facts about the Wheldon Heart, and wrote them down for his wife:

> Her name is Celia. She is 33 & married, but has had only 6 months of married life with her husband, a stupid [. . .] colonel now overseas. She is in love with Huw & has nervous breakdowns when he leaves her. He says she is a very fine person & so on but there is no question of his marrying her.

Two letters soon after gave more details:

> They agreed to part some time ago but when Huw heard that she had volunteered to go to Burma with a canteen or something, he reopened contact & persuaded her not to. He said she'd never survive it & anyway it was too fantastic her going off into the jungle to forget him, couldn't allow that . . . He tells me that this Celia business is his first love affair. The first time, as he put it, that the elements of lust & companionship were for him combined in one person.

These reported conversations give an odd picture of the affair. They are second-hand information and have to be viewed as such. But they strike the same dismissive note as Wheldon's remark in his January 5 letter to Leeper about 'endless troubles over silly trifles'. Celia's importance had to be denied.

Some details of what Leeper remembers hearing need clarifying. Celia's husband was not a stupid man. A Cambridge graduate, he was a senior instructor at the School of Signals between the wars, and an expert in communications and radar. According to Celia, 'my husband knew of my great affection and friendship for Huw and indeed admired the man.' He died in 1988, aged ninety.

The 'nervous breakdowns' are not true, either, according to Celia; she agrees she did have a breakdown of some kind towards the end of the war, but it was due to exhaustion and not eating enough. By this time she had left Bristol and was working in London as general secretary of the National Council for Unmarried Mothers.[1]

As for vanishing into the jungle, this is Celia's comment in 1989:

> [The Burma story] has set me giggling – we sound like something out of Somerset Maugham!
>
> Burma! Ye Gods! Nothing would have induced me to go off to Burma, it was in Mountbatten's bailiwick and I wouldn't join his circus for anything! It just did not happen.
>
> [Huw and I] were in close contact at that time and I was in the running for a senior post with the Save the Children fund – in Yugoslavia. Huw was greatly against my taking it, he said I should stop 'doing good works.'

The last days of the war came. Wheldon had returned to his unit in time to join the Allied advance as Germany disintegrated. Like many officers, he saw the inside of a concentration camp. He told Celia that he thought the German character contained 'a strong streak of madness' (she decided his response was based on 'horror, not compassion'). As the 6th Airborne trekked towards the Baltic, breasting waves of refugees escaping from the Russians, Wheldon found time to write about the scenes of chaos and defeat. 'Nothing can fix this, O my Christ, no words' (to Celia, April 30). 'The retribution is in kind, & complete, yet unbearably sad' (to Celia, May 6). 'I have seen stick-thin children of five, born to an unspeakable world, playing King of the Castle on a heap of naked and rotting dead women' (to his father, April 29). 'The Russians are three miles away, inscrutable [. . .] They

---

[1] During the war, the illegitimate birthrate was high. The Council was especially concerned with middle-class women in the armed services who found themselves pregnant.

drink like hell, and did a nice business in rape when they came. There is no cheeribee' (to Celia, May 13, five days after the war in Europe ended. They were at Wismar, on the Baltic coast. Dr Rees says he and Huw shared a bottle of whisky with the first Russian officers they met, and the doctor sang them the Welsh rugby song, 'Sospan Fach').

As far as anyone knew, the Far East war might go on for years. Letters home from soldiers in Europe were headed 'BLA', British Liberation Army. Wags said that what it really stood for was 'Burma Lies Ahead'. The 6th Airborne was told to start thinking about Malaya. It was rumoured to have been given the risky honour of invading Singapore. Wheldon, passing through London on May 25 on his way to a month's leave, wrote to Celia that he had no option but to go to fight the Japanese; but even if he had, he would volunteer.

From Prestatyn, where he spent part of the leave with his parents, he wrote fretfully to Celia on June 6:

> 0550. I hope it catches a post. This, to the minute, is the anniversary of Normandy. Fleets of gliders quietly landing on sunswept fields. Memories crowd, & I mustn't start.
>
> I have my DEAH Mrs Henderson, received your ENGROSS-ING letter, and will follow all 15 instructions in minutest detail.
>
> Miscellaneous points:
>
> Onely. Except no no ExPect the Presence between lunch and tea. Daring all, I will phone the office. Or.
>
> Twoly. Ice. I am not much of a one for having my ice broken.
>
> I have *NO* friend seeing Plans: & I have been to no shows at all. Certainly, book entire theatres, if you feel like it & want to see something. Me, I like pictures.
>
> I would say no concert on Sunday. I don't really know.[1]
>
> Under no circumstances will I stand for HAPPINESS. I am utterly anti-happiness.
>
> Huw Gloom Wheldon.

[1] There is a drawing of a seesaw, with 'Yes' and 'No' at either end.

I might, under stress, move cautiously into cheeribee: even jolliwolly. Joy? Ugh! I HATE joy. So limpid.

GLANDS [encircled, with an arrow pointing to:] this is a dreadful business.

Dont blame me, he whined, blame me glands. My glands O God my glands are to say the least of it glandular.

I am NOT gloomy about the Pacific. I LOVE the pacific.

Note. If you fix me with a doting look & say I wish I were your mother I will strike you stone cold. I've GOT a mother, for one thing. Besides. Huw.

Length of stay unknown. Depends on Sister Mair & Brother Tomos. Must see. Phoning Sunday night. Wednesday probably.

The idea of marriage was still in play. It may have been now, rather than earlier, that the idea of Huw reading for the Bar, while Celia lived in Wales with his parents, was floated.[1] She thinks it likely. 'Mind you,' she says, 'the word "divorce" was never mentioned. I was in a very peculiar situation. I didn't want to let my husband down. And I couldn't be certain about Huw. He didn't know what he wanted. He didn't like the idea of husbands in the background. He didn't like the idea of what his father would think, though he didn't mind much what his mother thought. Divorce at that time mattered a lot to everybody.' Later in the conversation she says, 'I was never the woman for him.'

The Leepers heard talk of a divorce that June. Now the excuse for not thinking about marriage was Malaya. Wheldon's unit was ready to sail on July 15, but there was a postponement. They went on training; Huw went on seeing Celia.

His last intimate letter to her was written from Romsey, in Hampshire (where he had been doing 'another fortnight's Jungle Training in that well-known jungle The New Forest,' he told

---

[1] Plans for postwar jobs were in the air, despite the Far East. Kent offered to take Wheldon back as an assistant education officer, at £500 a year. Celia knew a headmaster in Bristol who would have employed him. He made no move to accept.

the Leepers). His next stop was to be Matlock, in Derbyshire, for an Eastern Warfare course due to begin on August 15. But on August 6 the first atomic bomb was used on Hiroshima, and four days later the second fell on Nagasaki. The Romsey letter is dated August 8:

> So now it's atoms. We enter, at last, into the world of 'The Boys Magazine.' Bound to happen I suppose. I am working on a bomb which, dropped onto a quarry, causes the stone instantly to reassemble and be formed into rows and rows of Jacobean houses.
>
> Difficult, mind you.
>
> Atoms, actually, leave me unmoved. What the hell. Facts are facts. Lucid, eh?
>
> Romsey LOVELY especially the beautiful brilliant raindrops splashing into the breadstove.
>
> A sweet weekend, thank you for your instruction. I wish my atoms had been slightly differently assembled on 7 May 1916.
>
> En route to Matlock on Monday I might possibly be on a tea-scrounge – I'll come up Sunday if I can. This very very problematical. 9–8 against. Don't eschew appointments on that slender chance.
>
> Huw.

'Tea' usually meant tea at Celia's flat in Dolphin Square, on the Thames Embankment. Dolphin Square has a pool. They sometimes swam there together, and walked in the gardens outside. Celia says he had been a frequent visitor that summer. But at some point – the dates are vague – her husband was back in England for three or four weeks, before returning to Vienna, where he was a staff officer with the occupying forces.

She remembers slipping out of the flat, when her husband was at home, to meet Huw nearby. Was that the last time they met? The dates suggest it was early in the summer. But they were in touch later than that. There was the 'sweet weekend' around the start of August. Did her husband return for a second visit soon after the first? Did Huw and Celia have more than one emotional parting?

It was fine weather; she remembers a warm evening, and meeting Huw in the grounds. He was about to leave. Was it for Palestine? If so, it must have been the autumn. The army hadn't finished with the 6th Airborne. Reprieved from a Japanese war, it was going to the Middle East as a strategic reserve, in case of who knew what developments.

Celia says he broke down and wept. 'It was the first time in my life that I had seen a man cry,' she says, expressing surprise as the English are supposed to, 'and I was shattered.' What did he say? She has no idea. All she remembers is telling him that her husband was upstairs, and that she had to go back; and Huw sobbing.

In the following month she wrote to him twice. He didn't reply. On October 1 he was on board a troopship in the Mersey, waiting for the tide, moving crabwise towards another life.

CHAPTER FOUR

Candidate

THE MOST LIKELY career for Huw Wheldon after the war lay in teaching or some other branch of education. Traditionally the Welsh-speaking Welsh respected learning for its own sake, with the teacher second only to the clergyman in public esteem. This ideal, outmoded now, hovers at Wheldon's back. But for the war he might have been shunted into a classroom; his father was already telling him while he was in Kent in 1939 that a teacher-training job could be arranged. What Wheldon came to enjoy was something else, managing people by captivating them with language and the will. But education was the family trade. The notion that Huw-might-do-worse-than-teach can be detected. There are hints that for all his son's wartime prowess, Sir Wynn suspected a lame duck under the skin.

In the new army of the Second World War, education touched everyone. There were many Wheldons, rebelling against privilege. The authorities sought to raise morale by at least paying lip service to the need for the rank-and-file to be better informed about the war, the world and the future they were fighting for. The Army Education Corps expanded. An Army Bureau of Current Affairs published bulletins and ran discussion groups for every serviceman, at least an hour a week. Cynics said they were popular because men could sit in the warm and smoke. Political diehards of the Right suspected the talking-shops of being the thin end of a socialist wedge, as they were, in some hands. But overall they were part of the appetite for knowledge and even the arts that the war fostered.

Some adult educationists of the time thought the millennium had come, with 'The People' at last glimpsing a cultural Promised Land that could be theirs after the war. Wheldon's sympathies were more patrician (he would probably have denied it at the time), and so were his father's. Neither thought much of the ABCA, though Wheldon had to do his stint of work for it. Writing to his father in September 1941, when he was organizing half-hours on such topics as 'China's War' and 'The Democratic Machine', he thought that 'judged as Education, the thing is feeble; judged as propaganda, worse.' What he objected to was the grey dissemination of knowledge, 'as passionless as brown paper, neither revolutionary nor patriotic, & not, I think, worth a sausage.' But in the last months of his army career, Wheldon tried his hand at serious teaching.

At the beginning of October 1945, six weeks after the war with Japan ended, the division had begun to embark for the Middle East. Waiting aboard a troopship at Liverpool, Wheldon was caustic about the stevedores, who had gone on strike for a pay increase from 18 shillings [90 pence] a day to 24 shillings [120 pence]: 'offensive sullen ill-mannered idle pigs', he wrote to Ben Leeper. A month later he was in a tented camp in Palestine, being caustic about the Jews. Was his temper on a shorter fuse than usual in 1945? A 'hellish' year, he described it in the summer. Civilian life was looming up. Celia had gone for good ('Finished, beyond peradventure,' he wrote to the Leepers late in the year, waving away 'the horrors of my private life' as beyond discussion).

They were unsavoury times for the 6th Airborne's soldiers, who found themselves embroiled with the Palestine problem. The division arrived just as the Jews of Palestine were beginning their fight to set up a State of Israel. The British, who administered Palestine under a pre-war 'mandate' from the League of Nations, came to be seen as oppressors. Civilian terrorism got under way, a new experience for the British troops. Like everyone else, Wheldon disliked the role of security police. He realized the Jews had a case, but itched (he said) to use force against the

63

extremists. One or two of his letters are bellicose. Other officers who were there shrug their shoulders and say that many of them felt as Wheldon did. By the end of a war, soldiers have got the habit of fighting. Wheldon's brother-in-law, Dr Rees, remembers an engagement near the end of the war in Germany, when a local commander ordered an air strike on a town. The mayor had come out with a white flag and said they were defenceless. But the Typhoons still went in with the rockets. 'One wasn't able to make fine distinctions,' says Rees. It was better to be on the safe side.

Wheldon, writing home from Palestine about 'bomb-throwing fools' who boasted of 'nights of terrorism', described with relish how easy it would be to crush these unruly young Jews:

> a word on my wireless set, a sentence to a DR on his motor bike, a familiar order to my platoon commanders, and I would have Artillery and Mortars blowing their area to pieces, machine guns only too ready to have a crack, spraying their poison, and three platoons bashing in under smoke and a familiar routine, ready and capable of knocking the daylights out of anybody not adequately armed. Twenty minutes would produce the appropriate armour, churning away wherever needed, and there you are [. . .] We have done this so often that any 'night of terrorism' description would not occur to us, but on the contrary, this chance to deploy once more [would] be sweet and even jolly to us.

Wheldon described how he enforced the curfew in a Tel Aviv street with two rifle shots, 'action on a Napoleonic dictum . . . Machine guns are machine guns.' To Ben Leeper he wrote still more explicitly on November 30, after his men had searched a village where terrorists were hiding:

> My own power is frightful: & I honestly believe that I was fractionally near having to use it [. . .] Not to do it is a restraint abnormal. It is easy, familiar: meat & drink to us in a way, and (there it is, Ben, you've got to accept these things) to give the order of deployment and immediate battle is fun in its way, to be enjoyed. We *wanted* to bash in, in the old way, to a man.

64

A few weeks later he seems to have got the belligerence out of his system. He heard of an instructor's job at Mount Carmel College, an Army Education establishment in Haifa, where a school had been taken over. Men waiting to be demobilized who were regarded as 'university material' could attend month-long courses at these army colleges, specially set up. 'I am intriguing like mad,' he told the Leepers. Before Christmas he had talked himself on to the staff of Mount Carmel, to his father's delight. He left his regiment, with the CO's blessing, and spent his remaining months of army service in Haifa, before his turn came to be demobilized.

His subject was political theory, mugged up from reliable texts so that he could keep one step ahead of his students with Hobbes and Plato. 'I have to sweat blood to get my lectures prepared,' he told his father, 'but I really am loving it.' The college buzzed with talent and informality. Rank counted for little. 'Fine cushy rich job,' he wrote to Desmond Leeper, 'and my God what a difference. Heigh ho. The Cricket, they say, the early Lark, Le bon Wheldon. I love laying down the law, like Haifa, like pretty well everything except the Palestine set-up [. . .] Demob in May.'

As a lecturer he is remembered for brilliant performances, drawing people out. Cheeribee was the order of the day. The commandant, Lieutenant-Colonel Alan Champion, became a friend who could find no fault with 'Bash-on Wheldon'. 'He would sweep into the mess, thump me between the shoulder blades and say at the top of his voice, "Tell me, Champion, what was it that Aristotle said about the nature of a gentleman?" or some such question, to which at that time of day I could but flannel some sort of answer. He would then lope off at the double, three-quarters of a mile up to our school at the top of Mount Carmel.'

Wheldon had a gift for taking an account of an idea or an incident, and turning it into a story in its own right, coloured with his style. Dai Rees remembers hearing him hold forth at Bulford about Gibbon's *Decline and Fall of the Roman Empire*, 'but *he* wasn't reading it, *I* was, and telling him about it.' Desmond Leeper heard all about the Battle of Ramillies, when they were in hospital at Brussels. Wheldon had picked up a book about the Duke of Marlborough, and read, at random, an account of the battle. 'This being in his mind [Leeper wrote at the time], he told me about it for perhaps half an hour, as vividly and with as much excitement as if he himself had been taking part in it last week.'

Excitement is what he conveyed at Mount Carmel. Among instructors and staff were a dozen or so Jewish girls who had joined the British Army, on the advice of Haganah,[1] and continued to work alongside the British friends who were now coming to be regarded as enemies. One of them was Judith Maro; she married a sergeant-instructor at Mount Carmel, Jonah Jones. They now live in North Wales, she a writer, he a sculptor. Both became friends of the Wheldons later on. The first time she encountered him, Maro was talking in Hebrew to her companions. This jarred with Wheldon, who demanded she speak English. She replied that they were her compatriots, so naturally they spoke their language. Wheldon turned to a Welsh sergeant and said something she couldn't follow. Grinning, he told her that this was *his* language, which naturally he spoke with compatriots. Maro thought him wittier than the English, who relied too much on sarcasm when they were trying to be funny; relaxed at lectures and tutorials, though a stickler for protocol in the evenings, spick and span, wearing his medal-ribbons, talking non-stop.

The mood of the place was reformist and hopeful. Literature and history were taught as well as politics. Many of the people there would go on to be involved in teaching and the arts. Books and music had found new audiences in the war, and there was thought to be a sporting chance of retaining them. As for political reform, the first British Labour Government to have real power was in office, creating (it was hoped) a new and

---

[1] Haganah was a para-military organization, raised for defence, and not directly concerned with acts of terrorism.

worthier society. Jonah Jones, who came from a poor Tyneside family, says Mount Carmel was 'a hotbed of socialism, Zionism and Britishness', with strong echoes of old-fashioned adult education. 'We were all fairly strongly left-wing,' says Champion, 'including me.'

Huw Wheldon is assumed to have shared these sympathies, but there is reason to doubt it. Because he had a fine democratic manner and got on with everyone, some of his friends (and not only at Mount Carmel) think he was to the Left politically. In 1942, when Beveridge pronounced on the postwar social system, Wheldon wrote to Desmond Leeper:

> The Beveridge Report, writes my Father, is terrific – and I suppose it is. My immediate reaction, of course, is one of distaste for anything so unromantic, but I fancy that this is a purely middle-class attitude, only possible to one who has never known want or poverty or the ugliness of life.

He told his son that he voted Conservative in the 1945 election that put Labour in power. That would have made Wheldon practically an outcast at Mount Carmel, if it had been common knowledge.

Politics as such never interested him. A year earlier there had been talk of him standing as a Liberal in North Wales at the postwar elections. His father had been approached on his behalf. 'Alas, it is beyond my scope!' wrote Wheldon, obstinately blunt about himself. 'With my shop-window character & general salesmanship qualities I have no doubt that I should revel in the electioneering, and, as they say, knock them silly! . . . I would make vast promises, be gentle to children, charming to women, sell myself, in fact, with the utmost composure.' But beyond 'election antics' he had nothing to offer, and he was 'quite without political passion'.

Socialism aroused his suspicions, or so he told his father in March 1946. He was teaching 'a gang who think of Socialism as the only possible thing to believe in, and regard it simply as passing the baby to the Government. The way chaps quite coolly vote themselves into tyranny defeats me.' Whether he meant all socialism or only the non-British varieties isn't clear. Decades later, Jonah Jones and Judith Maro, among others, were to see Wheldon as having lapsed from a faith he never held. Celia insists that even when she first knew him, in 1939, he was 'strongly Conservative and monarchist'. It was easier to let people believe what they wanted to.

Wynn Wheldon followed his son's progress with vicarious pleasure. He had retired from Whitehall now, to live permanently in Prestatyn. The lecturing was 'first-rate work . . . I do not see why you should not follow it up when you get back – not immediately – but something will crop up.' That 'something' worried them both. Behind the scenes, the well-connected father was looking out for jobs for his son. The little roundabouts of nepotism turned briskly. Hints came about the post of principal, or 'warden', at Coleg Harlech, the Welsh adult-education college, opened in 1927 for miners and steelworkers. Sir Wynn sat on the council. So did Thomas Jones, C.H., who founded it. 'We have not got a sitting candidate to succeed B.B. at Coleg Harlech,' wrote Wheldon's father – 'a few, but not a distinguished field. I have headed them off considering you – quite right I hope – but if you were a possible candidate you wd stand more than a chance.' 'BB' was Ben (later Sir Ben) Bowen Thomas, Warden of Coleg Harlech since it opened. He was now doing the Whitehall job that Wynn had recently left. Round and round went the mutual interests.

Wheldon said no, half sounding as if he meant yes. He was full of doubts. In February his father had more ideas. He knew the adult educationist who founded the Army Bureau of Current Affairs and ran it through the war, W. E. Williams. 'I think you might do well to have a talk with [him] when you get back,' Wynn wrote to Huw. 'The Carnegie Trust are off on some new line in adult ed. wh. may be promising.' But Huw wanted a stage to occupy, not a niche in education.

In March he had a week's leave, which he spent at 'Dai's place', in Lebanon. His brother-in-law – Captain Rees and Mair were now married – was the MO at an old army station in the mountains with skiing facilities, used for rest and recreation. Life in London was still remote. Then, when he returned to Haifa, another of his father's letters was waiting:

> The Arts Council (CEMA that was) are advertising for a general officer for Wales at a £1000 a year – does it interest you, because I think you wd be considered if you choose to apply. I am not suggesting this, because I do not know what you have in mind, and though the job and the salary are both in some ways attractive, I can well imagine that it may not at all be your cup of tea, & of course from one point of view you know nothing of music, drama or the arts – though this does not really complete the picture. There are not many Welshmen who do.

This was the letter that launched Huw Wheldon on his career and led him to television. 'It tempts me,' he replied by return, 'I must admit. (The salary, of course, not least!) If it is possible to have a crack at it at this stage I should like to do so.'

He was understandably vague about the job and the organization. CEMA, the Council for the Encouragement of Music and the Arts, was set up as a private undertaking in 1940 to promote concerts and exhibitions as part of the war effort. The State supported it, and for the first time became a patron of the arts,[1] driven to it by the need to keep up morale and show Britain smiling in the face of danger. Half the population were hanging texts on their walls that said, 'There is no depression in this house. We are not interested in the possibilities of defeat. They do not exist.' CEMA was part of the same endeavour. Concerts, plays and exhibitions were staged throughout the war, often in factories, and their success made it seem briefly as if 'people's culture' for all, run on middle-class lines, might become a reality. In 1945 CEMA was turned into the Arts Council and given a royal charter; people's culture didn't last.

---

[1] The Pilgrim Trust, a charity established in 1930 by an American railway millionaire to conserve the 'British heritage', put up an initial £25,000, matched by Government money. Tom Jones was secretary to the trust. He became closely involved with CEMA and its development.

Wynn Wheldon knew most of those concerned, among them the educationist W. E. Williams and Tom Jones, the latter always in the background, advising and fixing. The Arts Council had a 'Welsh advisory committee', and Sir Wynn sat on it, alongside his friend Ben Bowen Thomas. A junior official did the administrative work from an office in Cardiff. By the middle of February 1946, headquarters in London thought it was time to appoint 'a high-powered officer for Wales'. The advisory committee met in London on March 28.

At least one local candidate was already being considered. But by this time Huw Wheldon was in action. He had written to 'The Secretary, Arts Council, Coleg Harlech', vaguely aware of an adult-education connection. His father told him that the letter had been forwarded to the correct address in London, adding, 'I do not know at all what they have in mind.' The letter was written three days after the advisory committee met.

However things were arranged, Huw Wheldon got the job. No doubt it would be insulting to say it was fixed. 'The old pals' act' sounds kinder. In practice the old pals were right. They had found someone who understood about Wales but was already impatient with it. He would enlarge the job to fit himself.

At Easter, late in April, before anything was formally decided, Wheldon was preparing to be interviewed as soon as he returned to Britain. He and his father agreed that the situation was 'very musical comedy'. 'I am frightened of biting off more than I can chew,' wrote Wheldon, and once again devalued himself in his blunt, bitter way:

> All I want anyway is a quiet life, goodness knows: and there's a lot of vanity in these things. I don't know what the job needs: but I fancy it is a kind of salesman racket, and as such I feel on good grounds. Selling Battle Drill and Political Theory & so on is always pretty easy for me. Sermons and salestalk are pretty much the same thing, and I'd feel no hypocrisy in selling what I take the Council to supply. However, we'll see. Leads nowhere, I imagine: but to be frank I don't give a damn about that.

*

He left Palestine and parted from the army he had become so fond of. Mary Glasgow, a former schools inspector who was secretary-general of the Arts Council, interviewed him. His appointment was announced on June 10, after a weekend of national victory celebrations that he spent in London, enjoying the evening fireworks with Mair and Richard Rees.[1] The *Manchester Guardian* had a paragraph about him, which began, 'Mr Huw Wheldon, employed before the war by Kent Education Committee,' but left out his MC, 'an action which I heartily approve', he told his father, although 'at the same time I feel a sneaking irritation, bubbles of vanity emerging from who knows what depths'. Sir Wynn had tactfully resigned from the Welsh committee a few days earlier.

When he sailed from Haifa, Wheldon left behind another equivocal relationship with a woman. This time it was a Jewish girl, Ruth, a British Army sergeant who was at Mount Carmel with Judith Maro, and became an instructor there. Ruth came from a family of Zionist pioneers. She had no strong political feelings and got on well with the British. At an early stage, Ruth says, she realized there was something odd about the relationship, that dinner by moonlight in Haifa might have been expected to lead to a goodnight kiss, if nothing more.

Like Celia, whose story she echoes, Ruth claims to have been sexually inexperienced: a fatal shortcoming, in her view, since it placed her in the category of women to be put on a pedestal. Their friendship in Palestine was close but platonic. When he left, she and Alan Champion got drunk together, so upset were they to see him go. Ruth was to follow Huw to London, and endure a relationship that ebbed and flowed over

---

[1] People still felt the glow of having won a war. *The Times* wrote on June 10: 'Many who stood upon the bridges at dusk as the lights shone on dome and tower and the rockets flared, with the Royal Barge made fast at Westminster, must have seen in the mind's eye the sweep of a greater flood than the Thames. In this day's solemnities ... the waters of victory were flowing down to become one with the tide of English history.'

seven years, 'playing a game that we would get married', as she sees it now, 'pretending that everything would be all right'.

None of Wheldon's letters to Ruth has survived, and the affair seems more remote than the one with Celia. It lacks, too, the categorizable air of a wartime romance between a lonely wife and a brave young officer. Wheldon was now a not quite so young administrator carving out a career. 'My birthday – 30!' he wrote on May 7, in a diary otherwise empty of anything but appointments and addresses.

How he came to terms with this dichotomy in his life, between the man of action and the halting lover – who, according to Ruth, for years found his only solace with 'little actresses and shopgirls' – is impossible to tell. Until the right woman and marriage solved the problem, Huw Wheldon's sexual life was muddled and unheroic, its nature unguessed at by those who knew him in later years, and probably by most of those who knew him then.

T. Mervyn Jones, who remembered Celia as part of a man-to-man yarn about a pretty woman having a fling, said that when Huw came to the Arts Council in Wales in 1946 he was the very devil with women; there were the dances at Llanwern Golf Club outside Newport, for example; tales could be told. This is manly stuff, and it may have been true, or had some truth in it, like Ruth's actresses and shopgirls. Beneath it, though, lies the other story, of a man with doubts about himself, sexual and otherwise. A group of letters written to his wife in 1959 shows that he read pornography and had fantasies about women, especially prostitutes. Sexual fantasies are so common as to be hardly worth recording. But Wheldon, the moral man who sought to follow in his father's footsteps, saw himself diminished by the humiliations of lust. 'You are the lilac tree in the middle of my mucky back-yard,' he wrote to his wife in 1959, 'and how could I smile and beam ever again if the lilac withered at a touch?' His fantasies grated on him. If they had not, they might have left no trace.

*

Wheldon went off to his new job with the grand-sounding title of 'director for Wales', determined to enjoy himself while encouraging the arts with modest sums of government money. After a few weeks at the Arts Council headquarters in London, he took lodgings in Cardiff, spent the first week in August at the National Eisteddfod, held that year at Mountain Ash, and toured Wales to make his face known. His method was orderly, logical, even military. 'I am moving off like General Montgomery on tours,' he told his father. The first batch of Arts Council stationery overprinted with his name gave him the style of 'Major Wheldon MC'. It is said he sent a telegram to headquarters saying 'Eschew Major, eschew MC.'

His engagements diary is a roll call of little places – a Cross Hands, a Brynmawr, a Mold, a Portmadoc. Wheldon believed that Wales, with its difficult geography (because of mountains) and its narrowed outlook (because of poverty), had no chance of aping the English cultural scene, based on London and a monied middle class with pretensions. What Wales, or at least Welsh-speaking Wales, did have was a strong native appetite for home-made arts. Music, drama and poetry flourished in the hands of enthusiastic amateurs, performing for their own communities. Wheldon wanted to encourage these pockets of culture, at the same time finding ways to proceed in the rougher climate of anglicized, industrial South Wales.

All this might have turned into an experiment in financing 'people's culture' of a more down-to-earth kind, although there is no evidence that Wheldon was ever conscious of seeing it in those terms. He took a practical view of the problems, beginning with his lack of resources: they were about sufficient for the island of Anglesey, he told his father. The question of 'metropolitan' culture hardly arose. Cinemas provided the only regular professional entertainment in the big towns (which are not very big by English standards) of the south. Cardiff liked to think of itself as a metropolis, but the claim was not taken seriously anywhere else. 'There was a fabulous period,' wrote Wheldon in a policy memorandum to London, 'when coal streamed like gold into the coastal ports and wealth and authority gathered in Cardiff [. . .] it looked, for a brief moment, as if there was being created in Cardiff the kind of environment in which the metropolitan arts could flourish and thrive. Those days are gone, and massive and flyblown restaurants tell their own sad tale.'

Partly by necessity, partly by Wheldon's design, the Arts Council in Wales thought small. Music clubs and touring players, together with visits by orchestras and an occasional exhibition of paintings, got the money. Wheldon had doubts about choral singing. T. Mervyn Jones said that his file on choirs was labelled 'B.T.B.H.O.', for 'Bawl their bloody heads off'.

The biggest matter Wheldon dealt with in his three years at Cardiff involved saying no to £20,000 that headquarters in London was offering, to set up a Welsh symphony orchestra. Wheldon disagreed with his committee. He thought a permanent orchestra would create a monster, always hungry for money. Mary Glasgow in London wanted Wales to have the £20,000 and did her best to outmanoeuvre him. But he persuaded the committee to reject the offer, so smartly that when she saw the minutes, Miss Glasgow took offence at the bald statement and asked, 'Was that all there was to it?' (Wheldon said he was afraid so.)

As a result of Wheldon's firmness, money was available for smaller enterprises. Visiting orchestras were paid for, a theatre in Swansea was subsidized, the struggling Welsh National Opera Company had £100 to help it survive.[1] Wheldon continued to operate with style, making friends and few enemies. Mary Glasgow apparently bore him no resentment. If he had arguments, he came out with them at the start. He gave the impression of being at ease with the world. Writing to Eric White, the number three in London, to say he hadn't finished some minutes, he

---

[1] In the long term, things turned out differently from the way Wheldon anticipated. A BBC orchestra became in effect the national orchestra, with Arts Council support. The Welsh National Opera has become famous. Audiences have changed. Cardiff is a sort of metropolis. Film companies work in the old Coal Exchange, and the restaurants are no longer flyblown.

said, 'It is now 12 Saturday, and I have decided to send everything to the devil, consign the entire Council to the everlasting flames, and push off until Monday morning.' Writing to his brother Tomos (June 1948) he said, 'As for me, unmarried unhonoured and unsung, pitiful creature, I carry on, slave to duty. In fact, I am as busy as a bird, and enjoying it.'

The letter to Tomos describes a European trip he has made, 'I am just returned from Istanbul and Rome. I thought it was time to quit this little parish for a few weeks, & as I both knew some people in Istanbul and also was able to fix up five rather bogus lectures (with beautiful expense agreements) I plumped for Turkey. It was superb . . .'

Wheldon's reason for making the trip was to see Ruth, the girl from Haifa; only the word 'unmarried' in the letter hints at that side of his life. She was now living in Istanbul, and he met her family. According to Ruth, he told her during the visit that he had gone there intending to ask her to marry him, but found that he couldn't do it. His manner was 'uncomfortable and uneasy', and he used a strange phrase to her, saying that 'we are both displaced persons'.

Ruth came to England later in the year, to be met by Wheldon at the railway station. She lived in a boarding house, earned money by teaching English to Turks, and French to the English, and enrolled for evening classes at the London School of Economics. When she realized that it would take her five years, at that rate, to get a degree, she began a full course at LSE. Huw tried to press money on her, she says, but she refused it.

By the spring of 1949, Wheldon himself was back in London for good. The Welsh interlude was over, not to be repeated. Ties of family and sentiment took him back, but he never lived or worked there again. What freed him from Wales was the Festival of Britain, that noble if eccentric gesture of hope for the future. Economic privation, the unkempt ruins of bombed cities, still framed everyday life at the end of the 1940s. A note from Wheldon in 1948, when Mary Glasgow was due to visit Cardiff and stay at one of its leading hotels, warned a secretary to 'remind her that the Angel does not supply towels'. The festival was like a day-dream of a different Britain, with modern design and technology at the main exhibition on South Bank, previously a marshy site near Waterloo Station, a fun-fair to end all fun-fairs at the Pleasure Gardens up-river in Battersea Park, and a summer of local festivals throughout the country.

Planning began in 1948. Despite efforts to make it a nationwide event, what the festival meant to most people was South Bank and the Pleasure Gardens. In all, it cost the Government £10 million. The Arts Council came in for only a small slice of this. It was given £400,000 and told to spend it on the cultural side of things. This boiled down to supporting the regional events and a two-month 'season of the arts' in London. By 1949 it was apparent that someone had to represent the Arts Council on the executive committee that ran the festival. Cleverly, the council looked among its regional directors, to show that the festival was not just a London affair. Wheldon was put on a short list, interviewed at the end of January 1949, and chosen within a week.

For the best part of three years, he was in the cultural swim, helping to spend the £400,000. His engagement diaries shift from West End theatre managers to the arts critics of newspapers, from the Dean of Westminster to the sculptor Barbara Hepworth. They are dense with committee meetings, lunches and railway journeys. He was forever travelling to Bath and Manchester and Swansea and Stratford, to meet festival organizers and mayors. Paul (now Sir Paul) Wright, who was the festival's director of public relations, says that 'Huw was never *doubtful* about anything.' Sometimes the two would act as minders for the director-general, Gerald Barry,[1] when he paid diplomatic visits to distant

---

[1] Gerald Barry, 1899–1968, journalist, wrote to the new Labour Government after the war to propose a 'trade and cultural exhibition' in 1951, the centenary of the Great Exhibition of 1851. Others had the same idea. Herbert Morrison, a prominent member of the Government, inherited the proposal in 1947. He saw it instead as a popular festival, and Barry, who had been editor of a London daily, the *News Chronicle*, was invited to run it.

cities. 'It was always Huw's party. "It's all right, D-G," he'd say. "All you have to do is tell them so-and-so. Money for old rope. Like falling off a log."'

Wright envied Wheldon's certainty and ease of manner as they toured the country, trying to enliven sleepy local authorities, or placate those who thought they were being left out. Communities seethed at what they took to be slights. (Wheldon's father, who ran the festival committee in Wales, left behind a file of these ancient complaints. Why were wives not being invited to the party in Cardiff Docks aboard the festival ship *Campania*? Why was Princess Margaret not visiting the Eisteddfod? Why was Barmouth having a warship but not Holyhead?) Anecdotes were added to Wheldon's stockpile. Arriving late at a Cheltenham hotel, the Arts Council party demanded supper, hoping for meat in those days when meat was still rationed. The local magic circle had been meeting; the magicians were just leaving. The party got rabbit.

Perhaps the festival succeeded as it did because confident, mainly youngish men were let loose to indulge themselves at public expense. Cheeribee was evident. On New Year's Eve 1950, Paul Wright and his wife gave a party at their house in Sussex. At midnight the french windows opened, and Wheldon, wearing a ballet skirt and a bra, was driven into the drawing-room, perched on top of a car. He was ringing a bell and throwing confetti. He announced he was the Spirit of 1951.

Celebrations began with a concert at the Royal Festival Hall, the only building on the South Bank site that survives from 1951. They played British music – Handel and Parry and Vaughan Williams and Elgar. That summer Wheldon attended dozens of plays and concerts where the Arts Council had lent a hand. The Old Vic had received a subsidy of £17,000, Sadler's Wells £18,000. Benjamin Britten had had an opera commissioned for £500, Saunders Lewis a play for £100.

On June 21 Wheldon was at Glyndebourne (£25,000, its first State subsidy) for a performance of Mozart's *Idomeneo*. It may have been on this occasion that Celia, who had reappeared on the scene, accompanied him – her name is in his diary several times during the first half of 1951, and also in 1952, when the diary shows he was at Glyndebourne again. She can't remember the year. After the war she and her husband had gone to Kenya. Bored, she went into partnership with a woman and began an antiques business in Nairobi ('the only antique shop between the Cape and Cairo'). Celia was back in England with her husband, who was on leave. By coincidence – another coincidence – she, or she and her husband, were at Covent Garden, and 'the first person I saw in the crush bar was Huw Wheldon'. The fires had faded; they resumed a more cautious friendship; he told her as he told the girl-friend at LSE, that if ever he married, she would have to be Welsh.

Ruth, too, is in the diaries, but not often. She says these brief mentions are the tip of an iceberg. Sometimes Huw was in a disappearing phase. He would keep out of her way for weeks or months; then, when they began to meet again, they saw each other constantly. Sometimes he would telephone her to say he had been to bed with a woman he didn't care for. One of his confessions, or fantasies, was about a girl he had met in the East End of London. For a short time they were engaged to be married. He had invited her to some function; 'it should have been you, not her,' he told Ruth gravely.

Wheldon's home in London since he began his festival job was Toynbee Hall, the East End 'settlement' in Whitechapel, established in Victorian times, where young men could live in a setting like that of a spartan university, and help the neighbouring poor with good works. This was the district where he met the girl. Ruth says she was a street-trader's daughter.

Toynbee Hall was an odd place for Wheldon to choose as lodgings, unless he was responding to the family tradition of 'service'. Under his father's influence he had helped at summer camps for unemployed youths in South Wales in the 1930s. The idea of social obligation appealed to him. It crops up in wartime letters, usually when writing to his father.

By 1949, when Wheldon became a resident, Toynbee Hall had

fallen on hard times. Between the wars its lectures and social services flourished under the warden, Jimmy Mallon.[1] After the war, Mallon was getting old, money was short, residents were scarce and the 'Welfare State', newly invented, was supposed to make charity superfluous. Wheldon was one of the first to go there when the place was refurbished after wartime damage. At thirty-three, he was well above the average age. Very likely it was his father who heard that Mallon was looking for recruits.

A plain bedroom, with breakfast and evening meal, and common-room facilities, cost about four pounds a week, a significant sum for a man just down from university, cheap for someone like Wheldon, earning eleven hundred a year. Cliff Tucker, a fellow resident, and a lifelong supporter of Toynbee Hall, says that 'to be quite honest, Huw made little or no contribution – I'm not criticizing, he wasn't alone. And he was busy.' The other residents elected him to the Toynbee Hall council. He was a notable organizer of Christmas parties. That was about it. What Tucker remembers is how like an actor he was – standing against the handsome fireplace of the refectory after dinner, under a portrait of the founders, Samuel and Henrietta Barnett, holding forth on this or that. Tucker remembers hearing about the shepherd that Wheldon met on wartime manoeuvres and spoke Welsh to.

Another contemporary resident was a medical student, now a doctor. He didn't do much in the way of good works, either. He recalls two things about Wheldon. One is the way he could demolish opponents in an argument. The other is 'an odd girl friend' who 'wasn't quite what you'd have expected'. She was working-class, an East Ender. 'Huw had some association with her. It surprised me.' It sounds like the woman Ruth heard about.

*

---

[1] James Mallon, 1874–1961, 'the most popular man east of Aldgate Pump', was a leading trade unionist before he went to Toynbee.

As the Festival of Britain came to an end, Wheldon told more than one person that he was worried about the future. Cliff Tucker heard him say it. So did John Drummond, who bumped into him that summer, and thought he was being asked if he had anything up his sleeve. Fear of unemployment had nothing to do with it. Wheldon was still Welsh director of the Arts Council; someone had been standing in for him, and his old job was waiting. But he had no intention of turning his back on London, or, if possible, on excitement. The post of secretary to King's College, London, in which he was briefly interested, promised little in the way of cheeribee. A reference from Bangor praised his 'trained administrative mind'. But Wheldon said he 'wanted to be one of the promising people the Arts Council was talking about, rather than one of the talkers'.

The BBC, 'glamorous without being silly', took his fancy. As a child he had gone to the studios to see his father broadcast. In his spare time at the Arts Council he gave radio talks and 'enjoyed them like anything'. Some were about the festival ('A nation of shopkeepers is no less a nation of shopkeepers by being a nation of poets and singers and actors as well,' he said in the European service. 'The taunt and the boast are probably equally true'). But radio was insufficiently exciting. Wheldon acquired a television set in 1951 and stared at it for hours to learn what it was about.

The Wheldons had BBC connections. Huw had a distant cousin by marriage, Major W. Gladstone Murray, a broadcasting figure of the 1930s, once thought of as a successor to John Reith. The Wheldons used to visit him in St John's Wood; though by now Murray had left the scene. Huw's father was known in BBC circles. He sat on advisory committees. He knew William Haley,[1] the director-general till 1952, and Ian Jacob,[2] the one who came next. Wynn Wheldon would not have needed to say

[1] Sir William Haley, 1901–87, was BBC director-general 1944–52. He left to be editor of *The Times*.
[2] Lieut.-Gen. Sir Ian Jacob, b. 1899, a professional soldier, was director-general of the BBC, 1952–60.

anything, and it is unlikely that he did; but the name 'Wheldon' was known.

Perhaps the significant connection was with George Barnes,[1] the director of television. Before his appointment to television in 1950, Barnes had been radio's 'director of the spoken word', a title from the very entrails of the old BBC. He had also been the first head of the Third Programme in 1946 – a civilized man, too civilized for some, who gave the impression of being self-conscious about culture and the need to have it in good supply. Barnes knew W. E. Williams who knew Wynn Wheldon. Williams, who became secretary-general of the Arts Council in 1951, had probably played a part in Huw's appointment as Welsh director. In 1976, when Huw was knighted, Williams wrote to tell (or remind) him how he, Williams, had told Barnes in 1951 to get Huw into the BBC because he needed a larger pool than the Arts Council to swim in.

Wheldon's account in a BBC interview of the 1980s was more straightforward:

> I had a hell of a job, you know. I went to see these birds and they said, 'You *must* join us.' You know what they're like, ghastly BBC people. 'You're *just* the chap we need.' That was as far as it went. Nothing actually *happened*. My father knew a lot of people. He'd mentioned me and so on. But it made no difference. I put in for a job as a producer but I didn't get it because they said I hadn't had enough experience. Well, I hadn't had *any*. So eventually I had to go before one of those boards. An old friend of mine called Hugh Burnett, who worked for the BBC, did a great cartoon many years ago of a BBC board behind a table. A candidate had just left, and one of them was leaning over to the others, saying, 'I think we made a very good impression on that candidate.' That's the kind of board I attended. Anyway, I got a job on the press side, with the publicity people, which I didn't want *at all*.

---

[1] Sir George Barnes, 1904–60, joined the BBC in 1935, and was director of television 1950–56.

Aged thirty-five, he found it all 'really rather humiliating'. But it was the job he had applied for, on October 1 1951, having been advised it was his only chance of entering television. What really happened was that he went to see Barnes, who told him to accept the post because it would get him into the BBC, and agreed that he could change jobs after a period – Wheldon said it was one and a half years, in fact it was two and a half. Thus he arrived in television as a man of promise, not least because his name was 'Wheldon'. The Arts Council said goodbye with regret. On January 4 1952 he reported for duty to the television studios at Alexandra Palace.

CHAPTER FIVE

Days of Innocence

MANY OF THE bright young names of future television were recruited in the early 1950s, already captured by intimations of glamour. Wheldon, not all that young, had no doubt it was the place to be. Yet looking back on it now, the BBC's service has an insipid look. Neither television nor its small audience had begun to teach one another the hard lessons of what was possible and desirable.

The BBC lacked the will to take its own television service seriously. Radio was regarded as the essence of broadcasting. Only a few years earlier, the war had brought it to maturity. Television was an upstart, slightly impure. Its development went ahead without enthusiasm. Official policy was to keep all television payments, whether to unions or performers, as low as possible, lest radio suffer. So the service, run from an inconvenient outpost on a hill in north London, was starved of money and quietly deplored by its elders and betters from their many-chambered mansion of Broadcasting House.

They were days of innocence. There were fears inside the BBC that the dangerous trivia of pictures would undermine literacy; whether or not this proposition ever had any truth, it was unwise for a television service to heed it. William Haley, who was still director-general when Wheldon joined the BBC, once gave a dinner party for his senior television staff and told them that if they were doing their jobs properly people would be watching less, not more.

George Barnes, in charge of the television service, was equally unhelpful. He said, 'You can't put thought on television.' It was generally assumed at Alexandra Palace that he had been sent over to restrain the scallywags. His manners were charming, and he had been known to attend meetings in a friendly old suit with an elbow out. Wheldon may have been his protégé. But he perceived that the director was contemptuous of his own service, seeing it, as Wheldon observed, as 'a kind of *Daily Mirror*'.

Part of the BBC's appeal to Wheldon before he went there was its standing as an institution. He had a streak of reverence for 'greatness', whether in men or organizations. It was disappointing to find the new service headed by duds, well-meaning but ineffectual – as he recalled them, they were ageing, dignified, nice, 'magnificently honourable'; and not very keen on television.

Wheldon, though, was diplomatic and got on with people. He fitted in. Since Reith's time, the BBC's ideal recruit had been a man who already possessed a professional qualification, or the self-confidence that went with one. Wheldon not only had his war service and decoration, he now had an OBE for his work at the Festival of Britain. His woman friend from LSE days, H., wrote to congratulate him, and tell him about the birth of her son. 'I am now in this TV thing, which is a jungle,' he wrote back (January 5 1952), adding that 'I have no idea what I'm doing. I have a few chaps to make up a department, but so far I have avoided them like the plague.'

In later years he preferred not to talk at all about his time in publicity. Did he fear that Wheldon the publicist sounded too much like Wheldon the salesman, as he had called himself to his father? The job was not as humble as all that. The television service was already simmering with talent, anxious to be known about and taken seriously. Fleet Street had always found broadcasting a good source of copy and general mischief. Television promised new treats. As usual, publicists had to distinguish between short-term news and long-term opinion. An internal memo Wheldon wrote after he had been there a year feared that the small number of people who made up 'informed opinion' had no time to watch television, and so were ignorant of its problems and its future. They needed to be got at and enlightened. This meant encouraging 'responsible articles in responsible journals', which in turn meant a larger staff for Wheldon's office, which was the point of the memo.

In matters of policy, Wheldon dealt with Barnes, the director, and Cecil McGivern, the controller of programmes. McGivern was not in the defeatist mould of Barnes, who once referred to him, in Wheldon's presence, as 'that maniac McGivern'. He brought to television a tormented nature (Wheldon called him a 'free-thinking Roman Catholic') and a devotion to his job of devising a schedule with scarce resources. McGivern was no fonder of Barnes than Barnes was of him. The director liked to have windows open. McGivern went to meetings wearing his hat and coat.

In those days, what later became the part science, part black art of 'programme planning' was a hand-to-mouth affair, looking barely a month ahead. 'The public' was still small enough to have recognizable features. A memo that reached Wheldon via McGivern (December 4 1952) began:

> *Letters from Viewers.* Over 100 letters came in from Shift Workers complaining that they could not see 'Victory at Sea' and requesting afternoon showings, and this has been arranged to start in 1953. An example of Viewers' keenness is that a number spotted an incorrect calendar, a prop in a play 'Island of Cipango', and the error was rectified in time for the repeat.

The simpler service of the time was entirely controlled by McGivern. Colleagues marvelled at the length of his working day; some thought he never went home. At weekends he would still be there, alone in his office, a faint smell of drink on his breath. He and Wheldon once discussed Lourdes in a pub. Wheldon, who had been there, remarked that even as a Presbyterian, one had to be aware that there *might* have been a miracle. McGivern looked worried and said he would never go to Lourdes. Wheldon asked why not. 'What would happen if I saw a miracle?' demanded McGivern. 'What do I do then? Buy a pair of sandals and desert my wife?' It was not a joke.

Wheldon liked him but felt the edge of his tongue more than once. Later on it was Wheldon who kept people at work till after midnight if it suited him. In 1953, McGivern saw him as the idle fellow, and reprimanded him accordingly.

A couple of the memos survive. The first is dated July 20, headed 'Subject: SUNDAY NIGHT, JULY 19: 8.50 p.m.', and says:

> I have just phoned your address as I wanted you in a hurry. A rather bored voice told me that (a) you were away for the week end (b) you might be back later. While I was asking if I might leave a message, the phone was hung up.
>
> I envy anybody the ability to go away for the week end and would not deny him this period privilege. If, however, he works in the Television Service and is any sort of a senior official, or an aspiring senior official, he must make better arrangements than bored voices.
>
> All the above just in case you are interested.

The second memo, written the following Monday, was even less cordial:

> Because of the Korean Truce and the necessity to alter our programmes considerably, I wanted you urgently this morning. By 10.20 you had not arrived.
>
> This is the fourth time you were not available when I wanted you urgently. I think perhaps we had better get together on this matter.

Most of the programmes that Wheldon had to publicize were modest enough. A day's viewing on Monday December 7 1953 began at 3.15 in the afternoon with an old comedy movie. An hour later the service shut down, restarting at five o'clock for forty minutes of children's television, after which the screens went blank again until the weather chart and *Newsreel* at 7.55. Then came four main programmes: *Blindness*, a documentary; *Shop Window*, subtitled *a display of new television ideas and personalities*; an outside broadcast from wine vaults in Bristol, *Wines for Christmas*; finally, at 10.15, a BBC film about the artist Graham Sutherland. *News* (sound only) at 10.45 ended the evening. Television news as such had not been invented.

But television was on the move, and had been since earlier in the year, when the coronation of Elizabeth II was seen by an audience that was guessed to have been twenty million, most of them watching on other people's sets. At a press conference afterwards, when it was announced that an overwhelming percentage had enjoyed what they saw, a stony-hearted reporter asked what it was that the others hadn't enjoyed. Wheldon retaliated with the witticism attributed to Hilaire Belloc, 'If Christ came back to earth, you'd always get someone saying, "There he goes again, walking on the water".'

Already Wheldon was a bit of a turn in the television service, with his brisk self-assurance and an aggressive good humour that fell just short of frivolity. To the amusement of some of his colleagues, and the envy of others, the publicity officer, instead of being content with the role of anonymous servant, had become a television performer at the same time. After the Conker King programme in October 1952, Freda Lingstrom hired him as a presenter, and he led a double life. One Wheldon sometimes wore a bowler hat, in those days still the badge of civil servants and bank managers. The other appeared regularly on the screen, a lanky figure, stooping to talk to children and looking as if he might topple over any minute, a joke uncle bursting with boyish enthusiasm who wants to be allowed to play with the model railway.

His vehicle was a late-afternoon programme, called at first *It's All Yours* and then *All Your Own*, where children sang, played instruments and showed off their hobbies. Novelty was easily come by in early television, and *All Your Own* was often repeated for adult viewers in the evening. The way Wheldon remembered it, he avoided a 'procession of precocity', and insisted that every programme include a failure, a disaster or a confession of some kind: the girl who ruined a trumpet solo, the boy who made a model boat but had to admit it sank. Little of *All Your Own* is left in the archives. One fragment records an episode that went through the mill of Wheldon's memory and came out as the tale of a boy who laboured for years to build a harpsichord, which he was to play in the studio. Wheldon leaned on the instrument and it collapsed in ruins. 'What are you going to build next?' he asked, and the wretched boy said, 'Another harpsichord.' In the recording, Wheldon slaps his hand on the instrument, produces a small cracking noise, and mutters 'Oh hell, now I've leaned down on something.' The boy plays on.

Wheldon worked diligently behind the scenes, helping to select performers, talking to parents, preparing the interviews. One of the producers was Cliff Michelmore, still some years from fame, whose job it was to restrain Wheldon from lashing out on sandwiches and cake. 'We have received a complaint from the Hotel Meurice,' he wrote. Ten extra people had tucked in, crying 'The BBC will pay!' This wouldn't do. Wheldon sent the memo back with 'OK, OK, I'll pay them next Saturday!' scrawled in red.

His performances have a hint of self-caricature. A pair of bird-watching schoolgirls (referred to as 'you two chaps') tell him about plovers. 'Do you have lapwings around there?' he wants to know. They tell him it's the same bird. Astonishment fills the earnest face. 'Lapwings and plovers are the same thing? Well, you *have* taken me by surprise! You see, I'm an old ignoramus, that's my trouble. That's my trouble.'

But had he read a bird book beforehand, and was the astonishment one of his effects? Certainly he liked to put on an act. People remember self-conscious gestures. Michael Gill, who became a television producer, saw him at a cocktail party, around the mid-1950s, lying on the carpet with a cap over his face, ostentatiously pretending to be asleep. George Campey, who became head of publicity, remembers how Wheldon, visiting his flat one evening, declined an offer to drive him home. 'No, no,' said Wheldon, 'I shall take a taximeter cab.' Campey murmured that taxis cost money. 'Money?' cried Wheldon, 'what's money?' He took out a ten-shilling note and ripped it up. Campey was fond of him. But 'was he thinking that one day, George can tell that to my biographer?'

By January 1954, Wheldon was into his third year as publicity officer, and seemed no nearer a job in television production. *All Your Own* remained an attractive sideline. It earned him money as well as celebrity, thanks to a punctilious rule that let BBC employees be paid for work not connected with the post they were engaged to fill. Each appearance was worth fifteen guineas, the archaic form in which the BBC went on paying fees until long after everyone else. By this means Wheldon collected a couple of hundred pounds a year. But the longer he remained on the publicity staff, the greater the danger that he would be promoted in a branch he didn't care for.

Meanwhile BBC television faced an upheaval. By 1954 the case for a rival network paid for with advertising had been argued and won by the Conservative Government. Independent television, or 'commercial' television as the BBC insisted on calling it, was to start in 1955. Publicists were in demand to help make the BBC's case. A few years later Wheldon was pressed to make a television career of public relations and refused. Programmes were like battles: they were where the glory could be found. By 1954 the BBC's programmes were improving. The first *Zoo Quest*, made by a young David Attenborough, was in the offing. *Dixon of Dock Green* and *Sooty* were not far away. Money was trickling through. 'The Competitor' (the other name for ITV) was coming.

In July, two vacancies for producers in the television talks department were advertised. Wheldon applied for the more senior post and secured it, with a salary of £1,400 a year, plus a further £200 thrown in to cover the work for *All Your Own* that he went on doing. Probably he had George Barnes to thank. The promise of an apprenticeship that wouldn't last too long could have been made only with the intention of finding him something better when the moment arrived. For the last time the influence of his father, ghostly and indirect, may have helped him. Thereafter it meant nothing.

At once he was thrown into hectic programme-making, based at Lime Grove, the old Rank film studios at Shepherd's Bush, in west London. He was one of a dozen or so producers in Talks, a misleadingly titled department. A discussion was a Talk; so was a documentary. Leonard Miall ran the department, an honourable man, but its storm-centre was the assistant head, an actor's widow called Grace Wyndham Goldie, a clever tyrant with a flair for politics and political programmes. People remember her as a compact lady with a smart handbag, talking about television as 'the medium of the actual', making dissidents quake; to one participant, 'the Stalin of broadcasting'. She is said to have used her elbow to knock Miall's papers on the floor, hoping to confuse him. Programmes about current affairs were her speciality, among them *Panorama*. Her protégés went far, not always happily. Her domain was probably the most creative in television, and 'Grace's young men', among them Donald Baverstock[1] and Michael Peacock,[2] were marked out for progress.

Wheldon was not one of her acolytes. He was older and as a rule had no time for women in television, though he had to acknowledge her talents. 'Ruthless but very feminine' was his view of Goldie, and his approach was mildly flirtatious; she had beautiful legs, and a delight in power that was itself a sort of sensuality.

Goldie's empire in current affairs was growing. Wheldon stood on the edge of it. He did programmes as they came off the shelf. *Facts and Figures* was a ten-minute spot of diagrams and graphics, an attempt to make information palatable. 'Chart 2,'

---

[1] Donald Baverstock, b. 1924, was in BBC radio before joining television in 1954. He began the *Tonight* programme and rose in the hierarchy, before leaving the BBC in unhappy circumstances.
[2] Michael Peacock, b. 1929, joined the BBC in 1952 and rose to be the controller of BBC 1 before leaving for richer pastures.

says a Wheldon memo, 'Defence expenditure in terms of personal tax (e.g. eight High Court Judges have bought a tank between them in the last four years).' *Asian Club* was Asians in a studio with a guest. *Press Conference*, one of Goldie's serious interests, put a public figure up against four journalists; Wheldon handled it occasionally, learning the craft of studio direction as he went along. As he admitted, he had no apparent qualification for a producer's job. Michael Peacock had been surprised that he got it in the first place: 'After seeing him in *All Your Own*, we took him to be rather lightweight.'

But Wheldon was good at managing situations. He was one of life's enablers. An early success concerned a programme to celebrate the eightieth birthday of Winston Churchill, who was still clinging to office as Prime Minister, in November 1954. Goldie and Baverstock had set it up, against opposition from the director-general – now Ian Jacob – who thought it would sound too much like an obituary; Churchill was enfeebled, his powers failing. The programme was planned around the presence of Churchill, at home in Downing Street[1] surrounded by his family, while friends on film or in the studio spoke their tributes; among them was Lord Ismay, one of his generals. Wheldon was in charge of the Downing Street end, reporting on whether the cameras would be able to watch Churchill watching the television set. Goldie planned three endings, depending on whether Churchill neither watched nor spoke, or was seen watching but remained silent, or was seen and said something. A television set had to be supplied. Wheldon stood by, in his element:

> Presently his family turned up, Duncan Sandys and daughters and people, and Randolph. But no sign of the great man. And then just before the programme started, he came in with his wife. I'd been told that he looked old, but I had simply not been prepared for the sight of this pterodactyl coming very slowly into the room. He looked about eight thousand years old, incredibly

---

[1] For technical reasons they were not at No. 10 but next door at No. 11.

old, and his skin was like yellow leather. He shuffled to his chair, sat in the wrong one I need hardly say, and paid no attention to his children, all of whom said 'Hello' – paid no attention to them at all. Still less to me, he didn't see me. The News was on, and near the chair was a camera, looking at him. He looked at the News and in a very broken, switched-off, childish voice, he said, 'Is this the programme?'

And in a reverential bellow, because it was clear to me that you had to speak very loudly to get at the old thing at all, I said, 'No, this is the News. The programme,' I said, 'will follow in a minute, and Lord Ismay will be there in Shepherd's Bush talking to you.' He said, 'Ismay is in Paris.' And I said, 'No, Ismay has come over especially for this programme.' Then I said, 'You'll be here watching the programme, and when at the end they wish you God speed and best wishes, if you want to respond in any way, all you have to do is to look into the camera over there, and you can speak directly to them, and I will give you a signal for doing that if you like.' To which he paid no attention, none. So I was very apprehensive. I went round the back of the chair to Clemmie [Lady Churchill] and said, 'Do you think he'll say anything?' And she said, 'It's difficult to say. He's very tired.'

I rang Grace up in the studio and said I had no idea what was going to happen – he looked like an old tortoise – and it wasn't at all clear to me that he would speak. Anyway, the programme took place, and he betrayed no emotion of any kind, of pleasure or displeasure – except that whenever Clemmie was mentioned he looked slightly in her direction, but whether to say 'How nice', or alternatively 'Why should that be said?', it was impossible to draw any conclusion.

The programme came to an end, and I was just preparing to signal Churchill towards the camera, Ismay having said 'So best wishes for the future, dear Winston,' or words to that effect, when I looked towards the great man. He was sitting up in his chair and his eyes were fixed on me, and it was exactly as if I'd come round a bend in a Pembrokeshire hedgerow in 1934 in one of those little Austins, and run into a gigantic red lorry. It was like running into searchlights full on. In some curious way he appeared to have switched on. I nervously signalled him towards the camera, and he then moved his entire chair so that he was facing it, and instantly spoke in this great diapason, 'I have been delighted' and so on, 'This remarkable . . .' and a great sonorous sentence came out, Gibbonesque, very good, very much to the point, extremely rounded, very masculine, very virile, very Churchillian. So he came to the end of his peroration and looked away from the camera to me, glared at me and said 'Good night!'

Then I heard the trumpets blowing, so I knew we were off old Churchill. I rushed up to him, and so did his family, and everybody said, 'You were wonderful,' 'You were marvellous,' all this sort of thing, but he paid no attention, he'd switched off again. He said to his wife, 'I hadn't had time to prepare,' and she said, 'You were very good, Winston.' He said, 'But I hadn't had time.' He shuffled to the door, and then did look round for a moment at his family – not at me, he never paid any attention to me from beginning to end – and he switched on for a minute. 'I'm going to have a bath,' he said, and pushed off.

Soon after this, Wheldon produced a *Press Conference* where the guest was the American actor Orson Welles, the only person in the entertainment business who took the wind out of his sails. Welles had a casual air of largeness that put him, for Wheldon, in the same unlikely bracket as Lloyd George, a comparison that Wheldon was heard to make. Having planned the *Press Conference* for an ordinary mortal, he was mortified to find it inadequate for the occasion, and wrote to tell his father so. The correspondence between father and son was sparse after the war, and by now it had almost come to an end. But this letter (January 15 1955) has the characteristic note of confession:

I put Orson Welles on a programme last night, Friday. He led me a terrific dance, & the programme was (from my point of view) a flop. But he impressed me enormously. He had to come from Paris; & I expected him in London on Tuesday. He postponed his journey five times. We re-arranged things as many times. By Friday lunchtime, he still had not arrived. No one in Paris had any idea where he was, and I was anxiety personified. He finally turned up at a London Club at 4, having arrived at Victoria & slipped past several people who were meeting each train. He rang me, & I met him at 4.30. I stayed with him till 7, & he drank whisky (& so did I) steadily & quietly. I was enchanted by him, but afraid of the unreliability I knew attached to him, & of the whisky.

I left for the studios at 7, feeling the effects of the whisky; & leaving him on his way to take a bath. I had carefully chosen a panel of four people who were accustomed to the wide cosmopolitan ways of stars & theatrical eccentrics. We had sorted out questions which seemed appropriate. In the event, he turned up, on the minute; & within two minutes of the start of the programme I knew I had made a first-rate error. I had forgotten that, theatricality or no, unreliability or no, he was a big man. The panel was wrong. The questions (the only ones of which they were capable) were wrong. Altogether, I felt that the whole structure of my programme – the placing of cameras, the technical as well as the purely programmatic approach – was simply a cheap, second-rate, second-hand progression of intentions, shown up vividly as such by what by now I was recognizing as a really outstanding man, a singular & a great person, whose stature would not respond to the twittering tempo of what I had set up. I think the programme itself was probably quite interesting – but for me it was one of the most depressing experiences of my entire life. I was doing less than justice, a shoddy *in*justice in fact, to one of the most remarkable people I have ever met. As you can see, I was most moved by the whole business.

Wheldon's deference towards the actor, which lasted for years, was remarked on by colleagues. Ken Russell, the film director, thought he debased himself unnecessarily. Wheldon went on to produce a series called *Orson Welles's Sketch Book* in 1955. He had a story about Welles at rehearsal, finding he had no ink for the sketches he used in the programme, throwing down his pen in irritation. Wheldon left the control gallery to see what was wrong. By the time he reached the set, Welles had disappeared, having told a stagehand he was off to Paris. This turned out to be true.

It may be that the mixture of unreliability and talent was part of the attraction: forbidden fruits, beyond the reach of an upright Welshman. The time came when Orson Welles offered him a job as his European manager. Wheldon refused, in one version because he was afraid he would never be paid; in another, reported by Melvyn Bragg, because 'Orson would have eaten me up'.

Wheldon spent his time in 1955 hopping from programme to programme, often having two or three on the go at once. Gilbert Harding, an early 'television personality' whose speciality was being rude, was passed to Wheldon with the request that he develop an investigative series. A simple formula was worked out. A couple of 'investigators' would bone up on questions or complaints sent in by viewers, dealing with the 'interesting things' of popular journalism as Lord Northcliffe invented it seventy years earlier: assorted topics such as queues for hospital treatment, railway sandwiches and the sparrow population of Great Britain. Harding would present answers and comments. Like many series, it was devised as a way of finding work for someone with an expensive contract that was based on an earlier success: in Harding's case, the long-running panel game *What's My Line?* His private company, Gilbert Harding (Exploitation) Ltd, was guaranteed a minimum of £7,000 a year, big money for the time.

Six programmes were made, with the title *Harding Finds Out.* 'I did my very best. They went from bad to worse,' said Wheldon. After each transmission he waited for colleagues to make some comment, but next morning it would be 'Hello, Huw' from all quarters – 'all you could hear was the programme not being mentioned'. The time for consumer journalism, which this tended towards, was not ripe. 'I shall be glad when this series is over,' wrote Cecil McGivern. 'It should be called "Harding Mutters".'

Wheldon looked back on it as a salutary experience – 'one learned how easy it was to fail, and how terrible it was, too' – but it was not the only programme he found trying. *Is This Your Problem?*, which he was saddled with in the same year, embodied another idea whose time had not yet come, the airing of private dilemmas in front of millions. Commercial television was to begin in September 1955, and this was one of the BBC's responses. 'Controller of programmes is very anxious that autumn programmes should be designed to catch and hold audiences,' wrote Miall. A series about personal problems had been decided on by March, hedged around with warnings about 'exhibitionism' and the 'violation of personal privacy'. Wheldon was chosen to produce it, the format having been suggested already by the presenters. These were Edgar Lustgarten, a writer and broadcaster who was a barrister by training, and his sidekick Edana Romney, an actress.

Each programme dealt with three or four people. Lustgarten did most of the talking, outlining a case-history and then questioning the person with the problem, who sat in a winged armchair, invisible except for an occasional shot of hands. Finally a panel of three 'experts' gave their views. It was Wheldon's responsibility to see that the programme was sober and clinical. Stage props hinted at the consulting room or headmaster's study: three framed prints, two ornaments, one leather desk-blotter, two dozen leather-bound books, oak bookends and bowl of fresh flowers. Lustgarten had a cold-fish manner and a bow tie, and was fond of phrases like 'beyond a peradventure'. The experts were extremely sober, typically a doctor, a clergyman and a magistrate, but from the start the series was suspected of titillation. Jacob ruled that it was 'experimental', which meant it was under permanent threat. The Religious Broadcasting Department, which carried more clout in those days, was anxious about the 'apparent insincerity' of the presentation and the 'exploitation of human emotion'.

In 1955, the prevailing standard was still a proper reticence, so perceived, about personal intimacies in general, and sexual ones in particular. The fury that was to descend on television later came from those whose conservative values had survived the war more or less unscathed, and expected reticence to go on for ever. Wheldon himself was deeply involved in *Is This Your Problem?* Lustgarten troubled him; he thought his approach meretricious. The BBC naturally stood for modesty across the board. Artificial insemination had been complained of in a science film in 1952. A year before *Is This Your Problem?*, McGivern had occasion to pronounce on male dancers in tights:

> The DG has received a very strong letter of protest (with a copy to the Home Secretary and the Archbishop of Canterbury) on the embarrassment of male dancers in ballet.
>
> I have drafted a reply but it is an almost impossible charge to refute. The fact is that to certain people and their families (and they include quite intelligent and ordinary people) the male body in tights, especially white tights, is quite shocking.
>
> I have raised this matter before and I must insist that great care is taken. The dressing of male dancers *must* be supervised and producers of ballet must shoot male dancers so dressed in such a way that the risk of offence is minimized.

Against such a background, the problems that Lustgarten and the panel dealt with were chosen with caution: a father whose son kept embezzling, a wife with a jealous spouse, an unmarried mother in her thirties who wanted to get a husband. But the reticence of the times was against it. However hard the panel tried, the genteel setting somehow trivialized the skeletons that emerged from cupboards.

Wheldon agonized over the series. The few surviving memos don't make clear exactly what he is agonizing about. In one of them (October 18 1955) he quotes a letter from his father, who had just seen the programme for the first time: 'nothing very excruciating I thought – do not like the young woman [Edana Romney], neither does your Mother, who is a better judge of those things. The medico was sensible and the parson decent. The others are what they are, I fancy [. . .] but they do not know this and never will!'

Cases involving people 'in any way psychotic or abnormal' were unwelcome to Wheldon, and there are hints of conflict on this score with Lustgarten. By the spring of 1956, Wheldon was talking about 'distortion' in the way problems were presented, and asking to be taken off the series.

The producer who inherited it was Hugh Burnett, who created an influential series of the 1950s, the *Face to Face* interviews by John Freeman. Burnett is an ascetic and an iconoclast who broods over his memories of television with a certain bitter amusement. He remembers the Lustgarten programmes as 'hilarious and very BBC', and Wheldon as being 'not the sort of man to tune in to those chaotic situations. Why he didn't like it, I don't know. Perhaps he wasn't interested in people's quirks and madnesses.'

As a television producer, Wheldon was not much concerned with that side of human nature. He liked positive attitudes. When Grace Wyndham Goldie wanted a programme about the centenary of the Victoria Cross, she chose Wheldon to make it, and his documentary *For Valour* went out on January 29 1956.

Wheldon liked to be seen as a plain man, with no nonsense. *TV Mirror*, a weekly magazine, put him on the cover, in colour – tweed jacket, cleft chin, intense eyes – on December 17 1955. The article inside was headed 'From Chapel to Cocktails'. Asked for the story of his life, he had replied with 'Well . . . nothing to tell. I'm a very straightforward chap.' But he was hardly that.

When Huw Wheldon joined the BBC in 1952, he was still living at Toynbee Hall. That spring he and two other residents moved to a flat in Upper Phillimore Gardens, an agreeable neighbourhood off Kensington High Street, sharing the costs. The warden wrote Wheldon a sharp letter complaining that three of them should have deserted at once.

People remember Wheldon as the single man at social engagements. He liked male company, a 'man's man' who kept his love life quiet, if he had one at all. No one could have been more sociable. Bob Sheridan, a fellow officer in the war, went with him on what was meant to be a camping holiday in Switzerland, probably in 1952 or 1953. Before pitching the tent on their first night, he called on the farmer, who ended up by insisting they sleep at the farmhouse. The same thing happened at other places; they didn't unpack their equipment.

Back in London, he gave a 'cheese fondue' party at Phillimore Gardens, having been introduced while on holiday to the delights of molten Gruyère, crisp bread and swigs of kirsch. Using rationed Cheddar, English bread and insufficient heat, the dish was somewhat different. But accompanied by cheeribee and Huw's insistence that his version was a refinement of the stuff served in Switzerland, its deficiencies were overlooked. Celia, visiting London from Kenya, went to the flat, and thought him 'very unhappy in his home-life, such as it was'. He seemed content enough at the BBC, though unsure about his future in it. Celia had passed into the category of 'old friend'.

Only now and then was he seen in female company. Sandy Smith, another 6th Airborne friend, was to dine at Wheldon's club, the Savile. They met earlier in the evening at a pub in Shepherd's Market, the corner of Mayfair where prostitutes flourished. Wheldon was with an attractive woman. When she went to powder her nose, Wheldon told Smith, 'She's only a tart.'

He and Ruth, the girl from Haifa, were still conducting their uneven affair; the only detailed evidence is hers, together with entries in his engagement diaries. But with Celia's story in mind, Ruth's account of his dilatory ways sounds likely enough. After coming to Britain and enrolling at the London School of Economics, she returned to Turkey for a year, probably 1951–2, because, in her words, in London she was short of money, refused to take any from Wheldon, and 'nearly starved'. When she returned, she resumed her studies at LSE, and saw Wheldon, when he was not avoiding her. 'He would sleep with women whom he considered were of the easily available kind,' she says. 'Little ballerinas – little actresses.' He claimed to have got engaged for a second time.

The suggestion that some of this may have been fantasy on Wheldon's part, or a means of keeping her at arm's length, doesn't appeal to Ruth. When Huw telephoned to say, 'I thought I would just call and tell you I spent the night with an actress,' she took it to be one of the plain statements he was capable of.

They went away for weekends, which were all negative in a sexual way except for one occasion, at a seaside resort whose name she has forgotten, where 'afterwards he was suicidal. I had to get him out of the hotel and walk with him along the front, he was in such a miserable mood.'

The strangest part of Ruth's story concerns an episode in 1953, when 'he told me he had been diagnosed as a clear case of an Oedipus complex, which is one of the reasons our relationship for years was off and on'. As a 'diagnosis' it is meaningless. Ruth took what she heard as fact. As a result of it, she says, 'Huw underwent deep analysis.' He told her he had regular appointments at 8 a.m., before going to the BBC, but gave no further details.

While this was going on, he asked her to marry him. 'We were both very moved. We were at the stage of saying, "Where shall we look for a place?" I was supposed to go with him to meet his parents. The engagement was being put in *The Times*. A friend was making a wedding hat for me. But just before the weekend, he called me and said he had a high temperature, so we couldn't go to Wales.'

Soon after this, Ruth returned to Turkey. By now she had taken a degree at LSE, and wanted a job. What she didn't want was to 'hang around London like some sort of displaced person'. She insists, however, that she meant to return in a year, in the hope that Huw would have benefited from his psychoanalysis.

In one sense, nothing could be more out of character than Huw Wheldon on the analyst's couch. But friends often thought that 'something' lay behind his vast exuberance. There is some evidence to support Ruth's story. One is in Wheldon's engagement diary for 1953. On August 29, a Saturday, he had a morning appointment with a Dr H. V. Dicks in Harley Street. He saw him twice more in September. Henry Dicks was a leading psychiatrist, an authority on sexual matters, and a Freudian therapist who was consultant to the Tavistock Clinic. As a major in the army during the war he helped look after Hess. Dicks died in 1977.

The other evidence is from G., a woman who knew Wheldon both through mutual friends and professionally. In the course of a long conversation about Wheldon, she gave an unprompted account of an incident that took place in 1955 or 1956. Following a traumatic episode (unrelated to Wheldon or his circle) in 1954, G. was having psychoanalysis with a woman at a house in Hamilton Terrace, north-west London. Her appointments were at 9 a.m. One morning as she arrived, Wheldon was leaving. They passed on the steps. He pretended not to see her. The incident was not referred to afterwards. G. spoke to her analyst, who made an equivocal remark that suggested she knew Huw Wheldon came to the house for treatment, but that she was not the therapist. The analyst is dead. At least one other analyst practised in the house, but she too is dead or untraceable. The simple explanation is the most credible. Huw Wheldon saw a psychiatrist in 1953 and thereafter underwent some form of treatment. He may have presented it in more colourful form to Ruth.

A further strand needs to be unravelled. Ruth's closest friend in London was Jacqueline Clarke, known to her friends as Jackie or Jay. She first met Wheldon about 1950. According to Ruth, it was Jay who made the hat for her to get married in. Until about 1954 Miss Clarke and Huw Wheldon were casual acquaintances. Thereafter things changed. They were married in 1956, had three children and lived happily until Huw's death thirty years later. Miss Clarke is now Lady Wheldon.

Jacqueline Clarke was ten years younger than Wheldon. Her father was an engineer who invented a gasket. He died when she was a child, and she was brought up in west London by her mother, a robust woman who went out to work, and her grandmother. A spirited child, clever and perhaps a trifle eccentric, she had a short, unsatisfactory education, made even less adequate by a serious illness when she was about twelve – possibly measles, possibly complicated by a tubercular condition – which led to an operation that left her hearing impaired. This made her isolated and single-minded, or encouraged tendencies of the kind that were already there.

During and after the war she worked at the Town Hall in Ealing. In 1946, as chairman of the Labour Party League of Youth in the district, she met Harold Laski when he came to address a meeting. She noted his curious accent, in which he seemed to address her as 'Madam Charwoman', and the fact that he was professor of politics at the London School of Economics, of which she had never heard.

Soon after, Laski summoned her to the school, offered her a secretarial job, and told her to attend lectures in her spare time with a view to a degree course later on. This duly happened, and she had a late but successful academic career, graduating with an upper second in 1952. Then followed postgraduate studies in nineteenth-century politics.

Her friendship with Ruth began before 1950. Jay saw her as 'rootless', echoing the remark that Ruth says Huw made to her, 'we are displaced persons, you and I'. Perhaps Ruth detected a comparable trait, an apartness, in Jay. At any rate, Jay says that 'we clung together'. Ruth lodged at the home of Jay's mother in Ealing. Like Huw, Jay went to Turkey and spent a holiday with Ruth's family.

Her first sight of Wheldon was at a café in Charing Cross, attached to the little Watergate theatre, where Ruth pointed him out. He was leaning back in his chair, shouting with laughter. 'What a curious chap,' she thought. Over the next two or three years, she was aware of a difficult relationship between her friend and the man with the laugh – 'If he wasn't running away from her, she was running away from him.' Among Jay's men friends in the 1950s was Norman Podhoretz,[1] then doing post-graduate work at Cambridge. The four of them once made up a party to see the Boat Race; it was 1951, the year Oxford sank.

Jay's memories of the period are shadowy and largely dateless, even more so than Ruth's. She remembers being asked by Ruth to intercede with Huw. Of the message she recalls nothing, but she is clear about what he said to her when she had finished: 'If I wanted advice, which I do not, you are the last person I would come to.'

At one point, Ruth has returned to Turkey, 'very sadly', and Huw asks Jay to go to the theatre with him. He is perturbed because he has heard from Ruth of a bizarre accident, in which a pencil has been driven through her eye. They go to see T. S. Eliot's *The Cocktail Party*. In the interval she makes intelligent conversation about the play. Huw says, 'I didn't bring you here to get a lecture on T. S. Eliot.' Jay thinks, 'Bloody hell, you've got to be on your toes with this chap.' She takes him home for supper, giving him whatever is in the larder. Huw says, 'What's this, a dog's dinner?' (But *The Cocktail Party* opened in London in September 1954, which doesn't fit the dates. Ruth says the pencil-in-the-eye story is exaggerated: she had written to Huw to say she had stuck a fingernail in her eye. He wrote back, 'What do you do with a one-eyed wife?' She doesn't have the letter.)

Three letters from Huw to Jay, and a few diary entries, provide fixed points of a sort. He had dinner with her ('Jackie – Ealing') on May 8 1953, the day after his thirty-seventh birthday. He sent her two letters in quick succession in December 1953, friendly but unrelaxed; perhaps Ruth and her bad eye were offstage. Both letters are on Savile Club paper. On December 10, a Thursday, he wrote:

> My incomparable Jackson!
> You certainly write a hell of a letter. Also, you use big words.

---

[1] Norman Podhoretz, b. 1930, American 'neo-conservative' writer. He edited the magazine *Commentary* from 1960.

I hope you remain invigorated for a decent time. Life passes in jerks, some wounding, some refreshing; but damned jerky.

The abiding thing is your generosity. I am very conscious of it, & feel most grateful, feel glad, that it flows my way. And certainly I shall jump into that stream; (not that I'm really sold on those records. It's the tea that gets me!)

And thank you for the nylon comb. Also W. H. It has a small table & I give a reverential bob as I pass it ('Take away that Wuthering Height' – do you remember Churchill on Reith?) I have now recollected that it is, in fact, Middlemarch [Jay says she had sent him the novel to cheer him up. Eventually he returned it unread.] I naturally only pass at a respectful distance.

You will not forget January 6. Foyer of the Old Vic fifteen minutes before advertised Curtain Up. Arrive unfed, and dressed as for Evensong at Uttoxeter Parish Church.

This is only for the record. I will ring you, if I may, before then.

The Oakeshott [1] news sounds good: I hope the work goes well & that the days don't drag. That sciatica must certainly be fixed.

Don't think me casual; but I see no point in labouring my thanks & feelings. You are more generous than you know, in my opinion. This is a hell of a thing to be.

3 Hogarth Rd my diary says. Can that be right? I simply cannot believe it. LSE it must be.

As ever, Huw.

His second letter, dated December 13, is not very clear but sounds like a brush-off:

Dear Jackson

It was nice hearing your voice on the telephone. And I realized afterwards that I'd sent my cool reply to LSE. So that's where it is, I suppose.

Also I wondered whether I had not written altogether *too*

---

[1] Professor Michael Oakeshott was professor of political science at LSE 1951–69, succeeding Harold Laski.

coolly (I can't remember what the hell I said!) In case you get that impression, please dispel it. I was touched by the way your mind had whizzed round; in a sense by the work you had done; touched by your sympathy; & touched by your friendliness. But the thing that counted was the generosity which poured along every line; & this was more important than any resolution, any understanding, any explanation.

So far as I am concerned, the fact that the only persistent thing is my sense of you as a generous person implies that our walk last Sunday was largely & primarily a walk. I was not really very impressed one way or the other with our common bad behaviour. I am used to it in myself, & not surprised at it in others. It was nothing, in fact. To me, that is. And I was concerned with your pottiness because it suggested that you were a bit potty, not because it affected any relationship between any of us. Like being concerned about your sciatica.

Life goes in leaps & bounds sometimes, and drags along at other times; and I don't expect either you or myself (or indeed, many others) to remain consistently sane. And in my heart, I have no doubt that your balance has only returned for a short time. Your circumstances are not easy, as it seems to me. On the other hand, it is good to know that potty or not, understanding cannot but be yours, because generosity has that curious reward.

I dare say that this does not really add anything to what I said in my earlier note. It remains pretty cool. But there you are: it is my nature to discount, in some degree, the moments of penetration which emerge out of these various little upheavals – not because the discernment & the emotion is wrong or inaccurate, but because they seldom persist. A quality of character is a different matter: & it is this that has impressed me.

So there you are Jackson. Forget it. Concentrate on darling Oakeshott!

For me, this is positively a major statement! I fly, flee this kind of letter like the plague! I mean to say!

I'll see you, with luck, during the week; or anyway, one of these days. I'll give you a ring.

Reduce Smellie [another LSE professor], seduce Oakeshott: &
that Doctorate is yours! Read nothing, think nothing, be simple –
& they'll make you Master of an Oxford College.

As ever, Huw.

The third letter was written from Cornwall in August 1954.
Wheldon's friend Brian Murphy was staying there, with his two
children and some of his wife's family. She had died a year
earlier, still in her thirties. Wheldon did what he could for his
friend. The weather that summer was dismal. The family were
at an isolated guest house. Wheldon hired an ancient car and
organized things; cheeribee triumphant. 'Is it your thought that
I am a poorish correspondent?' he wrote to Jay. 'Dismiss the
unworthy reflection!' Gales and rain kept them busy, 'Drying
this, fixing that. "Can I have a sweet?" "Why are some pigs
black but not many sheep?" Tea up & so on.'

By Jay's birthday the following May, 1955, he was bombarding
her with joke telegrams ('Heavy condolences on regrettable
annual occurrence. Stanley.' 'Much love and congratulations.
Marlon.'). In the summer they went camping in France. 'Bring
suitcase for J.C.,' says the diary. The tent was shabby. They saw
a bullfight and did some wine-tasting. It was the year of Gilbert
Harding and *Is This Your Problem?* Wheldon was now living at
the Savile Club, as though hinting still that he had settled for a
bachelor's life. Ruth says she stayed briefly in London on her
way to Harvard. Huw saw her off at the airport; they had
breakfast; he wept over his bacon and egg.

Jay was working for a doctorate. At the same time she was one
of a group contributing to a Nuffield study on the effect that
television had on the young,[1] and toying with the offer of a job
in the military histories section of the Cabinet Office. In November she was offered a place in the Joint Intelligence Bureau
at the Ministry of Defence. She also wanted to be a novelist, and
thought of becoming a full-time writer.

---

[1] *Television and the Child* was published in 1958 and quickly forgotten. It was
the work of Dr Hilde Himmelweit, who taught social psychology at LSE.

As for Wheldon, she was more ardent than he, to begin with. Eventually, she says, 'it was I arranged the whole thing. There were times when he backed off from me.' Ruth was not discussed. 'I never asked questions. He never supplied information. I suppose something like that seeped into the entire marriage. I don't know much about Huw between the time we first met and the time I married him. And when you're married, the opportunities aren't there.' In any case, they had little to discuss. She knew of no psychotherapy and no history of sexual problems. In later years, when he spoke of Celia, as he did, it was to recall a wartime romance, a young man's first love. The rest was buried. Huw and Jay got engaged in August 1956, three months after his fortieth birthday.

It was Jay who went to see a psychiatrist before finally deciding to get married. She wanted to write her Ph.D. thesis, and thought it incompatible with marriage. It is not easy to understand the problem. In the event, soon after her marriage she began to write an enormous novel, and published it ten years later. Much of her life was to be consumed by writing. Perhaps the true problem was her knowledge of this passion. As she remembers it, 'I was at my wits' end because I couldn't do two things at once. [The psychiatrist] said, you will always have this problem.' The thesis was not written.

In October, the month before he was married, Wheldon visited the United States for the first time, gathering material for programmes. Researchers were not at hand in those days to do the producer's bidding. Two documentary series were involved. One, *Portraits of Power*, was to profile contemporary figures. The other, *Men in Battle*, recounted tales of the war, and had already made a name for the retired general who presented them, Brian Horrocks. Horrocks travelled to America with Wheldon, seeking film and interviews for a new series.

Nothing suited Wheldon better than working with a general, on programmes that told stories about fighting men, stories with, by and large, happy endings. Lieutenant-General Horrocks commanded an army corps in the war. After it he was given the sinecure of 'Gentleman Usher of the Black Rod' in the House of Lords, and began to write for newspapers. When television caught his interest, he wrote off to his old pal Ian Jacob, one lieutenant-general to another, 'Dear Jake', in Wheldon's anecdotal version, 'I'm quite sure I could do something, should I come to see you?' Jacob passed him on to McGivern, and it was he and Leonard Miall who saw his potential, saying yes to Horrocks before Wheldon was brought in as the producer.

Wheldon's anecdote rearranges this, as anecdotes do, and has him visiting the House of Lords to see if the old warrior will be any good at television. Wheldon thinks not, but at the last minute Horrocks shows him his stall in the chamber, with red despatch boxes on a shelf. The boxes contain football-pool coupons. Yes, says Horrocks, he does them all the time while the noble lords are speaking. His only anxiety is whether, in the event of his winning a fortune, the pools company will respect the clause about confidentiality. He has consulted the Lord Chancellor, who considers a tick in the request box a sound legal instrument.

This insight into the private Horrocks (said Wheldon) changed his mind – 'a very rum chap, and no wonder he won battles'. They worked together on many programmes, which Horrocks found the most enthralling things he had ever done, and more exciting than being a corps commander.

In America, Wheldon was frustrated at poor interviews and worried by the cost of archive film. Being far away, he wrote about it to Jay, saying, 'I badly want your shoulder to weep on, or bite, or anyway, have by me.' She was furnishing the flat they already had in Notting Hill Gate:

> Buy away, my sweet, buy hard, buy fast. I claim the right to grumble increasingly! But bash on. Yours is a far better wicket than this dreary quicksand of ineptitude. Unprepared, of course: but holy God, one had some right to expect *something*. From him that hath not with bells on.

I must obviously stop this dismal hymn of lamentation. Jeremiah Wheldon, the cheerful chappie. So what, is the watchword. It all comes out in the wash. Who'll care, ten years hence? (I'm not so bloody sure about that).

Anyway, having sicked that up, I feel better.

One day he felt 'vaguely randy out of pure tedium'; another, staying at the Cosmos Club in Washington – 'old men, silver, enormous dining-rooms, aridity' – he assured her that his clubman's arrangements prevented

> any brighteyed jolly excursion into the carnal fringe [. . .] Not that I need any barrier, but I thought it might provide you with a moment's preening satisfaction to know this. All men are much more trusting than all women, especially you, although, in fairness, what you distrust is perhaps yourself rather than me, which is of course even more fatuous: never trust a man.

In the same letter he speaks of wanting her to be 'happy & well-occupied [. . .] It would be nice to reflect that I had provided someone in the world with something real. Not that anybody can *provide* these things.' He still had a Welshman's home thoughts. A Sunday letter reported a visit to church:

> Text from Deuteronomy; theme: the ageing Moses. All exactly like Presbyterian Temple, Bournemouth in, say 1893. I prefer sermons from the Old Testament, for all that. They assume & create an enormous myth which gives life to the proceedings. Once sink into Old Testamentitis, you enter into a tremendous world, & giants walk across your horizons.

The following month, on November 24 1956, they were married at St John's, Fulham, the church that Jay attended as a child. A few days earlier he had written from the Savile Club to thank H. for her wedding present. 'We get married on Saturday – so today finds us flapping round, two wet hens in a storm, no curtains, no money, no carpets. However, the storm will pass, no doubt, & leave us in some quiet corner, two mice, peering out at life.'

109

At work, he was busier than ever. The BBC was agitated. After a year of The Competitor it was drifting towards humiliation or worse. Where viewers had a choice – I T V's network was still being extended – the BBC attracted on average fewer than two-fifths of them. Hundreds of staff were lured with money. The core of the BBC as a programme-making organization was intact, and so was its sense of itself as the repository of 'good television', whatever that was. But it was badly shocked, and the old contempt for 'commercial values' rang hollow as audiences declined.

The BBC was driven to restating the obvious. Ian Jacob told the programme board in confidence (January 25 1956) that the BBC must serve 'the mass of the public' or there was no reason for its existence; at the same time, 'every programme, of whatever type, should have the stamp of quality and achieve distinction in its own field'. Wheldon's new documentaries were stamp-of-quality stuff, vivid essays (the series began with Hitler in April 1957), using archive film at a time when this was still a novelty, made on less than a thousand pounds a programme. Small as the budgets now appear, they were grudgingly approved. At best, they were steps in the right direction.

The real solution to the BBC's dilemma – competitive scheduling and a lighter touch with programmes – took years to achieve. The corporation had an official fustiness that audiences fled from when given an alternative. Why (one tiny instance) was Cecil McGivern so adamant that women announcers were 'too hesitant' to be used in political programmes? 'This is essentially a male job,' he wrote in 1955, and was saying the same thing a year later.

George Barnes was still not inspiring confidence. At a weekend retreat he told senior managers that he thought a one-third share of the audience was satisfactory. He added that he felt he lacked the ability to 'lead his people in that direction at all'. Before the end of 1956, Barnes took himself off to the calmer job of running a university, and a robust countryman, Gerald Beadle, replaced him as director of television. Beadle had spent his life at the

110

BBC, most of it in charge of the West Region in Bristol. At the new Television Centre – which was coming into use bit by bit – he liked to wear tweeds to show the kind of unmetropolitan fellow he was. Wheldon found him none too keen on watching programmes.

Some of the staff, Wheldon among them, thought McGivern deserved the job. But by this time he was drinking heavily. Not only was he passed over as director of television, he was eased out of his job as controller of programmes and made Beadle's deputy, a move that upset him deeply. So he drank still more. On Monday mornings his secretary would find his hospitality cupboard bare.

Where the reshuffle succeeded was in making Kenneth Adam, who had spent five years running the Light Programme on sound radio, the new programme controller. No doubt it was felt that his popular touch would be balanced by Beadle's *gravitas*. Adam made a good start and ultimately won back viewers, though drink did for him, too, in the end.

These high-level to-ings and fro-ings were of no more general interest then than now, except that they define the frame within which programme-makers like Wheldon operated. The picture he gave later was of a man indifferent to promotion; but whenever promotion appeared on the horizon, he was quick to take it. By nature, too, he was an enthusiast for whatever came to hand. One of the marginal duties of Talks producers was to help with political broadcasts. At the time of the Suez crisis, David Attenborough was present when Lady Eden was putting mascara on her husband's moustache, 'in case anybody should think he hadn't got one'. Wheldon did his share of such broadcasts, and was in charge of Harold Macmillan's first appearance as Prime Minister, a few days after he took office in January 1957. (It should have been Donald Baverstock, that other Welshman, but he was too busy planning a secret weapon against The Competitor; this emerged a month later as *Tonight*.)

Thereafter Wheldon became 'Macmillan's man', of which he was proud. In July he produced Macmillan again, and told the

Downing Street advisers that their master's scripts were poor stuff. In a letter to Leonard Miall he wrote about 'this convention in ministerial broadcasts of speaking sentences into camera which no human being could possibly speak direct to a postman or a professor or a housewife or a child'. Wheldon's memos circulated among BBC chiefs, and Macmillan listened to what he had to say. Wheldon implied it was he who eventually steered Macmillan into broadcasting unaffected English to the nation.

Whenever possible Wheldon still went before the cameras himself. From making highly praised programmes about Stalin or the Battle of Arnhem, he would turn to interviewing yodellers or a boy who built a cathedral from matchsticks. *Facts and Figures* needed a presenter; Wheldon would do it. He chaired a discussion about British working practices, and provided a commentary from the Royal Welsh Show. *Panorama*, part of Grace Wyndham Goldie's empire, ran an item about boy scouts for Baden-Powell's centenary: who better than Wheldon to interview modern youth and discourse on loyalty and service?

Some thought he made these appearances because he needed the money. He had married late, and his finances were undoubtedly a worry. But he liked performing for its own sake. Even in the corridors and canteens he had a filmic presence. 'He looked at people and knew about them,' says Michael Peacock. 'Those eyes! That nose!' A colleague speaks of the camera transforming him – 'a kind of magic, like a laying on of hands'.

The more odds and ends of camerawork he did, the more it drew attention to his uncertain status. Producers were beginning to specialize. Empires were taking shape. The same evening he interviewed boy scouts, Baverstock and Goldie launched *Tonight*, a crucial venture that gave the BBC a new voice. Wheldon admired *Tonight*, like everyone else – 'commentaries had to be written as if they were being spoken by human beings, pomp went out of the window'. He had no part in it, though, or in any other comparable enterprise. *Portraits of Power* couldn't go on for ever. General Horrocks was asking for more money, pricing himself out of the market.

Since earlier in 1957, there had been talk of inventing a magazine programme for late-night viewing. 'I am sure that "Panorama" and "Tonight" are producing at their best *real* television,' Adam wrote to Miall in March, 'and if it has been done twice . . . then there is no reason why it shouldn't be done a third time. I think it should be a highly sophisticated type of magazine, without necessarily appealing only to Third Programme types.' By the summer the idea had become an 'arts magazine' of some kind. No urgency was apparent; Goldie, the mover and shaker, was not much interested in the arts. They were still talking in the autumn. Wheldon had been drawn in as presenter.

At the end of November 1957, he was away from London for a week, on a lecture tour in the north. His audiences were women's groups of some kind, and he was presumably doing it for money; an entry in his engagements diary the previous June says, 'Huw earning money to buy clothes for Jay by lecturing in Bournemouth.'

From York he wrote calling it 'my Economy Tour!' Four hundred 'vast impassive women' heard him lecture. Back at the Royal Station Hotel he read 'a rotten book called the Psychology of Sex'. In Cheshire there were 'dinner jackets and fur wraps, grey nodding heads'. Staying at the Black Bull in Ripon, he lurched suddenly into confession. 'My past caught up with me in the most displeasing way this morning,' he said. He had met a woman, whose name he couldn't remember, whom he knew when he was stationed in Yorkshire in 1941. This 'Mrs Something' spoke to him about two other women he had known there. One was a Mrs A., 'enormously stylish and rich and fast and glamorous', whom he used to regard 'with a mixture of fear, dislike, fascination & desire'. She had a drunken husband. The other, Mrs B., was

> a girl who then lived in Wensleydale. Her husband was in the RAF. She seemed very desirable * [*marginal note*: *in an undeniably nasty sort of way . . .] to me, and undoubtedly wanted me to have

an all-out affair with her. I was shy & gauche & embarrassed & never got anywhere – indeed I was humiliated by the whole business & subsequently cursed myself for being so fatuous. There she had been, a pushover, and I had not pushed. Mrs Thing told me this morning that she often sees [Mrs B.] – & at the very name that old, shaggish, frustrated excitement stirred, willy nilly, in my blood. Christ! I thought. I instantly told myself to pipe down & simultaneously I was creating a little fantasy about my nobility of character; & deeper down seeing that it was only a fantasy; & under that again feeling the memory of the jungle; then the whole foundation collapsed because Mrs Whatsit was telling me how this [Mrs B.], this memory of the inviting, forbidden apple, was now a Grandmother twice over, & had been suffering badly from pleurisy for many years.

All flesh is grass.

I am late for the bus.

I do hope all goes well. All my love

Huw

Wheldon was back in London by the end of the week. While he was away, Goldie had made formal proposals for staffing the new arts magazine, as yet unnamed. Wheldon would have overall responsibility. His own empire was in the making.

CHAPTER SIX

Letters from America

THE IDEA OF A regular programme about the arts was not high among BBC priorities. Now and then a painter or sculptor would have a film devoted to his work. John Read, son of the critic Herbert Read, had been making them for years. They were well thought of but grudgingly paid for; management grumbled at the time they took.

The history of how the new programme came about, already touched on in the previous chapter, suggests that it was another response to competition. In 1957, when Adam (and his boss Gerald Beadle) became interested in the idea, the goad of commercial television was still at work. A draft paper to the governors, seeking more money for programmes in general, used gentlemanly language. 'Natural growth,' it said, was taking place in the service; apologetically, it added that 'the need to compete with the ITA has been borne in mind'. This was followed by the brave promise that the proposals would 'increase the number of programmes of intelligence and programmes of distinction' – in other words, we are fighting for viewers, but we shall not stoop to The Competitor's level. The next sentence said as much: 'It is not proposed to add to the cost of light entertainment programmes, whose number may also decrease.'

How much of this was sweet-talk for the board is impossible to tell. Compromise was in the air. Kenneth Adam, as controller of programmes, knew that the BBC had to claw back a million or two viewers. The trick was not to be caught doing it in a vulgar way. A paragraph was devoted to the arts programme: 'In order to strengthen Sunday night viewing, we propose to establish as part of Talks development a regular magazine of the arts of a comprehensive kind which would attempt to do in this field what "Panorama" has done in the field of current affairs.' It was a useful idea, both in itself (if it could be made to work) and as evidence that the BBC was still run by people of taste.

The board approved a fortnightly series, and a producer called Catherine Dove [1] was put in charge of the project. Dove worked on *Panorama*, one of the young Turks, or Turkesses, in Grace Wyndham Goldie's domain. As a trainee in 1954 she had worked with John Read on his films. From then on (she says), every year when it was time for her annual staff interview, she would propose an arts magazine. Goldie was sceptical. She remarked, 'If people want to have plaster ducks on the wall, Katie, who are we to stop them?' In 1957 Dove was delighted to learn that her annual idea had been adopted, or had coincided with someone else's idea.

By the middle of October, Dove's was still the only appointment. Someone had drawn up a hopeful list of fifty free-lance interviewers and writers. Among them were Peter Ustinov, James Morris, John Wain, Lindsay Anderson, Malcolm Muggeridge, Peter Brook, Robert Robinson, John Gale, Hugh Casson and John Mortimer. The fourth name was Huw Wheldon. Someone, perhaps Dove, put a question mark against him. Dove had always found Wheldon's style on television patronizing. Unless instructed she would not have used him at all. To her annoyance, word came down that he was to be the presenter.

Leonard Miall says that finding a vehicle for Wheldon was one of the reasons for having an arts programme in the first place. He was a successful presenter, and they wanted something better for him than *All Your Own*. But it was thought wrong for

---

[1] Catherine Dove, b. 1931, was twice married to broadcasters, first Charles Wheeler and then John Freeman. As Catherine Freeman, she was for many years controller of features at Thames Television.

a BBC staff producer to appear in a sensitive context like politics or current affairs. The arts were non-controversial.

At first Dove assumed that as producer she would be in sole charge of the show. Wheldon made the opposite assumption, that he was a senior producer in his own right, and had to be at least a co-producer. They fenced and manoeuvred. Dove and Goldie were both keen on topicality: the new play, the new exhibition. 'That wasn't my disposition,' said Wheldon later. Topicality, yes; a topical magazine, no. He hinted at other differences. 'The row', he said, 'was gigantic.' By early December, when Wheldon returned from lecturing to women in the north of England, Dove knew that she had lost. As yet he had no title ('editor' was decided on later), but the final authority was his. With a power-broker's touch, Goldie ruled that on the day of transmission, Wheldon would turn back into a presenter pure and simple, and Miss Dove would be the boss.

Looking back on the episode, which left her somewhat bruised, Dove says, 'No doubt I was exasperating. I was fifteen years younger, not long out of Oxford, still pretty green about production. But I was committed to the arts, and worst of all I was a girl. He was very much a man's man, not keen on women as equals at work.' Nor, she thinks, was he keen at first on the idea of the arts on television ('It was a case of coming to scoff and staying to pray'). She thinks a magazine about battles would have been more his line, but 'this was the only one going, and he badly needed a power base'.

She found him uneasy with much of the material she suggested. 'He said to me once, with great emphasis, "The public won't care what these people wrote or painted. What they'll want to know is, were they queer or did they have women, and if so, who." I burst into tears and he slammed out of the room.'

Dove recognized virtues – 'a bringer-out of talent, inspirational in his rhetoric, often very funny. Someone, let's say, who could have been the beak of a slightly eccentric school, dashing into hall in his gown – a bit of a bully, not intellectual at all, but a brilliant performer. The sort of man who would live in all their memories.'

She and Wheldon co-operated uncomfortably. Ann James,

117

their secretary, can't remember them at work in the same office. The programme would not be ready until Sunday February 2. Wheldon didn't think beyond the first six editions. Whether or not he was pulling Dove's leg about the artist and his sex life, he had little faith in a programme about the arts, and thought it likely to fail. An associate producer, Peter Newington, was brought in from children's television.

Two and a half weeks from transmission a team of nine sat down with Goldie for the first formal meeting. Wheldon and Dove were both present. A title was discussed. Dozens of ideas had been circulating, among them *Vista*, *Argus*, *Arena*, *Around*, *Silhouette*, *Mirror*, *Monitor*, *Lens* and *Periscope*. Goldie favoured *Periscope*. Wheldon wanted *Monitor*; as it happens, so did Dove. Various projects were reported. A keen young actor and film director, John Schlesinger, whom Dove had known at university, was making a four-minute film about Tom Arnold's circus at Haringey. John Read was dubbing Epstein's voice on to film of his sculptures. The theatre director Peter Brook was to show *musique concrete* in action. Another friend of Dove, Kingsley Amis (who was later a friend of Wheldon), would talk to Simon Raven in a Swansea pub.

The next meeting should have been in a week's time. Over the intervening weekend, Catherine Dove had a bizarre accident when her husband-to-be, Charles Wheeler, jumped back into bed with the Sunday papers and landed on her knee. The cartilage was damaged; she was admitted to hospital. Goldie assumed that 'Katie's bad knee' wouldn't keep her away for long. But Dove was only twenty-six, a woman, up against a resolute campaigner just entering his prime. She was not anxious for more in-fighting. There were other options. She married Wheeler and went with him to India, where he was the BBC correspondent. The knee, and having to share power with Wheldon, did for her career at the BBC. As a talks department official wrote about another matter, 'Sharing a bed with Monitor is never possible – Huw Wheldon kicks in his sleep.'

Monitor was launched as planned, on the first Sunday in

Major Wynn Wheldon, his wife Megan and their first-born, Huw Pyrs, a First World War baby. The birth certificate calls him 'Hugh'.

Mrs Wheldon with her second child, Tomos, born 1919, and Huw, aged about three.

(*right*) The preacher in the family, the bearded T. J. Wheldon, Huw's grandfather, and his wife Mary Elinor. Behind them are their son Wynn and (middle) daughter Gwladys.

(*below left*) Megan Wheldon, Huw's mother. He inherited her knack for mimicry.

(*below right*) Wynn Wheldon, the educationist. As children, his sons Huw and Tomos had Latin lessons when they were on holiday.

(*above*) Where they came from: kitchen interior of Llwyncelyn (in English, 'Holly Grove'), the farm below Snowdon where John Wheldon, the 'old sinner', scraped a living in the last century.

(*left*) In the garden at Bangor, 1933, just before the family moved to London: in ascending order, Nans, Mair, Tomos and Huw, now aged sixteen. He said his boyhood was 'a waking day-dream'.

Huw Wheldon as a young officer, early in the war.

'Celia', about 1942, when she and Captain Wheldon were having their wartime romance.

Spirit of youth: Wheldon, still a publicity officer with the BBC, listens to a performer in a 1954 edition of *All Your Own*, the children's television programme where he made his name as a presenter.

Cliff Michelmore, whose own career as a presenter was yet to come, was a producer of *All Your Own* when Wheldon was appearing in front of the camera. Between them is Michael Westmore, one of the production team.

Huw Wheldon marries Jacqueline Clarke, November 24 1956. On her right are Sir Wynn Wheldon and the bride's mother, Mrs Stroud – the 'mother-in-law' cited by Wheldon whenever he wanted to typify the 'ordinary viewer'. On his left are his mother and the bride's brother, Kenneth.

Sunday February 2 1958, before the first edition of *Monitor* went on the air. Second from left is Jack Ashley, associate producer, later an MP. Then: Grace Wyndham Goldie, the hard woman of television; Allan Tyrer (seated), senior film editor; Wheldon; Peter Newington, producer; Natasha Kroll, designer.

Sorcerer's apprentice: Wheldon and Ken Russell, still learning his trade as a director, look at rushes for *Monitor* in a viewing theatre, flanked by film editors.

Russell and Wheldon had some heroic arguments. Melvyn Bragg remembers a row that went on past midnight in the 'lavatorial, green-painted corridor by the cutting room'.

Father and son: Huw Wheldon and Wynn, about 1960.

February, at 10 p.m. Earlier in the evening was *What's My Line*, with Gilbert Harding. After that came Shaw's play *Heartbreak House*. *Monitor*, forty-five minutes' worth, was the last programme apart from News, Weather and Epilogue. Wheldon began with a cough and a statement: 'What we're interested in, in the end, are the people in all the arts, and what they do.' Schlesinger's *Circus*, the first item – the absent Dove's idea – was like a dream of circuses, bright-lit, with dark edges. The synthetic music was taken seriously but not too seriously. Amis, whose third novel *I Like It Here* had just been published, spoke fondly of South Wales, adding that 'I used to be basically much keener on being a socialist than I am now, really,' and so would the Jim of *Lucky Jim* be, if living in 1958. A play was reviewed; a pianist improvised.

Wheldon spoke briefly, with exclamation marks, recognizably *All Your Own's* uncle. Instead of 'We start with a stamp collector from Chelmsford!' it was 'And now, Epstein!' His brisk authoritarianism was joked about as long as he ran the programme. In a *Private Eye* cartoon (1962), he leers down at a little man in his hand – 'So much then for Jean-Jacques Pissoir, the world's greatest playwright.'

For better or worse, *Monitor* was made in Wheldon's image. But to begin with he was less confident than he seemed. Goldie backed him in the crucial months before *Monitor* became impregnable. 'He used to flirt with her,' says Baverstock. The early programmes crammed in too many items. Audience research reported modest 'appreciation' figures, around sixty on a scale where sixty-five was regarded as goodish.[1] Money was scarce. The minute *Monitor* was on the air, administrators were groaning. Five trips to Paris and Vienna were planned or, worse, had already taken place. As a result the programme's foreign-travel allowance for the quarter had gone. They were even begged not to take taxis, a sure sign of desperation.

---

[1] What used to be an 'Appreciation' Index later became a 'Reaction' Index; attempting, in both cases, to quantify likes and dislikes.

119

Wheldon had other distractions. Horrocks and Harold Macmillan and *Portraits of Power* were still his concern; so, irregularly, was *All Your Own*. In the spring his wife was expecting a child. A boy, Wynn, was born at the start of April. Shortly before this, H., Wheldon's woman friend from LSE days, called to see him at Lime Grove. They had exchanged occasional letters over the years.

The visit puzzled him at first; then he responded with a wry 'Note on a Meeting':

> What the devil was this about? Had she got an idea for a programme, or a husband's idea or a student's. If so, she would simply say so and not prattle on about dropping in for tea like a P.R.O. There never was anyone less like a P.R.O., & more direct, for all obliquity. So what was it about?
>
> She looked startlingly less than her age, & finely drawn. Age would continue to improve her. And brainy of course in that wary way. What had she in mind?
>
> The thing to do was to talk, reduce everything to the totally expected, totally acceptable, so that no fencings, no openings were necessary. Nothing emerged. Could she really want to see the studios? One's mother did. Many did. It was reasonable but seemed most unlikely. She was suddenly desperate and unhappy. What the bloody hell was this about.
>
> No, she must go at once.
>
> 'Hampstead.' A taxi all the way? Why not to a station? How could she afford it? What did it mean?
>
> Three children, & a real home, obviously. Not a flat. Occasional teaching. This was solid, & not surprising. There never was any cheapness in her. Was television then so cheap & life so gimcrack? There was Jay & her child, that was real; & for the rest of it, you've made your bed Little Brother so lie on it & don't grizzle. She seemed taller. It was baffling.
>
> He wasn't to know poor booby that it was friendship. Not simple friendship but something in that area. How could he be so blind? Friends are not so common, nor friendships so easily disposable. He'd got much to learn.

*

120

Monitor belonged to Wheldon as entirely as *Tonight* belonged to Baverstock. Rivalry existed between them. The two ends of Wales, North and South, have ancient jokes about one another. Wheldon was from the untrustworthy North, Baverstock from the rowdy South. Baverstock was television's version of the angry young man. Seen from *Tonight*, which paused only at weekends, the twice-monthly *Monitor* was soft and self-indulgent. 'What rubbish are you putting out this week?' Baverstock asked Peter Newington. The Wheldon style, which became the style of *Monitor*, was affable and conservative. He presided over the place like a stern but kindly uncle. One or two secretaries in other departments were said to have fled there if they wanted a refuge from harsher temperaments.

But the style could be deceptive. Wheldon held the programme in an iron grasp. He believed in authority. 'Nothing was ever done that I didn't agree with from beginning to end,' he said. 'Nothing was done which I found boring or tedious or tiresome or meretricious or wrong.' Three items to an edition became the standard. Film was the backbone – about Rodin, or Japanese action painting, or Korean ballet, or the Madonna. Some came from outside sources, especially in Eastern Europe, where copyright wasn't recognized. As time went on, *Monitor* made more of its own films and could stockpile them. John Schlesinger, in his early thirties, was their most imaginative director. He was a refugee from *Tonight*, thankful for the friendliness of *Monitor*. Baverstock is supposed to have said, 'When it works, we're happy to have you. When it doesn't, you're not worth it.'

One of the things Wheldon sought was revelation: how a writer wrote, how a performance took shape. 'I don't much like the idea of simply getting chaps to say how wonderful it all is,' he remarked, in a memo about provincial theatres. The word 'middlebrow' was used of *Monitor* by its critics, sometimes in the way that reviewers have, of putting a distance between themselves and the common crowd. No doubt art makes snobs of us all, since who can be sure of his own judgement? Wheldon's air of – at times – enthusiastic reverence itself suggested snobbery,

121

a sniff at the idea that *Monitor* might soil its hands with anything but Art and the Artist. 'The *Monitor* programme that I handle on their behalf was originally started by the BBC as very much a prestige programme,' he wrote to an acquaintance of the composer Darius Milhaud, who was being lined up for a programme. 'The intention has never been to deal in gossip or stuff about Gregory Peck having breakfast with the kids and such. Our business is to illuminate the creative process in the arts and to handle artists purely in terms of their product.'

In its severest form, such a doctrine would have led to no *Monitor* at all; few creators are keen on illuminating the creative process. But Wheldon's real aim was to offer glimpses, however humble, of artists and their curious ways. His 'links', learned by heart but backed up by a crib in his palm, were unpretentious. He always wrote his own material, as well as interfering with other people's. Here he is on March 16, Programme 4, introducing a film about the painter Bratby:

> This is a painting by John Bratby. It hangs in the Tate Gallery, where there are several more of his paintings, paid for, of course, as usual, by you and me. Bratby is very much a man who paints what he sees around him – in the kitchen or scullery or wherever it might be. Some people think he's marvellous, others think that he's wasting his time and ours, not doing a good sort of work at all. *Monitor* cameras saw him at work at home and at a film studio.

This was middlebrow Wheldon in action. But what other brow was possible on television? The audience was two or three million. For *Tonight* and *Panorama*, this would have meant disaster. For the arts it was very large: as it needed to be, if the programme was to justify having money spent on it. In its decline, years later – after Wheldon had left – *Monitor* did become cleverer. Its charms faded, and it was quickly closed down.

When explaining *Monitor*, Wheldon could turn on the current and make the platitudes glow. The relationship between art and artist, he asserted, was 'as important as anything else in life'.

Perhaps Catherine Dove was right and it could just as well have been battles. It hardly matters; art it was. He would have the arts writ large for the British, who were Europe's philistines. Colleagues knew it was Wheldon who gave *Monitor* its emphatic style, but some of them went on having reservations. Peter Newington thought Wheldon viewed the arts as 'a sort of huge Sistine Chapel ceiling populated by geniuses'. David Jones, who joined the programme in the spring of 1958 as a novice, saw 'a Welsh puritan streak in Huw that wished artists would shape up a bit'. But he also saw the gift for conveying enthusiasm. It could be parodied, but it was what people remembered.

Jones, who was at home with theatre and books, had expected to work for *Tonight*. But Goldie told him he had to go and help on 'a little magazine programme about the arts', adding that it would probably be short-lived. It suited him better; he became an old hand, and went on to be a Royal Shakespeare director. According to Jones, Peter Newington was 'the artistic conscience' of *Monitor*. From the Jones-and-Newington position, the straight-forward Wheldon was too straightforward, preferring the arts to be orderly, not unexpected.

Big men appealed to Wheldon, so he made an early start on creaming off the big names. No one had ever done it for the arts on television, at least on his scale; his successors grumbled that Uncle Huw had swept the board. In the first year his catch (on film or in the studio) included – besides Amis, Bratby and Epstein – Yehudi Menuhin, Arthur Bliss, Charles Laughton, Maria Callas, Michael Ayrton, Leonide Massine, Aldous Huxley, Tyrone Guthrie, Duke Ellington, P. G. Wodehouse, Aaron Copland, William Alwyn, Peter Brook, E. M. Forster and Georges Simenon.

Wheldon himself did many of the major interviews. Not all the big men were willing. Ralph Vaughan Williams's wife wrote sharply ('an emphatic no') to say her husband never spoke of his own work, and disliked the idea very much. Forster made difficulties at first, but eventually let himself be filmed at King's College, Cambridge, in time for his eightieth birthday. Laughton refused to do it unless Wheldon was the interviewer.

123

'We are dealing with rare birds,' said Wheldon. 'Can you, in fact, name a hundred English poets? Can you personally name seventy painters? The authentic voice of genius comes rarely. We dwell among the eagles. We are above the earth and sometimes find we are only dealing with sparrows, but they are at least trying to fly.'

One of the rare or rarish birds who provided a comfortable interview, filmed by Schlesinger in Switzerland at the end of 1958, was Georges Simenon. 'The Organization Man rushes through the dark air,' Wheldon wrote to his wife, flying to meet his subject. Discussing the film later, he was anxious that no one should regard the domestic details of Simenon at work, on which the interview dwelt, as journalistic gossip. Simenon had 'manias' before each burst of activity that produced a thriller. He sharpened eighty pencils, had his wife clean dozens of pipes, sometimes was medically examined. Everything was ritualized. A book took eleven days, during which he lived in a turret, avoided everyone and didn't change his shirt.

All this was significant, said Wheldon, because it showed us how Simenon needed the discipline of ritual to make his subconscious operate. Thus the ready pencils and the precise eleven days 'ceased to be gossip or an interesting sidelight and became relevant to a story or a film about a writer. And so we filmed it accordingly.' To which one might reply that 'gossip' about the creator doesn't need to be apologized for: the trivia of a life, past and present, may be as relevant as anything else. Either everything matters or nothing does.

To David Jones, Wheldon's delight in the well-organized Simenon was revealing, especially in view of what later became public knowledge about Simenon's sex life. When he left the turret with his dirty shirt and finished manuscript, he made straight for prostitutes. 'Here was an absolutely obsessive sexual performer,' says Jones, 'who behaved appallingly in domestic circumstances. A black tension existed between the man and the work, which never got into the "Monitor" film.' No doubt, as Jones concedes, Wheldon knew nothing of all this. But it is a nice irony that the bouts of disciplined writing he so admired went hand in hand with bouts of lust.

124

After Wheldon had been running *Monitor* for rather less than a year, Ian Jacob asked him to take charge of the BBC's public relations, with the title of 'assistant secretary'. According to Wheldon in his Oral History account, Jacob wanted him in Westminster, 'not on a programme basis but on a basis of getting the politicians friendlily disposed to the BBC'. Wheldon places the story several years earlier, and makes it part of the BBC's campaign to rally support when independent television was about to begin. The papers contradict him, as they often do. There is a cheerful egotism in much of Wheldon's reminiscence that makes it unreliable. He smiles and talks, and history is recast. He knew how to package himself for maximum effect.

The 'assistant secretary' job, as described in letters at the time, was offered at the end of 1958. Tahu Hole, Director of Administration, wrote in January that 'the idea is that . . . you should be the main agent and motivator of public relations activities, cultivating relationships inside and outside the Corporation, acting always, of course, within the framework of an overall plan that would be approved by me and operated by the Secretary'. Wheldon didn't fancy being a cog in someone else's publicity machine. In bed with jaundice in January 1959, he replied that experience has 'taught me that, as far as I personally am concerned, work of this kind cannot be regulated by "an overall plan".' He thought that 'nine-tenths of the success of any public relations job, high or humble, consists in being totally and directly and continuously in the confidence of the person or persons governing the organization, and particularly being truly in the mind of its Chief or Leader'. He declined the offer.

Soon after this, Wheldon applied for a job in America. He wanted a change, or, just as likely, wanted promotion and used restlessness as a way of getting it. In a memo to Grace Wyndham Goldie in March he wrote:

As you know, I have been restless over the last few months. I have been casting around for possibilities of promotion . . . I have now applied, as you also know, for the post of BBC

125

Representative in the United States. The Board is next Tuesday,
12 March. The job has its obvious attractions and challenge, and
I believe I could handle it were it offered to me.

I remain however in a serious and painful dilemma. The
stubborn fact is that I prefer the work I am doing at present . . .
[but] if I stay where I am, I do so (at present) to all intents and
purposes at the expense of advancement in either status or salary
or both.

The BBC structure didn't allow him to be recompensed as his
skills matured. Already he was nearly at his ceiling. Yet his
'particular combination of faults and virtues . . . does not grow
on trees'. He was being driven to look elsewhere.

The ploy worked. New jobs were forgotten. They fiddled
about with grades and titles, as he must have hoped they would,
pushing up his salary past £3,000 a year. That summer the
Wheldons bought a family house in Kew, south-west London.
In the autumn he went to the United States for two months on a
travel grant from the English Speaking Union, very likely spon-
sored by the BBC as another sweetener. The object of such
grants was to help 'notable Britons from all walks of life' learn
about America. On eighteen dollars a day he was shunted up and
down the United States, saw the affluent side of things, attended
a conference or two and told everyone about the marvels of
British broadcasting.

One result of the visit was a long, intense correspondence with
his wife, at home in Kew with a new house, small child and,
frequently, her formidable mother – now a widow for the second
time, having married a Mr Stroud, who had died after a few
years. Forty-five letters from the visit are extant (and one to Mrs
Stroud, 'My dear old Madam'). It was his first real separation
from Jay since they married.

The letters are a commentary on a relationship and on Wheldon
himself not found elsewhere. The contents are straightforward

enough: a man in love with his wife writes her letters from abroad. But it is the undertone of a conversation that one hears – the loneliness behind the itinerary, the need to confess behind the cheeribee.

In 1959 the Atlantic liners had not yet been driven out of business by air travel. Wheldon sailed from Southampton for Canada in the Holland-America ship *Maasdam*. The postscript to his first letter (Monday August 24 1959), written in his bunk, apologized for his prolixity:

> it is so hard to stop, but so impossible to commit the mind's wanderings to paper. I no sooner stop than I want you to know that I am thinking how rotten it is for you for me to be preoccupied with 'Monitor', how comfortable the ship is, how eagerly I think about our house [. . .] how I wonder what I should do, this side of fantasy, to be properly helpful, how you are creative but I am not, how my teeth [he had been seeing his dentist] are now only really a small semi-detached in my mouth & no longer a parish hall, how you will read for signs of love and loss, how I feel warm and wondering at the thought of our being in bed together – I want you to know all these things together with all the other innumerable pelting things: how at this moment I want to get up because I want to smoke a cigarette, how I despair of ever being in a position to let my mind be totally relaxed because the only target of its totally liberated journey is an area of darkness where knowing sly hands move through underclothing and mad faces speak a shared obscenity, how this prevents the writing, the free sought for expression for the deeply felt undiscovered thing, how I decided not to change for dinner, how I feel curiously ill-at-ease in a big English-speaking crowd not one of whom has ever heard of me, how none of this could even be begun to be written to anyone in the whole world except you and how I rest on the belief that, even if bored or irritated by it, you will in fact read it and that you are with me – and how this could go sprawling on for ever and yet get nowhere and it's because of that, all of it, that I am only at

ease, even if I am looking at the television, when you are there, and how that very statement is not enough because for me to be at ease is not the end of life, and how I know that and wonder how to be different – and all these things are flooding all the time in this one moment which simply goes on, circulating round the main single stem of your absence. So now I'll seal it Mrs Harris, and please don't quote me. O Jay.

The 'area of darkness' must be his sexual imagination, intruding into his thoughts whenever it has the chance. The writing that is prevented seems to mean writing in general, not letters to Jay. He wrote scripts and speeches; nothing, though, that committed himself in the way a novelist, say, is likely to do. As a young man he thought of writing fiction. Later he laughed at the idea. 'I could no more write a book than fly,' he told a reporter in 1968, when talking about his wife's achievement as a novelist. Jay Wheldon says only that 'he had a great awe of great and good writers. Possibly what he would have liked to write about was outside his capacity.' In any case, the question of 'being able to write' had been settled long ago. What mattered now was that he had someone he could tell about the 'darkness', releasing his energies to get on with his life.

Two days nearer Quebec he was describing 'pornography day, a day spent on an eiderdown of delicious fantasy', reading a nineteenth-century novel by the French Joris-Karl Huysmans, *Against Nature*, and Henry Miller's *Tropic of Capricorn*. The Huysmans, just published in an English translation, he found 'terrific . . . a work of art'. The Miller also pleased him. It

> seemed to me in no way whatever disgusting, but delicious. I
> don't really follow his Outsider line – perhaps because I was so
> keen on getting to the next time that a music teacher tore open
> his flies and grabbed his balls – but even that is swampy rip-
> roaring stuff and in some way RELIEVING. Huysmans reveals
> and Miller relieves. Between them they gave me a hell of a day
> and a day in which you were forever popping onto the page and
> walking cockily or quickly or thoughtfully or grinningly between

128

the lines [...] because for all my comings and goings and twistings and turnings you are the only woman with whom I have ever had the hot, slavering magnificent Miller moments [...] I thought of you, clever and penetrating and appreciative; and I thought of you abandoned and randy & demanding; and I thought of you one [and] all the same, and a woman full of flaws & fears, total & yourself.

So to hell with the rest, I forget even what they were.

And the letter plunges on: 'The whale. I saw a whale.'

After a brief stay in Canada he went to New York, and spent the next two months travelling the United States. He was in board-rooms and on ranches. In Hollywood he 'ran into Richard Burton'. At a San Francisco conference on public service he talked about the BBC and 'knocked the buggers cold'; 'Frisco Feels Some New Tremors as BBC's Wheldon Tosses a Zinger At WBC Pubservice Windup Meet,' said *Variety* newspaper. TV and radio stations pressed invitations on him to appear, but, to his disgust, offered no fees. He described one radio interview:

> an absolutely hopeless set-up recommended by the E-S U – handled by a very nice, human, fat chap who, as soon as the microphone was put in front of him, pushed his voice into an absolutely unnatural register, a complete stereotype of the Radio Voice, saying 'Assignment – People: and your host, Charlie Holmes. Today we have distinguished Huw Wheldon, senior television programme director of famed BBC England.' At one moment, driven into frenzy by the extraordinary feeling of being shaped & battered & chiselled into a packet of Tide Soapflakes, I said in reply to [his] deep throated pseudo-dramatic pseudo-friendly totally stale canned voice, 'For God's sake, the question doesn't make sense' & he went pale, & the thing had to start all over again. Tape, of course.

In the small town of Bangor, Wisconsin, founded by a Wheldon immigrant in the 1850s, he spent two days on a farm with distantly related Wheldons; John, the founder, he was told, avoided hard liquor, disliked slang and held that 'words is valuable'. In Oxford, Mississippi, he noted with relief the 'absence of oppressive plenty', and was captivated by faded glories: 'the lost, aristocratic, impossible set-up present, like mist'. William Faulkner (whose novels Jay was reading in Kew) lived nearby, too aloof and famous, Wheldon decided, to be netted even for *Monitor*. But he had been given an introduction, and looked forward to a talk – 'being here without meeting him is like being in Lime Grove & not meeting McGivern'. In the end he had to make do with Mrs Faulkner. 'They were burning cedar in the fireplaces,' he told Jay, '& the aroma spread through the house.' She was '58, delicate, survivor of two husbands, fragile, once a Southern Belle':

> She was adorable, and, of course, quite impossible I suppose. She does not vote, ON PRINCIPLE: and what the principle is, as you watch her holding her cigarette between her fourth and little finger, her hands moving exquisitely on the fulcrums of her thin brown wrists, as you watch her alert, lovely head, and take in the lace and the fragrance, what the principle *is*, who can tell?

Most of the time Wheldon was in high spirits. 'I put my shoes outside, my brown ones, to be polished,' he wrote from Chicago; 'and they came back RED. What next! Holy cats. Yrs, Clovis.' 'Me, I like a laugh to keep the jungle at bay,' he said in a letter the same day; although to his father he wrote that he was 'sick to death of my very limited fund of funny stories. I am typed as "an interesting man" & it's the very devil living up to any such description . . .' If there was a battle between cheeribee and reticence, cheeribee usually won. In Plainview, Texas, he sat in his hotel looking over Main Street, waiting to have dinner with some lawyers and their wives, and wrote to Jay that 'I really quite enjoy this kind of thing. It suits my temperament to live on the surface of things, to make friends quickly with people & then forget them, & be forgotten.'

The love-letter content is agreeably earthy. 'You married a

coarse horse, Mrs Harris,' he wrote (New York, September 5), 'and it's no use beating about the bush – and just consider that turn of phrase for a hot & silent moment.' But it is in their evocation of sexual fantasy, and his need to exorcise it, that the letters say most. From Washington (September 9) he told Jay how he 'lay naked at midnight', dreaming about

vicious women and desirable orgies, and not, my darling love, of Thee, of Thee. Earlier, restless and confined, at 9 or so, I had gone out into the warm Washington night, vaguely ready for anything. I would have slipped into a Striptease joint, had I seen one. I would have been arrested & tense at the sight of a brothel, were such a thing possible in Washington which is like York or Bath; would have considered entering, would have gone through the familiar compulsion of breaking into the soft vicious world, only to find a woman either untouchable & repellent, hard business-like & joyless or, even worse, a woman silly or soft or smiling or neurotic or motherly to whom & with whom only gentleness or rudeness or a total ignoring would in actual practice be possible & that on the cup of tea level, & certainly not the level of nakedness and desire. And so, driven by vague fantasy I wandered about, then felt thirsty, a real feeling, hard and definite. At which, I turned into the first hotel I saw, and found myself, with Sigmund S. Freud Esquire holding me firmly by the elbow, in the foyer of the only place I knew at all in Washington, the foyer of the hotel in which Horrocks and I stayed so long ago. And I knew where I could drink coffee, quietly; & there it was, the familiar corner; & there I sat, at ease & at rest, drinking the bad & never changing coffee & reading (God be praised for lovely living minds) Forster's Room with a View. And then, at last, you were there, because the impersonal, clean, efficient coffee bar in the enormous hotel was home to me, & Forster was you, Kew with the television set with Peter Dimmock doing Sportsview, and the waitress was lovely, & black, & kind, & cheerful. So I sat there in Kew Gardens, reading my evening away. Then back to the hotel, to lie vapidly in the fag ends of the early evening's desire. And this morning there were people to see . . .

If the 'Oedipus' diagnosis has any relevance to Wheldon, it would help to explain the pornography, which is supposed to separate 'sex' from 'love'. But a taste for pornography hardly needs explaining today. The significance is not that he read it, but that his taste for it worried him so much: the puritan with unworkable ideals, ashamed of his strong sexual appetite. Unlike those who get along with both the appetite and the shame, he went on suffering almost into middle age. So what mattered to Wheldon in his forties, as he makes clear, is his freedom to let his wife see him as he is. There is a parallel with Tolstoy, making his fiancée read his diaries with their accounts of his sexual affairs. Wheldon was shifting a burden. He could be himself at last, as he had failed to be in his earlier relationships.

There had been fear as well. He spoke to a colleague once of 'the abyss'. Perhaps it was the need to check his sexual desires that made him anxious to keep control of himself. Something seethed under the skin and gave his character its edge. By the time he was tramping about the New World, he was learning to come to terms with what he was. He can see himself as cultured and common in the same breath, as when he writes that he 'spent two hours in a bookshop reading a magnificent (& magnificently short) book or essay on Leonardo da Vinci by Freud, looked glancingly at Sex-Pulp, interesting of course to a bloody maniac like me, but not all that interesting really, and read two essays by Cyril Connolly written in the vintage 1943/4 years' (Chicago, September 14).

The same letter includes this paragraph:

> My letters you say have quietened down, the reflection gone – '& I hope the feelings haven't seeped away.' – I don't think so, I don't think so. Besides which I am only concerned to share the brimming mind, and it does not bother me that what brims over is only tripe and onions. I find it incredibly easy to write to you, but only because I have discovered that nothing is expected of

132

me except myself. It would be better for you if my name was Monet or Van Gogh or Henry James in some ways, but I cheerfully dismiss the piteous thought with no trouble whatsoever, and rest on the thought that what you've got in solid fact is me; and I therefore take my corsets off, put my false teeth in the bowl of water, belch & fart a little, wriggle my yellow feet, and take it absolutely for granted that this is OK by you, & that, poor sweet, you are reconciled to the fact that I am not Ernest Hemingway, although I wish to God I were. So I am not bothered to write reflectively *or* unreflectively, but simply to slop over, come what may. I haven't read that over, but I bet it's as bland as bland can be. Huw Bland Wheldon, the boy from Llanfaircaereinon. Be bland & see the world.

At the end of the month he was in San Francisco, writing on a marble-topped table in a North Beach café about lust:

Yesterday, somehow, was a lost day. I left myself free to enjoy leisure, but freedom is not my friend, and it was a dirty wasted day. I must tell you this, & disgust & disappoint you, and bore and bewilder you, but how else to share my life? And how else to share the burden? So nothing happened, except that I padded around, like a G.I. Joe in Tottenham Court Rd, reading the pulp in the drug stores, eyeing the 'Fun with the Nudists' film ads, longing for some unimaginable circumstance in which I would be snatched from the streets by some virago bent upon seduction, bent upon exposing my risen flesh to the fascinated gaze of her cohorts. This kind of thing can waste a whole day, a total day committed to waste & shame – can and does. Mercifully some dull party took me up in the evening, and the spell of blank-eyed, somnambulist lusting was over, and I came back into a real world, no matter how footling, & drank beer, & chatted . . .

Tomorrow I spend the day in the TV station, tomorrow night dine with a barrister who has clearly made a fortune out of being sardonic. Thursday I go to an Actors Studio, and I *must* write to these Los Angeles places so that I am not left there to my own devices, because that only means doing absolutely nothing in a waste of shame.[1] This must have been a tedious letter for you to read, and even as you narrow your eyes to criticise or shake your head in bewilderment or feel your stomach turning at the problem of being married to such a half-man; even as you say to yourself how self-pitying and dismal a letter this is, please grin and snap your fingers at the same time, because I just can't spill my life over in this way unless you are kind and cheerful, & because you are the lilac tree in the middle of my mucky back-yard, and how could I smile and beam ever again if the lilac withered at a touch? You said you missed my sense around the place, & I hope you do – but it is not your sense I miss or depend on, it is your whole totality, your breathing womanly being, no less, and I am living on the assumption that you are THERE, confident & cheerful & lively & to hell with all morbidities.

The next and final outburst was a few weeks later, when he was travelling between Mississippi and Virginia in bad weather that interfered with flights. From Richmond he wrote on October 15, beginning with a separate covering note to say this was a 'damned personal, sex-ridden letter', so 'Better take a glass of water . . . and a Tranquiliser or two.'

Yesterday ghastly all round. When I am active or taken up, things are alright. Boswell, bothered about 'dark imaginings' in his all too prurient mind, asked the great Doctor what to do, & got a stiff reply to the effect that he, the Doctor, could suggest nothing [at] all for this condition except that Boswell concern himself, as he should, with 'innocent pleasures and virtuous duties' or words to that effect. And he was damn' right. Yesterday, with so much bumping and wobbling that reading was difficult; with so much darkness surrounding the journey that there was nothing to be seen; with so much calculating about re-connections, and re-routings and so many stops on airports all

---

[1] 'The expense of spirit in a waste of shame/Is lust in action.' Shakespeare, sonnet 129. This footnote will irritate those who recognize the allusion. Wheldon would have understood the difficulty. See page 140.

over the Southern States; with these as the outward circumstance of the day I fell into that tetchy, hateful, self-hating, prurient mood where anxiety was king and there being nothing else to fill my mind, it swung as it does, of its own accord, like a magnet to the north, to a stale loathsome re-run of every infantile lust known to man, so that I sat there in the wobbling aeroplane, in the dim roaring light imagining hosts in unknown towns who would invite me to join them in their love-making; imagining contact men who would suggest rendezvous with slack faced men and women who, unclothed, were watching obscene films; imagining women who in some predictable unexpected circumstances would join me in an aeroplane or a bar or a bus or a meeting, and invite me in some lewd way to lechery, imagining chambermaids who, compulsive as their victim, would slip into my room, to draw the bedclothes down and stroke my red-hot body, gradually, eyes gleaming, stroking their way to the quick of me; imagining, helpless somehow as a baby, all possible variations on a theme which is so sterile and so positively absurd as to leave you exhausted. In one airport I got out of the aeroplane and marched grimly to the bookstall and bought all the rude, sex magazines I could see – five of them. Leafing them over in the aeroplane was at least better than being dragged along in the wake of my own thoughts, because while photographs of women holding their bosoms, and lying with invitation between their parted thighs are, God knows, part of a world of pure fantasy, they were at least women, and looking them over one, or I at all events, felt saner altogether. The straightforward pleasure of looking at all these bosoms and nipples and bellies was milder and in-comparably more bland than the confused, undefined images I saw or partly saw in my mind's eye. Besides which they had faces, some pretty which was nice; but mostly brutal which simply dismissed them from the world of my desires, as I saw them. So that in a way I got quite a pleasant, even a smiling, kick out of the fatuous magazines, any translation to a world anywhere near reality being so comparably better, more straightforward, than the mind's own journey. They pricked a balloon. But not

135

for long. The compulsion is like wind, you are blown along by it; like hunger and simply undismissable except by activity or things so absorbing that the situation does not exist.

It is selfish, ruthless of me, to write all this – because it is only, in some way, an effort to shift a burden or at least have it shared. And perhaps the burden is too big, for sharing to help – too big, that is, for you. And I don't want you to be anything but yourself and this kind of thing puts such a strain on you that I am afraid of telling you, and feel that it is unfair to do so. And yet, I cannot for the life of me sit down to write you a letter as if these things did not happen.

Anyway, it is morning now, and anger and purpose and so on drive the phantoms away more or less . . .

That afternoon he wrote in a lighter mood, to say that 'maybe a day with those fucking phantoms does me good, explodes the pressures, punctures the built-up pustules: anyway I feel very cheerful and full of affection; & you encircle my mind & inhabit me.'

Mrs Wheldon seems to have taken it in her stride. A week later, one of his presents from America arrived in Kew: petticoats. He was a great buyer of clothes for his wife, and had her measurements carefully written down in his diary, including hands and feet. 'Huw, you are the cat's pyjamas,' she wrote back, 'the girl's best friend, the one and only mostest.'

The trip was coming to an end. Back in New York, Wheldon stayed with Norman Podhoretz and his wife, looking for *Monitor* items and counting the hours. 'You are a God-sent funny writer,' he told Jay, reading one of her letters. 'You don't grow on trees. You are rare, Mother Grady, rare, rare, rare [. . .] Off now to see some Ballet bastard.'

In another New York letter:

> The Mail has just come – your note saying Please Please don't mind about the blown-back house. Why, Mrs Grady, Mrs Hush, dear, you just don't understand the feelings of a traveller returning from a suitcase, an animal house after a journey through other people's rooms. Quite apart from. And. Not to mention. It would take too long. Off now to the Alien Tax Division, the

Museum of Art . . . Make a speech to the St David's Society of New York tomorrow night, dine with Tycoons Sunday night, fly the Atlantic Monday night, sleep with my wife in my bed in my house in my country Tuesday night. And Wednesday night too thank God, & Thursday.

Monitor had been missing him. Jay had written more than once to describe items that, for her, fell below his standard. Professional watchers felt the same. Talks department's last-quarter report in 1959 said that '"Monitor", which had lacked the presence of Huw Wheldon . . . got back into its stride with a number of good editions.'

By the spring he was in New York again, in a different mood, with Humphrey Burton. Jay was pregnant again, and he wrote that 'I find it a frightful oppression not to mention your delicious burgeoning glory, but remain discreet as any poodle, thin-lipped to the last.' He and Burton were making a film about Rudolf Bing and the Metropolitan Opera. Wheldon wrote of

hideous difficulties with unions & with our own limited powers of invention & stimulus, made ironically plainer by the extreme & unbelievable helpfulness & patience of Bing & the Opera people. With the facilities given us we should have a gem. Instead, a lump of faintly glistening mud . . . (Yesterday we had to pay overtime to 10 men, TEN MEN to sit in cars while two men inside shot a few silent sequences with Humphrey tearing his hair & me going greyer.)

But he wanted no word of his pessimism to reach the *Monitor* office. 'Strong confidence the line, so help me God,' he ended.

In August 1960 his wife gave birth to a daughter, Sian; a newspaper quoted Wheldon as saying he regarded women as 'a more satisfactory piece of creation than men'. An undated letter, headed 'Midnight. The Dining Room', must have been written to await Jay's return from hospital with the new baby, in his absence on *Monitor* business. There seems to be a new certainty about his affection. He wrote:

137

I have been trying like anything to find some graceful act, some lovely and appropriate thing, some symbol, some token, and I can think of nothing. Were it the other way round, you would undoubtedly have arranged something. I have mad ideas, of course, like painting the front gate white for you, or handstitching and embroidering a suitable message. I ponder them, and cast them aside. It would be more helpful if I washed these bloody dishes and collected the day's newspapers.

A single rose on your pillow really would look ludicrous.

You must make do with the knowledge that the house has been as empty as the grave without you, and that only with your return does it assume any meaning. You must also accept the responsibility, like any other Pope or Queen or Lord Protector, of being the person round whom the set-up revolves. Not just now, but always. This is not just idle chat, Mary, but a number one piece of concrete fact, Jacqueline. You may be a B.Sc. (Econ) but I don't think you have any inkling of your actual importance – not as the person who makes things work (although of course you are that too) but as the person for whom it must be done, the person without whom no work is possible because it no longer means anything [. . .]

What counts is that you are back, and that without you nothing mattered except your return.

Is that bed comfortable?

Do you want any other books?

Do you want *different* flowers?

A glass of water?

Tea?

More cushions?

Ink?

A Mouth Organ?

Go on. Ask for them. I wish to hell I was there. I would give you everything, including love.

One day that winter the Wheldons and their two children were visiting Kew Gardens, half a mile from their home. As they left the Palm House he came face to face with Celia. He looked away.

Wheldon's career with *All Your Own* came to end in December, though not by his choice. His appearances had become infrequent, and payment for them had long since been consolidated into his salary; the only reason for going on was that he liked it. Now a new head of children's programmes decided to drop Wheldon, writing to him to praise his 'born actor's instinct for attack, timing and opportunism', but regretting that such virtues 'tended to make your performance unpredictable'.

Wheldon had outgrown the hobbyists. *Monitor* had raised him up to be a name, widely respected, laughed at a little. To the BBC he was valuable, the man who had brought off a brilliant trick. ITV, home of game shows (as its critics liked to say, in those days) had nothing comparable. The *Monitor* operation became another piece of evidence to impress the Pilkington inquiry into broadcasting, set up in July 1960, and help nudge it towards giving the BBC a second television channel – as it duly did.

Towards the end of 1960, when Penguin Books were about to be prosecuted over *Lady Chatterley's Lover*, the defence solicitors were busy making a list of witnesses, a few of whom might be called on to discredit the Crown's case. Wheldon was asked if his name could go on the list. He was anxious to agree, and join the other liberals ready to endorse the book's merits. Seeking BBC permission, he pointed out (September 2 1960) that 'if ever I were called, it would do the "Monitor" situation no harm, as it were'. His superiors took a contrary view. A note from Grace Wyndham Goldie (September 8) said tersely, 'As discussed. You felt that you would, on the whole, prefer not to accept this suggestion, since you would be vulnerable and might do yourself and "Monitor" harm by appearing.'

He was a public figure now, and that, after all, was what he wanted.

CHAPTER SEVEN

Arts and Crafts

THE WHELDON OF *Monitor* was a showman, telling viewers to roll up and look this way. It was one of his strengths but it laid him open to the charge that he was 'naïve' about the arts. He was accused of being 'melodiously out of his depth' and 'amateurish'. His habit of giving simple information was sneered at by some critics, anxious to be thought well-informed. To have it explained that Tolstoy renounced the world and died alone was to insult the well-read viewer. He was supposed to know it already.

Wheldon saw the problem but came down on the side of clarity. In the case of Tolstoy, he had a line inserted in the commentary to say that it was 'on this occasion that he made his famous renunciation'. When *Monitor* did its Milhaud item, it worried Wheldon that among his two or three million viewers there would be many who had never heard of him. For their benefit he spelt it out: M-I-L-H-A-U-D. Lips curled at once. A journalist wrote reprovingly about Mr W-H-E-L-D-O-N. 'Maybe he was right, at that,' said Wheldon charitably; adding that the problem remained. His mother-in-law had heard of Rembrandt, he said, but she would be unlikely to know he was born at the end of the fifteenth century, which might be information that a viewer needed. Mrs Stroud, or 'Madam', stood for the non-elite audience. He once described her as a kind and adventurous woman, who, when young, was not only an athlete but played the double bass. 'At the same time,' he added, 'her

best friend could not call her particularly literate about the arts.'
Colleagues became used to hearing her cited as an authority. He
was half serious. He liked to watch television with her. Writing
once to Jay, who was in North Wales with his family, he said
that he and Madam were

> all set up to watch
>
> Tonight
> Hancock
> Monty
>
> with a break for kippers at 8.

Monitor was not, in his view, a platform to let one elite address
another. People deserved to have the arts in their lives. The
public servant in him rose to the occasion. Like Mount Carmel,
like the Arts Council, like the Festival of Britain, *Monitor*
embodied some old-fashioned ingrained principle of 'betterment'.
Wheldon, the teacher, would pose straight questions and hope
for enlightenment. 'How is it that you know so much about
tramps?' he asked Harold Pinter, after seeing his play *The
Caretaker*. 'How do you become a conductor?' he asked Colin
Davis. Pinter was not particularly forthcoming; Davis was. Few
people were, or are, as ready as Wheldon to risk looking unclever
on television. His directness appealed to those of similar stamp
among his subjects. The filmed interview with Henry Moore
(November 20 1960) is remembered for that reason.

Not only critics were waspish about this powerful middlebrow
in their midst; traces of the same snobberies can be found among
ex-colleagues. One of them describes a meeting where the late
D.G. Bridson remarked, 'Let's do something about collage.'[1]
Wheldon muttered, 'Never heard of him, old boy,' while those
who had, nudged one another. Having spoken of it, the ex-colleague
added, 'It's a mean story, I shouldn't have told you.' The same

---

[1] *OED*: 'An abstract form of art in which photographs, pieces of paper,
newspaper cuttings, string etc are placed in juxtaposition and glued to the
pictorial surface.'

ex-colleague recorded the same story for a television programme about Wheldon when he was dead, and made the same disclaimer, 'I shouldn't perhaps have told that story.' (It was not used.)

Another colleague, this one more sympathetic, remembers the day Wheldon discovered 'Church Going', the poem by Philip Larkin, and 'went bananas about it'. He insisted on reading it aloud to everyone in the office, declaring they must make a programme about it – 'He could drive you batty like that,' says the colleague. But twenty years later Wheldon was still quoting the poem in speeches. What he felt was genuine.

His straightforwardness – together with his liking for the methodical and well-ordered – may have been why technically he was such a powerful editor. That was David Jones's impression. On one occasion Wheldon asked what he wanted to do next. Jones suggested a film about West Indian novelists in London. 'Are there any?' said Wheldon. He let Jones talk at length about five or six names, and was convinced. Then, having learned what he needed to know, he became the editor, already beginning to structure the programme in his head.

'In that kind of situation,' says David Jones, 'he would say without hesitating, "The ones I want to do are George Lamming and Edgar Mittelhozer, ten minutes on one, eight minutes on the other, start shooting in two weeks' time." I'm not saying the decisions were absolutely right, but there was an extraordinary decisiveness about them. Equally, when you brought back the film and showed him a rough cut [the "first assembly", the stage after the initial editing] he would say, "That bit's boring, that bit's in the wrong place." On two occasions he sent me back to shoot stuff that he felt was crucial to the story.' The focus of the story was never overlooked. Jones directed a film about the Irish writer Frank O'Connor (November 1969), who was interviewed by Wheldon in Cork city. O'Connor was making a return journey to the place he grew up in, and had long since left. Wheldon, says Jones, 'shifted the emphasis of the film from a trip down memory lane to an essay on provincialism'.

The *Monitor* team – about ten strong in 1960 – often argued with Wheldon, and sometimes won. Humphrey Burton, who went to *Monitor* from radio, with music as his special interest, had to work hard to arouse interest in an item about the Allegri string quartet, eventually much praised (March 27 1960). What persuaded Wheldon was hearing from Burton of a family tradition within the quartet – 'like a guild of Mastersingers, the torch handed from father to son'. Nancy Thomas, an associate producer, proposed an item about the French artist Marcel Duchamp, whose provocative work included old junk as well as surrealist paintings. Told about the bicycle wheels and urinals that were part of the opus, Wheldon said, 'Nancy, you can't be serious.' Convinced that she was, he let work proceed. Duchamp was interviewed on film, not by Wheldon, and he and his work discussed in the studio (June 17 1962). It occupied an entire edition. A critic praised Wheldon's introduction as a model of its kind: 'well thought out, concise and fluent'. But Wheldon had never heard of Duchamp until Thomas mentioned him.

To concede a case, Wheldon had to be seized by the art or the life. Otherwise the idea was dropped. He was older than them; most of the unit were children in the war. He was also sterner. The Lime Grove offices that had once been little houses might rattle with his laughter, but he never used his good humour as a way out of difficulties. 'The one thing Huw would never tolerate was any attempt to defuse a situation by charm,' says David Jones. His scrupulousness was noticed by secretaries. When he was out of the office, he always rang up to report where he was. He didn't fiddle his expenses – 'In later life,' says Ann James, 'I found it was normal for some people to do so, and I was shocked. He didn't even get any allowance for his suits on *Monitor*. He never used me for ordering dustbins or writing letters to the bank. I respected it very much.' Not everyone was impressed by this. It was said behind his back that he was a bit of a boy scout. Ann James adds, 'I was aware that those who disliked him disliked him intensely.'

David Jones found contrary things to notice. Sexual imagery would crop up in conversation. When Jones showed him the rough cut of one film Wheldon shook his head and said, 'The trouble is, you haven't actually fucked the story' – meaning, says Jones, that 'he didn't want something that was safe and nice and polished. He wanted you to commit yourself – commit yourself to communicating the centre of that person within twelve to fifteen minutes.' Wheldon liked to sit with his feet up on the desk, elaborately casual. Jones noticed 'the hand often *here* [on his crotch], or even down inside the trousers, when he was listening. I don't think this is particularly unusual. But I believe there was a link between the burning enthusiasm for the work and the sexual drive.' Wheldon himself made the point inadvertently when he said to a journalist some years later that *Monitor* had been a companion, a friend, an obsession. 'I had no need for fantasies,' he told his interviewer, a woman, 'very seldom even sexual ones.'

Jones recalls 'stories of how a woman looked at him in a peculiar way on a bus, or a respectable looking girl came up to him in a bar off Piccadilly Circus and said, "How would you like me and my friend to take you to an hotel and give you your pleasure?" I asked him, "What did you say, Huw?" and he said, "I told her I was terribly sorry, I was too busy at the moment." I would say he thought about such things a great deal. It was as if it was necessary to tell stories with a sexual edge on them.' But they always ended innocently.

In some cases it was no use arguing with Wheldon. At least one item about a novelist regarded as a homosexual was not approved – 'No, no, old chap, we can't have someone who's overtly queer on the programme.' Homosexuals in other spheres seem not to have been objected to. Perhaps Wheldon felt he knew more about the novel than about, say, painting, so he could be more confident about his prejudices. Patrick White was given the black spot on aesthetic grounds – he was 'one of today's most overblown novelists'; the fact that he was in Australia was incidental, since 'I wouldn't let you film him if he lived in Ealing.'

When it came to a big interview, Wheldon sometimes reacted

with or against a subject in a way that left traces of irritability or uneasiness in the film, to its benefit. This happened with Lawrence Durrell (February 1960), another writer about whom Wheldon had doubts. Wheldon and a film crew went to his house in Provence the previous month. The director, whose idea it had been, was David Jones. The interview was filmed over two days. Talking before the cameras started, Wheldon seemed on edge. He didn't take to Durrell. At one point he contradicted him, saying that 'you don't realize what you've written'. The novelist was taken aback.

The first day's material was adequate but without lustre. On the second day, Jones used the Roman amphitheatre at Nimes, which was nearby, as a dramatic setting for the remainder of the interview. Durrell was not keen on mounting the steps, complaining he had no head for heights, but agreed to do it. This time the place and Wheldon between them sharpened his manner. Jones says he 'gave Huw a hard time'. On the page this is hardly apparent, but in the film Durrell does have a glint in his eye. When a book of *Monitor* transcripts was published in 1962, reviewers noted how much was lost in print. One exchange in the book has Wheldon quoting a character in a Durrell novel, 'The thing to do is to laugh till you hurt, and hurt till you laugh,' to which Durrell replies, 'Yes. You have to.' The actual exchange was longer and more muddled, with Durrell saying pointedly, 'Yes – and you?' after 'Yes. You have to.' Jones's recollection, that Durrell said, 'If you want to be a human being, you'd better learn', is at fault, unless the words were edited out. The brilliant Allan Tyrer was *Monitor*'s chief film editor. He says that Wheldon marched into the cutting room and told him to keep the Durrell interview to ten minutes, complaining that he was 'an impossible man'. But he had second thoughts: the interview as transmitted was twice as long. In any case, the trace of conflict survived.

An interview with the American novelist Mary McCarthy was another instance of Wheldon and his subject grating on one another. When the *Monitor* book was published, a reviewer noted that the 'disdainful manner' in which she dealt with questions scarcely appeared on the page. At one point she remarked on 'the daily cant that pours in from everywhere, all the stuff that's piped in, including probably this programme with me on it'. When Wheldon queried the American fondness for 'intellectuals', she responded with a fierce smile, baring many teeth, and savaged non-intellectual writers like Hemingway and others – 'red-blooded young people whose minds would never be raped by an idea'.

Wheldon: 'Would you go so far as to say that Ernest Hemingway had never been raped by an idea?'

McCarthy: 'Absolutely.'

When Wheldon interviewed Orson Welles a month later, the exchange was less productive. With inserts from his films, the item lasted more than half an hour. No theme emerged; Welles smoked a cigar and enjoyed himself. It was hardly interviewing. At the beginning, Wheldon mused, 'Whether he's a prodigy who's now entering into a more stately maturity, or whether he's a genius not yet totally fulfilled, who can tell?' At the end, when Welles said that all the books written about him in America were derogatory, and he wished there was 'something nicer [posterity] could read about me', Wheldon replied, 'I hope, Orson, somebody writes it for you pretty soon.'

Sycophancy was not Wheldon's usual way. Talk was a serious business, what he did best, socially as well as professionally. He was aware of his dangerous facility. 'I talk away my ideas as I talk,' he said, comparing himself to Simenon, 'but *he* keeps them damped down.' He needed to be heard, to dominate a conversation. A wife remembers him trying to steamroller an old friend in a wine bar. There were BBC colleagues embarrassed to be on a bus with him, everyone listening. He could be curiously insensitive. Brian Murphy's second wife, Joan – he remarried in 1959 – remembers the doorbell ringing persistently on Sunday evening after *Monitor* had gone out, and Huw needed to talk about the programme. She was very fond of him. But 'no matter if the children were asleep or it was late and you were too tired

146

to talk. Huw had arrived.' He would upstage his peers if he thought he could. His anecdotes were large and powerful. 'He told his life in long paragraphs,' says Humphrey Burton, adding that it didn't matter if one had heard the stories already. Not everyone agreed.

Wheldon could use anecdotes like a weapon. A rival storyteller might set him off. Emlyn Williams, the Welsh writer and actor, was another raconteur. He was on *Monitor* twice in 1961, first in a live interview, later in a film about his childhood, when his early autobiography was published. Like Wheldon, he came from North Wales, although his background was one of poverty. He wouldn't revisit Connah's Quay with the film unit. While working on the material in London, he went, with a BBC man, to lunch at a pub near the Ealing studios where *Monitor* films were edited. Wheldon joined them, and at once launched into a comic narrative. Williams listened politely until the story finished, Wheldon's laughter piercing the air. Before he had time to start one of his own, Wheldon was off again. Another major anecdote followed, and a third. By then it was time to go. Wheldon left, and Williams and his host returned to the studios. They went up three flights of steps and were in the Gents before Williams said softly, 'He'll die laughing one day, that one.'

At the same time, Wheldon liked to explain that his was a modest role, and so was everyone else's on the programme. They were all artisans, doing their bit for the arts. He said:

> I am doubtful as to the extent to which a film or a studio item can, in its own eternal right, be a work of art, but I am in no doubt at all as to the extent to which it can serve as an artifact through which the artist speaks. While we are prepared to have pictures by Bellini or sculpture by Zadkine or music by Handel or paintings by Graham Sutherland, we are not prepared to put around those pictures [any] film or studio circumstances which themselves claim to be artistic, but rather studio or film circumstances that claim to be seemly. So that there is a curious little tightrope which gets thinner and thinner that you have to walk.

147

This tightrope is to be not arty, but not, on the other hand, ignoble. You have no right to film or to edit, or to direct in a studio, works of Moore, or works by Larkin, or works by any artist, in a way which is gimmicky.

Wheldon's most fecund relationship was with a creator in his own right, working within the unit. This was the film director Ken Russell, whose work shifted from being a framework for other artists towards being idiosyncratic art of its own. Because Russell was part of *Monitor*, his work had to be interfered with. Russell, who was learning his trade and didn't begin to make films for the cinema until most of his *Monitor* work was done, seems not to have resented this. He still affirms that through *Monitor*, Wheldon ran the only British film school. Wheldon returned the compliment when he told John Baxter, who wrote a book about Russell (1973), that 'Ken is a much abler man than myself in all sorts of ways.'

Russell got into television by sending the BBC some amateur films he had made, at a time when Wheldon needed to replace John Schlesinger, who was moving on. *Monitor* had been running for less than a year. Wheldon saw the work of nearly fifty directors. One of them was Russell, a nobody aged thirty-one, whose films, according to Wheldon, looked as if they had been shot on toilet paper. His first piece for *Monitor* was *Poet's London* (March 1 1959), about John Betjeman. Innocently, he tried to include a scene with some friends of his, dressed up in Edwardian clothes. Real people were not impersonated in television documentaries in those days. Wheldon thought it was cheating, and removed the scene at once.

This issue, reality v. fiction, remained on the agenda all the time they worked together, with Russell never giving up and Wheldon retreating a step at a time. The issue was important to Wheldon. Blurring the line between fact and fiction was a threat. Thirty years later, the argument is still going on in television, though it has moved a long way since Wheldon's time. It was another couple of years before Russell tried again, with a piece about Prokofiev and his relationship with the Soviet State. Wheldon wouldn't hear of an actor playing the composer. Russell went as far as he could. He showed bits of Prokofiev – someone's hands playing a piano, someone else's feet, and a reflection in rippling water. Finally he did a long-shot in which a distant Prokofiev lay on his death-bed. This meant seeing an actor's face. Goldie and Wheldon were in the dubbing theatre (where sound-tracks are added) when they viewed the unfinished version with Russell. The dying Prokofiev was too much for them and had to go; the rest was grudgingly allowed.

Russell was making seven or eight films a year. Like everyone else, he had to get his ideas past Wheldon. 'He'd call you into his office, and sit with his feet up on the desk, which was supposed to put you at your ease. It was rather like going to see the headmaster. It didn't put you at your ease at all. You knew he was acting. Having his feet up didn't seem a natural thing to do. He'd get you to tell the story, and on the merits of how you told it, he'd tell you to go ahead, or say, "No, no, old boy."'

Many of Russell's films had musical themes, like *The Miners' Picnic*, his impression of an annual brass band event in Northumberland. Once he had said Yes, Wheldon let him pursue his ideas, well away from the studios if Russell could manage it. The production secretary received a postcard from him when he was filming with the miners: 'Dear Ann, These fiendish Bingo tables & Housy Housy hells have been the ruin of us all. Could you ask Humph [Humphrey Burton] to bring me £15. Thank you.' Russell was kept out of sight in London. 'I was like the Jew in the attic in the Occupation,' he said. 'Grace Wyndham Goldie didn't really want me there. Every producer in talks department was supposed to go to the weekly meeting, but I only went once. Huw always made an excuse, because he knew if she saw me it was like a red rag to a bull. "We don't want film directors *manqué* here, we want television programme makers." So Huw spirited me into the attic.'

Another of his ideas was 'a look at the strange and varied world of the dancers of England', which he and Burton evolved as a film, shot in more than thirty locations. An extra five hundred pounds had to be begged from the controller of programmes. It was shown as *The Light Fantastic* at Christmas 1960. Wheldon was not particularly keen on the idea, or even on the finished product, but he was susceptible to other people's excitement, as he expected them to be susceptible to his. Russell says that 'what struck me as strange about Huw – and I've never met it with anyone else at all who had power – was that even if he didn't approve of an idea, if he felt that you were passionate enough, he'd let you do it.'

In one of his off-the-cuff dissertations, Wheldon rambled on about the dancing film, and in doing so threw light on the nature of his debate with Russell: the editor and the artist. They were both unhappy when making the film, he said, because they lacked a firm opinion of their ragbag of amateur dancers – were they to be seen as good or bad, feeble or vigorous? They had to *mean* something:

> The problem is, you are facing two chasms. The one is to be prissy, because anyone can make a prissy film about dancing, so that we can see all this lovely culture going on in Newcastle and Lewisham. Equally you can look sneeringly at all this activity and mock it. And neither of these will do. Russell and I were talking one day about old gentlemen in the Athenaeum who tut-tut about juvenile delinquents – and it's a terrible thing of course that young men should knock old ladies across the head. There is certainly such a thing as juvenile delinquency, and it's vicious. Then if you think for a moment of the old gentlemen tut-tutting, there is something a little disagreeable about that, too, because in some perhaps rather romantic but nevertheless true way, there is a sense in which the delinquents for all their degeneracy are innocent if only because they are young, while members of the Athenaeum for all their virtue are on the whole neither young, nor, in that sense, innocent. There is a sense in which a thing can be both degenerate and innocent at the same time. And Russell got the feeling that this was particularly true of dancing. If you go to a rock-and-roll place you see empty girls with empty vacant

faces, dancing together to noisy, pitifully abject tunes. You can see it as being a degenerate process, but at the same time there is an innocence as well. So Russell made the film with love, finding the degeneracy as best he could, and finding the innocence, too [. . .] We found a barrow boy who knew nothing about dancing except that he was a first-rate dancer, and got him to make the commentary, because at least he spoke with authority from inside. He communicated an innocence.

What mattered to Russell was that he himself was not articulate, and Wheldon showed him how to define ideas and turn them into scripts. That was the 'British film school' side of their relationship. 'He drew words out of me. I couldn't write a single bloody sentence. All the other producers and directors were university graduates. I was from the Nautical College, Pangbourne. When we were editing the Prokofiev film, he said, "Why have you put these pictures together like that?" I said, "It's obvious." Wheldon: "It's not obvious to me. What are you trying to say?" I said, "That he's a genius." Wheldon: "What do you mean, genius? These pictures don't tell me that." He channelled my woolly thinking, made me draw up an architectural plan.'

But the headmaster was not always at ease with the pupil. 'He could never make me out,' says Russell, 'because I was an ignoramus. I knew nothing. I don't know much still.' Perhaps Wheldon saw him as an innocent with a delinquent streak. He certainly wasn't safe. 'An artist among [Huw's] directors would be like a painter working on the programme full time,' Russell told Baxter, 'someone he would have to respect *as an artist* whether he agreed with him or not. He didn't mind extreme opinions if they didn't upset him. But I began to upset him.'

Pop Goes the Easel (March 1962) was about pop art, another idea that raised doubts. Russell told him it was about a new culture of painting: not *The Horse* by Stubbs, or Turner's *Sunset*. He was told to go ahead. What appealed to Russell was the idea of a popular culture, rather than the works of art

151

themselves – 'using pin tables, and Marilyn Monroe, and the twist with Chubby Checker, and rock-'n'-roll, things that hadn't been seen on television.' Allan Tyrer says that Wheldon kept looking in at the cutting room to see if the film was ready. 'I used to say, "Ken, he's after us again," and Ken would say, "Don't show it him till it's finished."'

'It was a flip film,' says Russell. 'No one spoke in it much, which was unusual for *Monitor*. When Huw saw the film, he said, "Brilliant, old boy, brilliant, but you don't show the artists at work. They just seem to be a lot of wankers drifting about, playing pin tables. Won't do, old chap, got to show a bit of paint on the canvas, a bit of pigment on the palette." So I went back and shot them painting, and he was delighted. He said he would introduce it by saying these were serious artists, they'd been at the Royal College for years, and graduated with honours. I said, "Fine, and do you mind if I pan down to you in the studio from a picture of Marilyn Monroe?" "Not at all, old boy." He wasn't crazy about pop art, but he wasn't a King Canute, either.'

Wheldon censored a scene at the end of Russell's film *The Preservation Man* (May 1962). This was about Bruce Lacey, an actor and theatrical props maker whose surburban house and garden were crammed with unusual objects – old military uniforms, obsolete vacuum cleaners, wax-cylinder gramophones, stuffed animals, working robots, a penny-farthing bicycle, a 'What the Butler Saw' machine. 'He and his family lived in happy squalor,' says Russell, 'and while I was making the film I saw the way he lived. He had just recorded a Victorian sentimental ballad called *Roses Round the Door*, about an ideal family living in a cottage. So I made a sort of television commercial. There were eight children. They sat around a bowl of custard with lollipops, dipping them in the custard. Outside the back door there weren't any roses, just beaten earth and rubbish as far as the eye could see. But it was [Russell sings] "Roses round the door, babies on the floor" – it was a marvellous satire on the television world. That was the coda of the film.

'Huw did a double-take when he saw it. He rang me up on the

day of transmission and said, "We've just had a run-through, old boy. Nobody laughed." I said, "They're not supposed to laugh, Huw." "Well, nobody laughed. I'm cutting it, old boy. I'm sorry. Goodbye."

'I thought he chickened out. It wasn't the image he saw for *Monitor*. It was satire. He didn't go much on satire.'

While making *The Preservation Man*, Russell got the better of Wheldon by producing a faked recording of Tennyson that he passed off as the real thing. The BBC archives have a wax cylinder recording of Tennyson reading *The Charge of the Light Brigade*, which Russell wanted to use with shots of Lacey's phonographs. But the voice is almost inaudible. Russell decided he could improve on this. One of Lacey's machines was an early office dictaphone, which recorded on wax cylinders. They stuffed a sock in the tube, to give a muffled sound, and Russell imitated the poet. 'Tennyson, eh?' Wheldon said when he heard it on the sound-track. 'Marvellous old chap.'

Apart from the occasional nude, briefly glimpsed, Russell's earlier films had little or no sexual content for Wheldon to object to. Like David Jones, now and then Russell caught a sexual tone in Wheldon's conversation. He heard him tell the same story (it was about Henry VIII's codpiece in his armour at the Tower of London) to two women, on occasions years apart, and each time watch closely to see the reaction. In a BBC canteen, when Russell and other colleagues were hunched around a table contemplating some crisis, he heard Wheldon say briskly that it did people no good to sit there wondering how big their cocks were.

Wheldon had a strong sense of what it was decent to let a mass audience see. No doubt he was over-cautious sometimes. Nancy Thomas did an item about an Indian painter, Avinash Chandra – 'He was influenced by temple art, and there were strong erotic themes. Huw didn't like it. He said, "You can't put that out!" "Why not?" I said. We did, and no one complained.' A dirty word, an erotic image in the wrong place, was not wise; it was not *right*. A clip from *Notti di Cabiria*, a film by the Italian director Fellini, was banned because it showed a prostitute.

Prostitutes were too near the bone. David Jones was present. 'Huw said, "It's quite clearly a prostitute." We said, "Yes, Huw, it's a prostitute." "But you can't show that," he said. "It's a Sunday. What about families? Someone will have to explain to their families what this woman does." He was adamant.' The clip came out.

Wheldon's father died in November 1961. His brother Tomos, three years younger than Huw, had died earlier in the year of leukaemia. Sir Wynn was buried in the churchyard at Nant Peris, the country where his paternal ancestors had farmed and quarried. The *Times* obituary spoke of the Nonconformist conscience. Huw wrote to thank H. for her condolences:

> My father died, in fact, very gently & almost, you might say, characteristically. He remained unbelievably vigorous & unchanging, not old, until the Summer; felt seedy as autumn came, collected his papers, saw to things; & then fell ill. They operated, he lived on, totally lucid & good humoured, his affairs in order, knowing for certain that the thing was finished, & thus composed, he died.

Monitor was making more demands than usual that autumn. The Competitor had decided to copy the BBC, and ABC Television, one of the original ITV companies, began an arts magazine called *Tempo* in October. The critic Kenneth Tynan was in charge. For the first time *Monitor* faced direct competition, having been threatened even before *Tempo* began by attempts to poach its staff. It's uncertain whether Wheldon himself was approached. The only traceable reference is in a talks department paper that mentions *Monitor*'s return in September, after the summer break, and says, 'An attempted take-over bid for much of the *Monitor* team by the organizers of *Tempo* had earlier been frustrated.' The competition turned out not to matter. Tynan had promised to defy the 'culture snobs' and prove that 'art is not a minority affair'. But *Tempo* seemed to prove the opposite, leaning towards the pretentious.

Any threat to *Monitor* was taken seriously. In October Wheldon was sent the typescript of a novel that included a fictitious programme called *Seven Arts*. Its presenter was described in unflattering terms, and bore a superficial resemblance to Wheldon. Outraged, he threatened legal action if the novel was not rewritten before publication. None of this became public.

The novel was called *The Birdcage* and the author was John Bowen. Then aged thirty-six, Bowen had written four previous novels, including the widely praised *Storyboard*. From 1960 he was for several years a part-time script editor for Associated Television, another of the old ITV companies. He had also appeared on ABC Television's *The Bookman*. The novel was about a television presenter, Peter Ash, and a script editor, Norah Palmer. They had lived together for years, tolerating one another. The birdcage symbolized their state. Ash, who insisted they break out of the cage, had been a practising homosexual before his affair with Palmer. Now his tendencies in that direction revived. But life outside the cage proved impossible, and he had to take up with Palmer again, destroying his self-esteem in the process.

None of this had much to do with television. But Bowen intended his protagonists to be 'in some sense public people', and television was a convenient setting. The woman was given a full-time version of his own script-editing job. As for Ash, Bowen says that 'I wanted Peter Ash, who was much given to self-delusion and self-importance, to have what I considered then and still consider to be a bogus job – the front man of a TV programme about the arts.'

Bowen says he neither knew Wheldon nor thought of him as resembling Ash. However, while he was writing the book, which took him about a year, *Monitor* was the only arts programme on British television. If the fictitious Ash, in charge of the fictitious *Seven Arts*, turned out to be a thin man with a prominent chin and an incisive manner – as he did – the thought might cross a reader's mind that Huw Wheldon was like that, too. The off-screen Ash, who was explored more thoroughly, was not at all like Wheldon.

155

An internal report on the book at Faber (August 8 1961) called it 'a good read, though one that leaves a nasty taste' – the characters were thought to be disagreeable. It added that 'the MS will obviously have to have a very careful libel checking. Peter Ash/Huw Wheldon is ... the most dangerous; but what about Fred Trent (the North Country novelist, page 91) and John Braine?' Nothing more was heard of Trent/Braine, but a great deal of Ash/Wheldon. Some early cosmetic work was carried out. It was made clear in the text that Ash worked for ITV (matters were further complicated when plans for *Tempo* were announced), and a reference to the real-life Wheldon was added, to demonstrate that Ash and Wheldon were not the same person.

Charles Monteith, a young director of Faber (and a Fellow of All Souls), was in charge of the firm's fiction list. When he sent the typescript to lawyers to be read for libel in September, he affirmed that Ash's private life bore no resemblance to Wheldon's. He went on, 'The trouble is that Peter Ash's television manner – as portrayed in the novel – is, without much doubt, an unkind but fairly recognizable parody of Wheldon's manner. Three people, including myself, who have read the typescript, have all been struck by this.'

The cosmetic changes didn't satisfy the lawyers. Their report concentrated on passages about the domestic Ash, with their allegations of promiscuity and homosexuality, the latter still a criminal offence. The publishers were not too worried. Libel readers are expected to be cautious. Peter Ash was a genuine fiction except for echoes of the Wheldon of *Monitor*; no doubt Faber, and certainly Bowen, expected Wheldon to take that in his stride. Monteith decided to write to Wheldon, which he did on October 5, seeking his help with 'a possible problem'. After describing the novel, he explained that 'since [Ash] isn't a very attractive creature, I'm very anxious indeed that there shouldn't be any misunderstanding in anybody's mind about the fact that he's completely and entirely fictitious.'

Wheldon was about to leave for Cork, to make a *Monitor* film. He agreed to read the typescript, and did so presently. The first thing he would have noticed was that on the pink folder enclosing the typescript, someone had given the game away by writing, '?Huw Wheldon identification'. He read on, making notes. He singled out phrases about Ash being a 'scoutmaster of culture' and 'eager to please'. He noted a sentence that said, 'But for him, millions of people might not have known that the arts existed at all.' He found references to Lawrence Durrell and John Whiting, both of whom had appeared on *Monitor*; to Ash's thinness and tallness, and to the abstract shapes that appeared in the *Seven Arts* titles, as they did in *Monitor*'s.

Within the next few days his wife read it, and so did Kenneth Adam, the controller of programmes. Adam advised him to demand substantial changes. On October 24 Wheldon sent the typescript to the BBC Solicitor, drawing attention to phrases that suggested *Monitor*, for example:

> He was a kind of scoutmaster of culture, presenting units from his troup to the viewers for 45 minutes every Friday night at a time only just after the peak viewing hours, with a two-month break in the summer.

Wheldon went on to say that the 'scoutmaster' sentence, 'together with another sentence on the same page, "eager to please and clean in thought and deed," is, I am afraid, the kind of thing that various people entertain about me, although it would be difficult for me to put my finger on any exact quotation.' Other resemblances were noted, including Ash's prominent chin, 'which God knows, I have'. Wheldon suggested that once the connection was made, 'there is a curious sense in which all sorts of other things become grist to the same mill of identification.'

The Solicitor consulted Dick Walford, the BBC's head of copyright, himself a solicitor. Walford thought Peter Ash couldn't possibly be regarded as a portrait or caricature of Wheldon on such slight evidence. But if Wheldon wanted to prevent publication, he should say he objected strongly without giving his reasons. This involved an element of bluff, but put the onus on the publishers.

Wheldon did as he suggested. Faber promised revisions, and Bowen produced them by the end of November. Ash was now plump and blond, and answered to the description of 'the Dirk Bogarde of television interviewers'. He wasn't eager or enthusiastic; nor was his chin in evidence. *Seven Arts* also underwent changes, but Wheldon insisted that the programme being described was still recognizably his. An arts programme could be run in various ways; this one was run just like *Monitor*. He pursued the argument and wouldn't give an inch. In the end Bowen came up with the desperate solution of abandoning television altogether, and making Ash a presenter of short films that were shown in cinemas. Agreement was reached in January 1962, and *The Birdcage* appeared in October.

Wheldon had reason to complain if he thought he might be identified with the libertine, Ash. Was that his concern? Or did the root of his objection lie elsewhere, in the parody of a 'scoutmaster of culture' and other hurtful digs?

In 1962 Wheldon's formal editorship of *Monitor* ended; he moved up to assistant head of Talks in the spring. Humphrey Burton took over temporarily. Wheldon kept a finger in the pie, sometimes all his fingers.

The year was marked by the most successful film ever shown on the programme, Ken Russell's biographical study of Edward Elgar. According to Wheldon later, he and Russell quarrelled violently over the making of it, although Russell isn't so blunt. He remembers only differences of opinion; perhaps the editor knew he was losing the battle with the artist, and so in retrospect had more to be unhappy about.

An item about Elgar was first suggested in 1958 by the composer Arthur Bliss, soon after he had appeared in *Monitor*. He thought 'a short film of Elgar's birthplace' would be feasible. Wheldon replied to say he would prefer a film profile of Elgar himself. The following March they were still exchanging letters. The year, 1959, was the twenty-fifth anniversary of Elgar's death. Wheldon now said it was 'rather a "museumy" thing to do, in the sense that relics are curiously difficult things to handle.' He did have tentative plans for an item using photographs, 'with Elgar's music permeating it'. But that was as far as Sir Arthur Bliss's idea ever went.

This was when Ken Russell first worked for *Monitor* as a freelance. He couldn't live on the money, and applied to the assistant head of films, Norman Swallow, for more work. It was Swallow who first saw Russell's amateur films, and was impressed enough to pass him on to *Monitor* and Wheldon. Swallow now paid him fifty guineas to research and write the outlines of six films. One of them was about Elgar, and the treatment Russell wrote is still in the programme files. So is a note from the head of music productions, who was asked to read it, dismissing it as 'gossip-column stuff'.

Three years later, in Wheldon's Oral History version, the hundredth edition of *Monitor* was approaching, so they decided to do an Elgar film to celebrate. But the script was inadequate. Russell kept trying to write dialogue, against Wheldon's wishes. If you had dialogue, said Wheldon, it had to be in a different kind of film: 'a real work of art', not a documentary that was 'full of lines like "There's a man at the back door who says his name is Brahms." "Good afternoon, Mr Chopin, do come in." "Hello, Debussy." I couldn't stand this stuff.'

Russell says dialogue was never part of the plan. Four actors were needed to portray Elgar at different periods of his life, but they didn't speak. Whatever arguments went on beforehand, the film that Russell went off to make is the one outlined in the treatment he had written three years earlier. The first paragraph said it would be 'richly illustrated with [Elgar's] music'. The second described the scene with Elgar as a child that everyone remembers from the film – 'A sunny but windy day on the Malvern Hills. A boy riding bare-back is galloping his horse over the countryside . . .'

The music was Russell's frame for the life. He worked with Humphrey Burton on the shooting script, while Wheldon supervised in the background. The editor and the artist had words (according to Russell) or 'an enormous great quarrel' (according to Wheldon) over a scene that showed victims of the 1914 war accompanied by Elgar's 'Pomp and Circumstance March No. 1', the 'Land of Hope and Glory' music. Wheldon hated the juxtaposition (this, too, was in the 1959 script). According to Russell, he said, 'What right have you got to make that bitter statement about war? A lot of people suffered in that war.' Russell says that Wheldon was ready to take out the war sequence but in the end relented. Perhaps this was the compromise that Wheldon the old soldier resented having to make.

Russell says he wanted to use four minutes of Western Front war film, from the Imperial War Museum archives, edited to 'Pomp and Circumstance' so as to contrast the optimism of the music with the misery of the front line. The row ended with him agreeing to use only two minutes. Russell says now that he thinks Wheldon was right not to allow the original length.

In Wheldon's Oral History account he still sounds angry, declaring that 'as usual', Russell went too far. 'He had got it into his mind that Elgar was not only sick and tired of hearing "Land of Hope and Glory" but that he was really disgusted by [it] because he was disgusted by the war. Well, he was made miserable by war, as indeed everybody was, but it wasn't right to make Elgar into a pacifist, which in fact he wasn't. And I didn't like the sanctimonious element that was creeping in.' Wheldon goes on to talk about 'absolutely horrifying' material, using actors in gas masks pretending to be soldiers floundering in mud, but he seems to be confusing *Elgar* with *The Debussy Film*, where Russell again fitted music to the horrors of war. In *Elgar* a line of blinded soldiers stumbles along to 'Land of Hope and Glory', but the sequence couldn't be called 'horrifying'.

The hundredth edition of *Monitor* fell on Sunday November 11, Armistice Day. That evening the programme celebrated with a party at the Television Centre. TV monitor screens were provided for guests to watch *Elgar*. Russell was with the telecine operators putting out the film, imploring them to keep the sound levels high so everyone could hear the music. When audience response was measured by the BBC, the Reaction Index was eighty-six, the highest for any *Monitor* programme since it began.

Russell continued to make films for *Monitor* and Wheldon continued to present it. David Jones became its editor in 1963. Around this time Wheldon recruited Melvyn Bragg from radio, where he was a trainee in Laurence Gilliam's features department. Bragg was sent to television as part of his course, and asked for an attachment to *Monitor* because it was the only programme he had ever seen. Wheldon asked him why he wanted to join *Monitor*. When Bragg said that he didn't, he preferred radio, Wheldon was delighted at such contrariness, and offered him a place.

At first he was a researcher – 'a dogsbody, the tea boy'. His first opportunity came when Russell was making *The Debussy Film* in 1964. The two had written it as a cinema feature, using the story device of a film about a director making a film of Debussy. For the first time Russell set about putting dialogue (which Bragg wrote) into the mouths of his actors. In Russell's account, Wheldon accepted this, though without enthusiasm, presumably because Debussy and the rest were only actors in the film-within-a-film. His objection was to a scene where two girls play tennis with a man, against the music of Debussy's ballet *Jeux*. They embrace. Wheldon was disturbed. 'What's all this about, old boy?' Russell explained that it was a lesbian ballet. 'Can't do that, old boy. My mother-in-law doesn't understand the meaning of the word lesbian, and I'm too old to start explaining it to her. Forget it.' The sequence was cut.

Bragg tells it differently. He thinks Wheldon let Russell make the film against his better judgement, probably because *Elgar* had brought them unexpected glory. But when he saw it in a viewing room at Ealing, he 'really went off his head'. Russell, Tyrer and Bragg were there. 'He leaped from the front row, turned round and said, "I will never show this!" You've no idea of the venom. It was barrack-room language. It was actually trench language. We had betrayed the basic idea of truth to the

161

artist.' After midnight they were still drinking tea and arguing – 'in that lavatorial, green-painted, sweaty corridor by the cutting room. We were leaning against the wall, exhausted, and Huw was going on about ruining the idea of everything *Monitor* stood for.'

Bragg says they convinced him in the end. Why Wheldon should have done an about-turn isn't clear. 'One or two sequences' were trimmed, and the film went out on May 18 1965 as a *Monitor Special*. Next morning the hard men of *Tonight* were rolling their eyes in the canteen. 'What did you think you were doing?' they said.

Bragg became a friend and protégé. The families were neighbours in Kew. On Saturday nights the Braggs would go round to the Wheldons for supper and conversation after the children were in bed; there was a second daughter now, Megan, born in 1963. Jay and Melvyn, both hoping to be writers, read bits of their manuscripts to the company, which might include the Murphys from next door and Wheldon's sister, Nans. 'And then Huw would destroy us all by reading something from Tolstoy or Gorky or Dylan Thomas. I had written a bit about my grandfather. Very good, said Jay. Huw just pulled out Dylan Thomas on "A Visit to Grandpa's" and destroyed my piece completely. Huw was a feisty person. Sometimes you liked him and sometimes you didn't, to tell you the truth, to tell you the real truth. But the reason we thought highly of him is because he was this complicated person who was nearly always competitive about everything. He had the highest regard for great artists, and if he thought you weren't up to it, he just cut you off at the throat.'

Watching Wheldon at work, Bragg saw 'a complex of worries' that made him so effective as an editor; he was a sieve, whose intellectual uncertainties made him sensitive to ideas and methods – 'plus the fact that he was a very cruel editor. He actually damaged some people. If you are going to say about him being cruel, you must say this, that I loved him. But I saw him being cruel, and with others on the team, told him not to be. And maybe that was his strength.'

*

Monitor kept going for a while. In 1964, by which time Wheldon was in charge of documentaries, he brought in Jonathan Miller as editor and presenter, and the programme was relaunched. 'Après Huw Le Deluge,' wrote Miller. 'Succeeding him is rather like taking over from General de Gaulle.' Miller said later that the invitation 'must have seemed mad to him afterwards, because I stepped deep into a swamp of criticism as soon as I took on the thing.' Perhaps the programme had already run its natural course; after Wheldon, decline was inevitable. It lasted until 1965, and was closed down.

Miller's impersonation of the Huw Wheldon of *Monitor* is still admired. He and others developed the caricature, he suggests, 'as a protective device because Huw had such control over us that the only way we could escape was by pretending that we had control over *him*, in the form of a working model . . . He was so discussed, so caricatured, that I think he took some pleasure in epitomising himself. Certainly over the years I knew him, I could see him gradually settling into a much more vivid version of Uncle Huw.'

The other side of Wheldon was still glimpsed from time to time. A colleague from the *Monitor* days noticed Wheldon's almost obsessive need to be in control of himself. He thought it helped make him so effective an editor, putting an edge on his decisions. But it was emotional, not intellectual. Wheldon once spoke to him of 'the abyss', a dark side of his nature that needed to be ruled. Wheldon was drunk when he said it, in itself an event. 'He was terrified of losing control. The terror was there, the abyss was there, and it had been very near.'

And did Wheldon speak, on this one occasion, about sessions on an analyst's couch? 'I would give that story credence,' says the colleague, but declines to elaborate.

CHAPTER EIGHT

War Games

THE MAN TO watch at the BBC in the early 1960s was the other Welshman, Donald Baverstock, the darling of a staid institution that was now busy embracing youthful energy, and even what the old guard would have seen as vulgarity, in order to survive. For all his achievements, Wheldon was still dismissible as a lightweight, who had damaged himself by his weakness for self-publicity.

All those *All Your Owns* and *Monitors*, together with random work as chairman and interviewee, had spread his image thinly across the land. Television producers should be craftsmen, not performers. The fact that Wheldon was a craftsman of a high order didn't affect the argument, to which many subscribed, including Baverstock. 'In the old BBC,' he says, 'where the rule was self-effacement, when I saw Huw popping up on *Monitor*, I knew he shouldn't be advancing himself like that. The *Tonight* producers didn't – Alasdair, Jay, me.'[1]

No one could call Baverstock's personality self-effacing. But he and almost everyone else acknowledged the line between producer and performer. Wheldon was the exception. In January

---

[1] Alasdair Milne, b. 1930, a Goldie protégé, was with Baverstock on *Tonight*, and has remained a friend and ally. He was director-general of the BBC, 1982–87, a difficult period. Antony Jay (b. 1930), also worked on *Tonight*. Later he founded an independent production company, Video Arts, and became a rich man. He was knighted in 1988.

1963, his colourful history was no bar to his appointment in February as head of documentary programmes, a new title within a new Talks group, run by Grace Wyndham Goldie. But Baverstock, already assistant controller of programmes, was made chief of BBC 1 in the same reshuffle.[1] He was at least two jumps ahead of Wheldon.

The BBC itself was in better shape. The shock of competition had been absorbed; before the end of the 1950s, programmes had improved and audiences were growing. In January 1960 a new director-general had taken over, Hugh Greene, Graham Greene's younger brother. By trade a journalist, by inclination agnostic, he was a considerable figure, mischievous and eccentric. In the background was a family business, Greene King, the East Anglian brewery; he liked to drink beer. He was also fond of women and cricket. One of his early acts as director-general was to set up a secret inquiry into the ramifications of commercial television and its financial and other relationships with commerce, in the hope of finding dirt that might be useful if the Pilkington inquiry looked like going against the BBC. A 'Black Book' still exists in some archive. It seems to have served no purpose; the ITA found out about it.

Genial enough when he felt like it, his style was more contemporary than the BBC was used to. It amused him that Malcolm Muggeridge, the irreverent journalist, had not been allowed to broadcast by the express decree of his predecessor, Ian Jacob. Once Greene took over, the Muggeridges were welcomed. Capable and persuasive with those he respected – such as politicians who might make trouble for the BBC – Greene was contemptuous of what he regarded as smaller souls. Many qualified. He was irritated by a lobby of faithful if barmy

---

[1] The new network, BBC 2, was in preparation, so from now on, each channel had its own boss. Michael Peacock, another of Goldie's protégés, was made chief of 2. Both Baverstock and Peacock were subordinate to a controller of programmes, in 1963 Stuart Hood, an enigmatic figure. Kenneth Adam had become director of television.

radio listeners who demanded that he drop plans to shift the main news and the accompanying chimes of Big Ben from 9 p.m. In private he was heard to deride the Big Ben Association, its members determined to 'think beautiful thoughts while the clock struck nine.' He brushed aside a Midlands schoolteacher who appeared from nowhere to castigate the BBC, Mary Whitehouse. Mrs Whitehouse, who claimed to speak for millions and was at first regarded as a joke, would have meant trouble however carefully she was handled, but Greene's thinly disguised contempt for her was a mistake.

Greene's permissive approach had small effect on Wheldon, whose sub-empire (presently enlarged to include music productions) was not pressing to push back the boundaries of taste, as some departments were. Wheldon's idea was to make solid, wholesome documentaries. Baverstock, who as chief of BBC 1 could say yes or no to other people's programmes, was impatient of the Wheldon approach – he had been critical enough of it in the *Monitor* days, and now he continued to see it as too indulgent and long-winded. 'He didn't come up with many ideas,' he says, 'and his producers used to take so long making them.'

But Baverstock was critical by nature, and people made allowances for his style. Where Baverstock was blunt and impatient, Wheldon was increasingly the affable gent. Yet he was direct, outspoken and unshakably reliable. However much he was perceived as putting on an act, old-boying his way from one florid anecdote to another, he gave every sign of being someone who could be trusted to say what he thought, to your face: tempered with a smile and expressions of goodwill, but a plain, truth-will-out approach all the same.

His ingenuity was admired even by those on the receiving end. John Read, the producer, whose own work had been overshadowed by *Monitor*, and who had no particular reason to be fond of Wheldon, took an idea to him, as head of documentaries, that meant sending a film unit to Australia. The subject was the Sydney Opera House. Read outlined his proposal to a silent Wheldon. When he had finished, Wheldon said, 'You actually want me to pay for a trip to Australia? I tell you what. Sit in my chair. Pretend you're me.'

They crossed over to one another's side of the desk. Wheldon presented the case for flying a film crew across the world. Read heard himself turn it down. 'I fell into the trap,' he says sadly. Hugh Burnett, who also heard the story from Read, says that 'such were the techniques whereby Huw defined a situation without being heavy-handed, and in the process screwed you up.'

The case of John Drummond is instructive. This is the arts producer, not Wheldon's friend the army officer. Drummond joined the BBC in 1958, when he was twenty-four, and was in the Paris office, 'a prissy young academic' (his own words), when he met Wheldon, who saw him as a candidate for a job on *Monitor*. Like Ken Russell and others before him, Drummond was cross-examined for a couple of hours at a pub in Ealing, over the road from the studios. He had a broad knowledge of the arts; perhaps too broad or too overt for Wheldon, who didn't take him on. Eventually he got into programme-making after *Monitor*'s time, when Humphrey Burton was in charge of music and arts television.

For years, says Drummond, Wheldon lost no opportunity to put him down. Had Wheldon earlier felt himself put down by the young man, eager to display his knowledge at the Red Lion? Drummond thinks it likely. He suffered years of snubs and slights. His *Tortelier Master Class* programmes were admired, but not by Wheldon. Wheldon complained that he let the camera see too many instruments and too few faces, and wouldn't hear about the need to demonstrate the players' techniques. 'You are absolutely an inhuman person,' he told Drummond cordially. He said he was submitting Drummond's film *Kathleen Ferrier* to a festival, 'but of course it won't win.' Long afterwards, when Drummond had left the BBC to run the Edinburgh Festival, and was about to return to be controller of music (he is now controller of Radio 3), he met Wheldon, ten years retired, who told him he was 'absolutely wrong' to be returning. Drummond said, 'I've known you for twenty-five years, Huw, and I can't think of a single occasion when you haven't reproved me.' Wheldon nodded. 'You see, you are one of nature's reprovees,' he said.

Drummond charitably sees the other side of Wheldon, who 'created the world in which I was working at the BBC.' They had a confrontation once, when Wheldon had risen in the hierarchy, and Drummond was among producers complaining about management's isolation from the staff. Wheldon lectured him, with frequent references to his own days as a producer. Drummond took his life in his hands and said, 'There are some of us more concerned with our future than your past.' Wheldon clenched his hands till the knuckles went white, and told him not to be so foolish. Then he asked if Drummond would represent him at an arts conference in Canada; though whether this was punishment, reward or tactical move to get him off the premises isn't clear. And when Drummond was applying for the Edinburgh job, Wheldon gave him a reference that said he was difficult to work for, but 'I have never met an artist who didn't respect him.' Drummond even sees traces of Wheldon in himself nowadays; 'a curious legacy' he calls it.

By the 1960s everyone in television was coming to know bits of the Wheldon philosophy. He was the chap who wanted people to face up to life and be manly. Antony Jay saw him at an appointments board for an administrative post with Talks in 1962. The candidate, an accounts clerk from the BBC in Bristol, was making a poor impression. Wheldon looked as if he might be asleep. Someone asked the clerk why he wanted the job. 'Er, well,' he said, 'that's the sixty-four thousand dollar question.' Wheldon woke up and said, 'No, *this* is the sixty-four thousand dollar question: you've got all these "O" levels, so why haven't you done better so far?' The clerk relaxed and started talking. He got the job. David Attenborough was with Wheldon in the street soon after a car crash. Most people would have said, 'How awful.' Wheldon said, 'It's a great event, old boy, something has *happened*. They'll go home knowing more about themselves.'

Wheldon was still looking for recruits. He said it was one of his vanities. With BBC 2 due to start in 1964, and needing new production assistants, he found (or, rather, Allan Tyrer found for him) 'a very contained and dignified young man' called Peter Watkins who had made an amateur film, *Forgotten Faces*, about the Hungarian uprising. One newspaper critic who saw the film was convinced it had been shot in Budapest in 1956. But it was made in Canterbury. Instead of actors, 'ordinary people' had been coached to re-live a part.

Watkins had persuasive ideas about the uses of fiction in making films about real events. In that respect he was reminiscent of Ken Russell and his dramatic biographies, which Wheldon was still tinkering with on *Monitor*. But Watkins had a more intense manner, and was more grittily concerned with 'truth' in a literal sense. From the start Wheldon seems to have accepted the principle of reconstructing events on film. Perhaps Watkins's air of deadly earnestness went down better than Ken Russell's jokes.

At his first interview with Wheldon, Watkins mentioned that he would like to make a film about a nuclear attack on Britain and its aftermath. This was so ambitious, not to mention politically dangerous, that Wheldon merely said it was out of the question. Watkins was offered and accepted a job as a programme assistant. There were some early misgivings. A film that Watkins made on his staff-training course, about the behaviour of French troops in the Algerian war, had violent scenes that troubled Wheldon. Stephen Hearst,[1] the producer he was assigned to, was worried about the way Watkins used archive material in a film – this time for transmission – about Tito's wartime campaigns; film of one event was used to suggest another, breaking the documentary code of literal truth. But the footage was brilliantly assembled. Within the department, some felt that Watkins held too zealously to his beliefs. Wheldon ignored this

---

[1] Stephen Hearst, b.1919 in Austria, was later controller of Radio 3 (1972–78) and a special adviser to the director-general (1982–86).

view. Watkins was to be encouraged to have ideas. Soon the department was overflowing with them. All were designed to 'capture the inside heart-beat of people and events'. One list proposed intimate biographies of Nelson, Luther, Atatürk, Joan of Arc, Cromwell and Napoleon, to name a few. An account of the Sharpeville killings would be 'a reconstruction in minute detail'. A suffragette's story would include 'what she underwent in prison'. An East Berlin family on the day they plan an escape to the West would be examined 'minute by minute'. These and many other films, using 'ordinary people' instead of actors, would be structured and shot to look like the real thing, not a representation. Still Wheldon gave his support.

Watkins's priority remained his 'nuclear' film. But he was also keen to reconstruct the Battle of Culloden, 1745, when 'Butcher Billy', the Duke of Cumberland, massacred the Scottish clans. The violent subject worried Wheldon, or so he said later. But he had to let Watkins make one of his films, or risk losing him altogether. He said yes to *Culloden*. John Prebble, who had just written a book on the subject, was hired as a consultant; a book made Wheldon feel safer. A draft script was written and approved.

Difficulties arose. Baverstock was reluctant to promise a slot on BBC 1 for a film by a man no one had heard of. The minimum Equity daily rate might have to be paid to the amateur actors, at an estimated cost of nearly £5,000. Even without this, the film was budgeted at £2,500, and eventually cost far more. Wheldon manoeuvred, calling the film a 'pilot' to keep it out of Equity's clutches. Money was tight throughout the filming, in the summer of 1964. Wheldon, away on holiday, received an urgent appeal for more funds to pay for the battle scenes.

No one could be sure what was happening at the locations on the moor of Culloden and elsewhere in Scotland. Watkins had about 140 'ordinary people', one cannon and a selection of uniforms and other props, which he had painstakingly researched: spectacles, clay pipes, bugles, telescopes. Most of the action was filmed with a hand-held camera. The cast, said Wheldon, would do anything for Watkins – 'Greengrocers, lawyers, teachers from Inverness, youngsters, he marched them in their clobber through heather and gorse and bog, twenty-three miles, and at the end of it they looked exhausted, and he filmed them, and it was quite brilliant.'

But Wheldon wasn't there. Like Ken Russell, Watkins didn't want anyone looking over his shoulder. When the twenty-one days of filming were over, the rushes were kept away from Wheldon as long as possible. He first saw parts of *Culloden* in the cutting room late one evening, after Watkins had left. Presently the first assembly was ready. Wheldon said it was the best he had ever seen, with only minor changes needed.

The fighting, the actors' remarks flung at camera, and the unseen narration were all meant to deglamorize war. People still remember the wounded man who turns and shows his slashed eyes. Wheldon saw Watkins as a man obsessed. According to Wheldon in private, and Grace Wyndham Goldie in public, trip wires were set up so that fleeing Highlanders would fall headlong, to add to the realism. This was denied by Watkins, who pointed out that you didn't get people to work for you by cheating them, and made the BBC apologize. But the myth of the driven man inevitably gathered around someone who could create such disturbing effects with a handful of people on a moor.

When the film was shown on BBC 1 (December 15 1964) it was extravagantly praised and made Watkins's reputation. Many viewers sampled by the BBC reported a 'tremendous anti-war impact'. At the programme review board,[1] Goldie said no historical documentary could ever be the same again, and congratulated Wheldon for backing a 'wildly impossible scheme'.

Watkins had already moved on. Having made a success of *Culloden*, he was now insisting that he be allowed to make his

---

[1] Television's programme review board, or weekly programme review, was (and still is) held on Wednesday mornings, and is an open forum attended by about forty senior staff. There is much gentlemanly criticism, turning nasty at times. Minutes are taken and circulated.

nuclear film. That story has to wait. By the end of 1964 Wheldon had other matters on his mind. A crisis within the television service had been threatening for months. Now it began to make itself felt.

Greene's BBC was confident enough, but the fact that he let new forces loose inside the place led to a certain amount of pain and anguish under the surface. The hottest of all his potatoes was the satire show *That Was the Week That Was*, or *TW3*, which gave unprecedented pleasure and offence on Saturday evenings from November 1962, until it was taken off just over a year later. For those who were offended, the programme meant filth, sedition and blasphemy. The BBC governors grew alarmed: their vice-chairman thought of resigning, and Greene, laid up with flu for a week, got depressed and decided to kill it off. But before that it had its glory.

TW3 was invented by Ned Sherrin, then a BBC producer. Baverstock and his aide Alasdair Milne (by now running a sub-empire called Tonight Productions) were its patrons, and much of the kudos went to Baverstock. In television terms, the programme brought in the noisy freedoms of the 1960s. At its height, twelve million watched it late on Saturday evenings. With this and the earlier *Tonight* as his achievements, Baverstock had the best track record of anyone in television. It strengthened his claim to run BBC 1 as he chose.

As chief of a network, he dealt with the heads of programme-making departments, powerful figures in their own right. Wheldon used to call them 'barons'. Baverstock made enemies. Some of his quarrels were with the baron who ran light entertainment, Tom Sloan. Sloan was not amused by *TW3* or by any of the new strains of comedy that drew their power from an affront to old values. He removed a Peter Sellers sketch from a programme on the grounds that 'to refer to someone who was obviously Lady Dorothy Macmillan as a great steaming nit was not in good taste'. Baverstock's view of Sloan was concise: 'He didn't have an idea in his head.'

Further quarrels arose with Sydney Newman, head of the drama group. Newman, a Canadian who looked like a Mexican, had been poached from ABC, where he made the weekly *Armchair Theatre* into the best play series on British television. He posed as a philistine (when a producer mentioned the playwright Ionesco, he is supposed to have said, 'Ian who?'), perhaps finding it a useful way of cleaving through BBC snobberies.

It was Greene's idea to recruit him, in 1961. Newman received 'one of those very English letters' from Adam, proposing lunch, and a series of clandestine meetings followed with BBC executives. He and Baverstock quarrelled at once. According to Baverstock, 'He said, "I've never seen any *Tonight*," and I said, "I've never seen any *Armchair Theatre*."' ABC were reluctant to let him go, and he didn't join the BBC until January 1963. At ABC his salary had been £8,500, plus a Jaguar and a free mortgage. The BBC tried to get him for £6,250, but eventually he settled for £7,250 and his expenses back to Canada whenever he left. Baverstock remembers the figures: 'They paid him two thousand a year more than me to become head of drama.'

Their professional differences revolved around the issue of 'single plays' versus 'series and serials'. Baverstock was cool about single plays; Newman saw them as crucial. A row between them in the summer of 1964 had to be resolved by Adam, the director of television, who ruled that 'temporary concentration' on 'such certain winners' as *Dr Findlay's Casebook* and *Z-Cars* was necessary, even if it meant fewer single plays on BBC 1. Newman was on the terrace of the BBC Club with a couple of drama producers. The producers were depressed at Baverstock's victory. 'Don't worry,' Newman told them. 'Donald's dead.'

Internal rows are part of normal business, but bad feeling and muddle were more rife than usual. Besides the Baverstock question, BBC 2 was under attack. The new network had been rushed on the air in April. Michael Peacock had devised a scheme called 'seven faces of the week', an attempt to cope with the limited amount of material he had, by dedicating each evening to programmes of a particular kind; Monday was entertainment, Tuesday was education, Wednesday was repeats, and so on. The idea was ingenious but not much admired.

Another problem was Stuart Hood, the controller of programmes. In theory he was the arbiter and dynamic of the service. But he was regarded as aloof and intellectual. A protégé of Greene's – they had worked together in the Overseas Service – he was a Scot with a clean desk and a disturbingly quiet voice who had undoubted talents but was unable or unwilling to cope with the daily grind of Baverstocks and Newmans. Stephen Hearst called him an 'inscrutable Trappist monk'. In 1964 he decided that the BBC was becoming too susceptible to political pressure from the Right; he himself had made a political shift to the Left. The story is that one morning in June he dropped his resignation into Kenneth Adam's letterbox, told his wife he was leaving her, had a restyled haircut, and went to join an ITV company. 'All true,' he says, when asked.[1]

With the departure of Hood, the management crisis came to a head. Adam stepped in to do Hood's job – that was why he was arbitrating between Baverstock and Newman – but he was past his best, drinking heavily and said to be too far gone to discuss anything after the middle of the day. In the end it was so bad that a senior staff member was deputed to keep an eye on him. Secretaries on the sixth floor of Television Centre, the 'Direction Suite', would see him with his door open, leaning down for the wine bottle in the bottom drawer of his desk.

Wheldon, meanwhile, was overseeing *Culloden* and the rest of his domain; and watching, like everyone else in television, to see what would happen next. For a long time nothing happened. 'It must have been seven or eight months,' said Wheldon. 'It was known all over that Kenneth was taking what he called "sound-

---

[1] Hood's book *Pebbles from My Skull* (1963) describes his life behind enemy lines in Italy when he escaped from a prisoner-of-war camp. It is also a remarkable exercise in the nature of perception and memory. No one reading it would be surprised that television management was not Hood's metier. He soon left ITV and has been a free-lance ever since.

ings" as to whom the service might accept as controller of programmes – rather a feeble thing to do. And the morale of the service went down.'

A senior secretary who was privy to these goings-on says that Greene used to 'urge Kenneth about it gently'. Baverstock was considered, but he was not in favour. She recalls him having tea in the Direction Suite, and being given it in an ordinary cup and saucer, not the 'rather nice bone china with a pattern' that the nobs enjoyed. 'This isn't right,' he said. Did Adam note such niceties of behaviour and add them to the debit side?

Michael Peacock put himself forward as a candidate. The observant secretary says he even suggested the salary he should have, a presumption that Adam found shocking. He, too, was ruled out. Then there was Wheldon. According to the secretary, it was some time before he was considered at all. 'You know what I mean, he was a *performer*. He wasn't taken seriously. And he didn't have a particularly good academic background. Kenneth Adam had been at Cambridge, at St John's. Greene was Merton College, Oxford.'

Do these miscellaneous objections about teacups and colleges reflect what was being said in Adam's office? In any case, Wheldon passed the test. He emerged from the 'soundings' as the man most likely to be acceptable to the barons. In the end there was no one else. He was sent for by Adam early in 1965 and himself sounded out. No offer was made, but Wheldon knew it was coming. Greene made it soon after, only to find that Wheldon said he would have to think about it. 'When he *did* think about it,' says the secretary, 'he gave them his terms for doing it. They were totally taken aback.' Wheldon said he would do the job only if he had absolute control – his words were 'the Controller and not the Referee', in a memo of February 2. When it came to taking power, he struck hard. The two-page memo outlined 'the basic context in which I can see myself operating as a CP Tel, and in the absence of which, I could not undertake the responsibility. I have discussed the point both with you and with DG.' He also wanted a sizeable cash reserve of his own so that he could intervene in programme matters, spending money where and how he chose.

He let a day pass and then told Adam that his personal salary would have to be at least £500 a year more than a network controller's. This memo began by saying that 'I have never been any good at negotiating my own salary. I hate doing it.' He was certainly successful at it.

The conditions were not a problem. The problem was Baverstock. Wheldon made it clear that he would be unable to accept the controller's job if Baverstock remained at BBC 1. No one argued with him; Greene and Adam had already told him they saw Donald as 'a great problem', which Wheldon was expected to solve. At the same time, the BBC didn't want Baverstock to go. Nor did Wheldon. Nor did anyone. There were great protestations about how much they all wanted Donald to stay in the fold, what a tragedy it would be if he left. No doubt everyone was sincere. Still, it was expecting a lot for a man with so many talents, who had been praised up to the eyebrows and who might be forgiven for supposing himself impregnable, to let himself be moved around like a piece on a board by a man who was still nominally his junior.

Wheldon became a focus of ideas even before he had accepted the job. Long authoritative memos about television management trundled out of his office. For Baverstock he proposed a job that would suit his creative gifts. He claimed to remember a conversation they had in 1962. Wheldon had said, 'If the BBC, instead of giving me initials, gave me [a salary of] £6,000 a year, a room with a blue carpet and the status and power to be able to lay hands on people and facilities, and then said, "OK, you're a star turn, we know it, and what we want is one new programme a year," I'd be delighted and they'd be better served.' Baverstock had replied, 'By Christ, you're dead right.' The suggestion now was to create such a post for Baverstock, invent a nice title ('assistant controller, new programme development' was suggested), put a couple of bright producers on his staff, and give him a budget of £50,000 a year to invent new programmes. If

Baverstock agreed, move Peacock from BBC 2 to BBC 1, and offer BBC 2 to Alasdair Milne.

Baverstock didn't agree. Wheldon, now being consulted as if Adam didn't exist, produced a new plan: swap Peacock and Baverstock between the networks, so that Baverstock would be running BBC 2. Anguished meetings were held, in offices and people's homes. For a while Baverstock toyed with the idea. But he suspected the mechanics of what was happening. He had reason to. The prizes he was being offered were less glittering than the one he had already. In a long letter setting out his position to Adam, he commented that 'I have been, I know, accused by Huw Wheldon, seeing it from below, of having too much assertiveness as Chief of Programmes – when the real problem has been the opposite – too little authority in the post.'

In another passage he said that 'Huw Wheldon, whose foibles and misunderstanding I can sincerely tolerate while still regarding him as a personal friend, has told you, I know, that I am a kind of maverick, a rebel, a radical originator etc. I know the line. I have heard it before and have always thought it amusingly wrong. But when this kind of gossipy nonsense combined with other less well intentioned talk about me is taken seriously, I have to become a little alarmed.' He defended his record as a disciple of public broadcasting and an enemy of complacency.

Wheldon himself defended Baverstock up to a point, saying that the circumstances were partly to blame. But it was he who made the final recommendation to Hugh Greene, in a six-page memo on February 23, that his own promotion and Peacock's move to BBC 1 should be announced at once, together with the fact that Baverstock had turned down the other network. 'I now distrust altogether his capacity to work with me,' he said, 'or with any CP Tel, however the job is designed.' He added that 'we in the BBC' had contributed to a situation that 'has its tragic and deeply unsatisfactory side.'

Wheldon sounded surprised, now and again, that Baverstock should not have fallen in with the plans. This was disingenuous. He must have suspected that for someone as clever and volatile as Baverstock, the alternatives on offer – all of which involved working under the control of Wheldon – would be unacceptable. 'Control' pleased Wheldon when he took it. Baverstock couldn't be expected to share his pleasure. In the Oral History, Wheldon seems to go out of his way to agree with Baverstock's view of himself: 'Donald, who has always been regarded as a kind of rebellious creature, was not I think himself a rebel at all, he was very much a BBC man [. . .] a very constitutional man, you know, Donald.' But that was long after the event.

For a week or two the papers were full of television politics. Bernard Levin, who had been a regular performer on *TW3*, battled in print on behalf of his 'dynamic and talented' friend, 'forced out' by lesser men.[1] The BBC in general, and Wheldon in particular, sought to limit the damage. He said how sad and disappointed he was that Donald had refused the kind offers. No doubt the regrets were genuine. But Wheldon, acting in everyone's best interests, had been a necessary executioner, or adviser to the executioners. He said of his own appointment that he had neither sought it nor particularly wanted it now, not wishing to work twenty hours a day. The evidence suggests that of course he wanted the job. Why should he not?

So the BBC lost Baverstock. The Fleet Street version was that hot-blooded talent had been crushed to make way for the old complacency. There is no doubt that Baverstock had a raw deal. His brilliance, though, was seen as unsettling. The BBC needed continuity; it always put that first. Wheldon, now they came to look at him, was stability itself.

---

[1] Baverstock's BBC career was destroyed in February 1965, at the age of forty-one. Alasdair Milne chose to resign with him, and the two joined Antony Jay in an independent production company. Later he went to Yorkshire Television, and was director of programmes there for six years. In the mid-1970s he returned to the BBC in Manchester for a year or two to run a David Frost programme and a short-lived magazine, *Terra Firma*. Today he and his wife Gillian (who is a daughter of Enid Blyton) live in a fine house at Ilkley, facing the town, with the moor rising beyond. He is up early most mornings, watching television before breakfast.

Was there, too, a feeling that the BBC, which seemed to upset more people than it used to, needed someone who would defend it in public, who would be aggressive but agreeable? If so, Wheldon was the man. As a performer there was no one to touch him in the upper echelons of the BBC. He was genuine, straight-up, look-you-in-the-eye, and the fact that he was a bit of a poseur as well only helped to make him human.

When the photographers came to see the new controller of programmes on the sixth floor, he posed like mad, one foot cocked up on his desk, lighting a cigarette or slumping open-mouthed with laughter. It is said that in one of the shots, you can see a hole in his shoe.

Wheldon's first year of power cast him in the mixture of roles that went with the job: banker, diplomat, technician, censor. New talents among programme-makers were at work in new climates of opinion. Subjects unthinkable half a generation earlier found producers and writers anxious to press up against the limits of what was becoming possible. Wheldon's own innovations had not been of that sort. Now here he was, the arbiter and helmsman.

Awkward cases arose so often in 1965, one might have thought producers were trying things out on the new controller to see what they could get past him. But good programmes are made in secrecy, within private worlds of ideas and imagination. Getting them past the bosses comes late in the process. Nineteen sixty-five was an interesting year because the time had come to raise the stakes. Someone was due to film a piece of low-life realism like *Up the Junction*, just as, at a humbler level, someone was due to look the camera in the eye and say 'fuck'.

No case was more awkward than that of Peter Watkins and *The War Game*, although its implications put it in a class of its own. Wheldon was much concerned with the affair. He allowed the film to happen, intervened continually in its making, argued for it at the highest level: and in the end was powerless to save it, implicitly conceding the need to put the corporate interest of the BBC – which would not have been served by transmission – before any other.

There were those who said he betrayed Watkins or Art or freedom of expression. But the only betrayal could have been of the BBC itself. That was where his loyalty lay. That was why Greene made him controller of programmes. Without the BBC (ran the argument) there would be one less advocate of the freedoms it did represent, which were many. Had Wheldon thought otherwise, he would have been unsuitable for the job. The same was true of his superior, Greene. Greene was regarded, rightly, as a liberalising director-general. But when it came to his loyalty, as it did with *The War Game*, he had no option but to be a corporation man.

For all that, the spectacle of pragmatists at work is not attractive.

If *Culloden* had been a flop, no problem would have arisen. Its success made Peter Watkins, who was twenty-nine, a desirable property for the BBC in general, and Wheldon, his patron, in particular. In October 1964, two months before *Culloden* was transmitted, Watkins was telling Wheldon that he was not to be side-tracked from 'a series of strong subjects that I want to tackle. If everything I film for the next two years or so is either a brutal or controversial subject, this is because it is this realm of subject I feel for most.'

At the top of his list was still the 'nuclear film', tentatively called *After the Bomb*. Wheldon agreed that a research assistant could begin to gather material, but made no firm commitment. On the last day of 1964, by which time *Culloden* had been seen and praised, Wheldon (still head of documentaries) sent a memo to Kenneth Adam to say that following much 'anxious thought', he wanted to agree to *After the Bomb*. In order to keep Watkins, 'I must certainly let him get this film out of his system.' Grace Wyndham Goldie, nearing retirement, had been brought into the discussions. Her view was that if the facts were accurate and there was no risk to national security, 'the people should be trusted with the truth.'

That sounds reasonable enough. So does Wheldon's view as put to Adam:

> The programme will, of course, be horrifying. It is being worked on with the greatest possible care. We intend to retain counsel on certain security aspects. The build-up, both of the attack and the reaction of the country, is being done well within the bounds of possibility according to the best authorities and the best calculations. That is to say, it is likely to be the more appallingly credible because it is not exaggerated.

Wheldon went on to examine a wider problem:

> Would the Russians make such a film? If they would not, why should we? Alternatively, is a film on this subject analogous to making a film about a man, say, dying of cancer? A programme *about* cancer is one thing. A reconstruction of a man dying in a long agony is another. What quite is the point? The answer is unfortunately not without ambivalence. On the other hand, can it possibly be held that the facts of nuclear bombardment are unimportant? Should we not all be aware of what is after all in some sense the major fact of this century?

Wheldon made his recommendation with 'the greatest anxiety'. He added that 'the film cannot be put out until it has been seen, and we must decide later precisely who should see it.' In making that statement, Wheldon trod the BBC path exactly. 'We must decide who should see it' sealed the fate of the programme.

The memo barely touched Adam's desk before it was passed to Greene. Soon Wheldon was called to the presence, to be told that the DG was doubtful whether such a film would ever be viable. Urged by Wheldon to reconsider, he agreed to move one step at a time, initially approving only research and a script. In February, on the strength of this cautious agreement, Donald Baverstock accepted the Bomb programme in principle for BBC 1. It must have been one of the last things he did accept, because by the end of the month he had resigned, Peacock had taken his place, and Wheldon was in charge of programmes. (Adam was still director of television, but he mattered less and less.)

The new head of documentaries was a reliable film-maker, Richard Cawston. Wheldon sent for him and said, 'Sit down, you're running the department, there's fuck-all to do.' Later Cawston found a file of letters, left behind by mistake, that showed Wheldon had been trying to get the director John Boorman, then with the BBC, as his successor. Cawston took charge of Watkins and his Bomb, but Wheldon was never far away.

Watkins's relationship with both his supervisors was good. Cawston once told a colleague that he thought Watkins had a natural, almost magical gift that enabled him to 'make films in the same sort of way that Mozart could compose music when he was four.' Watkins was also an assiduous researcher. Even by the best television standards, his preliminary work on *The War Game* – it had found its final title by the end of February – was impressive. His bibliography lists more than sixty books and a similar number of reports and articles. These include scientific and military appraisals, histories and polemics. Watkins had a private panel of nine informal advisers, among them a couple of scientists, Civil Defence officers, past and present, and at least one member of the Campaign for Nuclear Disarmament.

It was important that the film be seen as rooted in facts. This was Watkins's method in any case. But the more he knew about civil defence, military strategy, rocketry, bombs, fire-storms and radioactivity, the happier Wheldon and Cawston would be, should they be challenged. They commissioned a free-lance writer, Gilbert Phelps, who had been a BBC radio producer, to prepare a dossier on the making of the film. One of Phelps's tasks was to analyse the script and show the source of every statement in it. This was very Wheldonesque. In his *Elgar* film, Ken Russell was not allowed to show the composer flying a kite until he proved it had really happened.

To make things still safer, Wheldon insisted that when the

Donald Baverstock, who fell from grace in 1965 as Wheldon rose.

As controller of programmes, Wheldon now had his own driver to take him across west London to the Television Centre.

A view from the sixth floor: the new men of BBC television assemble in March 1965; Wheldon, in charge of programmes, with David Attenborough (BBC 2 controller), next to him, and Michael Peacock (BBC 1). Kenneth Adam, with pipe, survived a bit longer as director of television.

Wheldon with his daughters in tow, in front of their house on Richmond Hill, probably December 1970.

Family group, about 1966: the Wheldons and their children.

Power group, 1972: Lady Hill (extreme left), wife of the BBC chairman Lord Hill, greets Jay Wheldon at the BBC's 50th anniversary banquet at Guildhall. Hill, partly hidden, greets Wheldon. On Wheldon's heels is Ian Trethowan, who succeeded him as managing director a few years later, with Mrs Trethowan.

Huw Wheldon with Alastair Cooke.

Michael Checkland (*above left*) (now the BBC's director-general) and Joanna Spicer (*above right*) were part of Wheldon's planning team when he ran the Television Centre. With David Attenborough (*below left*) at BBC 2 and Paul Fox (*below right*) at BBC 1, they were his closest colleagues.

Royal accolade: Sir Huw and Lady Wheldon after he was knighted by The Queen, March 1976.

Royal Heritage: Wheldon at Chinon, France, filming for the BBC series.

In retirement: Wheldon and the view from Richmond Hill.

first assembly of the film was ready, it was 'essential to have the strongest advice possible.' He said this in a memo to Adam on February 22. It might involve consulting 'special people', including 'a Home Office official' – the Home Office being responsible for Civil Defence. But bridges must be crossed as they came to them.

When the first-draft script was ready, probably by early March, Greene read it and so did the chairman of the BBC governors, Lord Normanbrook.[1] They wanted to stop the project. Again Wheldon argued and won his case, still, of course, within the boundaries set for the game. Watkins was told he could start filming. During March he visited amateur dramatic societies in parts of Kent, and held auditions. Filming, with a revised script, took place throughout most of April, using derelict sites and an abandoned barracks at Dover. A fire-brigade helped unofficially with the fire-storm sequence.

Wheldon and Cawston viewed the first assembly on June 24. Phelps was there to make notes, and reported a cool response. Wheldon said he wanted the film to be so outstanding that it made a case for itself. This was another Wheldonism: policy didn't make programmes, it was programmes that made policy. (He believed that *TW3* was a success, not because Greene had said 'Let there be satire', but because the programme was so good that satire became worth supporting.) His reservations were partly aesthetic, partly to do with policy. He thought the virtues of the nuclear deterrent should be stressed. He didn't like mercy-killings by police or the summary execution of rioters.

Phelps wrote in his dossier that Watkins was 'only prepared to alter it in his own way.' Nearly a month later, on July 22, Wheldon saw a new assembly, and this time was enthusiastic. Among the 'policy' changes, the film now had an opening statement about the pros and cons of the deterrent. A speech by

---

[1] Lord Normanbrook, a former head of the Home Civil Service, was the BBC's chairman from 1965 until his death in 1967.

a Civil Defence worker worried him because it 'sounded too much like CND propaganda.' The mercy-killings and executions were still there, but in the context of the new version, he was less concerned, and would not insist on removing them.[1]

After further editing, the film could now be seen by the director-general, and recommended for transmission. A date was pencilled in, the week beginning October 18. *The War Game* had survived.

But antagonism to it existed from an early stage. The Home Office refused to help Watkins with his research, and complained to the BBC. The press, too, did its stuff. Once filming began, Kent newspapers welcomed a ready-made story on their doorstep, complete with faked riots, ghastly-looking make-up burns and lorry-loads of pretend corpses. 'THE WAR COMES TO GRAVESEND – WOULD THIS HAPPEN IN WORLD WAR THREE?' one headline wanted to know. 'WILL IT BE TOO FRIGHTENING?' asked another. By the end of April it had reached the national papers. 'Sudden death. Slow and agonizing death. Blindness and brutality . . . You will be able to see them all soon by courtesy of BBC Television,' observed the *People*.

It was September 2 before Greene and Normanbrook were able to view the film. The BBC secretary, Charles Curran,[2] was also present. Phelps wrote that Adam, Wheldon and Cawston waited in another room, and were called in afterwards.

In view of the Phelps account, it is worth noting the reason that the BBC, and Greene himself, gave later for not transmitting *The War Game*. He thought it too horrific. The official statement – in November – said the film had been 'judged by the BBC to be too horrifying for the medium of broadcasting.' Greene stuck to his story. He said in his Oral History recording (1977): 'I

---

[1] Wheldon was never happy with these scenes. He said later, 'It was a kind of attack on the police. It seemed to me that if you were going to bring about a mercy killing you'd have people in white coats or doctors or nuns . . .'
[2] (Sir) Charles Curran (1921–80), an administrator and not a programme man, was director-general of the BBC, 1969–77.

thought of some old lady watching by herself and being so utterly terrified she might run out of her flat and throw herself under a bus.' A letter he wrote to a periodical in 1986, not long before he died, said the decision about the film, 'right or wrong', was 'based on humanitarian grounds and not because of any pressures from the government of the day.'

On September 2, when Wheldon and his colleagues were admitted, Normanbrook was the first to say what he thought. The film had made him 'a wiser but sadder' man. The 'horrors' had been handled with more skill and tact than he expected, although he wondered if television was the right medium for them. He then made the point about possible effects on the old and lonely.

Greene, according to the account that Phelps was given for his dossier, was more concerned with the political implications. Harold Wilson's Labour Government, elected the previous October, had a majority of under five. A new election could be called at any time. If it coincided with transmission of *The War Game*, the film might inadvertently help the Left wing of the Labour Party, and the BBC be accused of influencing the result. This sounds far-fetched. But Greene had a mischievous interest in politics, and may have liked to feel he was more influential than he was.

Both Greene and Normanbrook said it could be argued that the film was questioning the defence policy of the West, and might be accused of affecting public morale. In such circumstances, Normanbrook said they must 'take soundings' at the Home Office and Ministry of Defence, 'and among members of the Government.' For the moment no decision would be made about transmission. Five days after the viewing, he wrote to the secretary of the Cabinet, Sir Burke Trend, to say he doubted whether the BBC should shoulder all responsibility for showing the film, adding, 'It seems to me that the Government should have an opportunity of expressing a view about this.'[1]

---

[1] Normanbrook's letter was quoted in an article in the *Guardian*, 1.9.80, by Michael Tracey, Hugh Greene's biographer. The letter and associated papers

Watkins was outraged, as most film-makers would have been, when he heard hints of what was happening. From this point his relations with the BBC deteriorated, though for a while he remained on good terms with Cawston and Wheldon, regarding them as his allies. On September 14 he threatened to resign. Wheldon tried to persuade him otherwise, but made no concession on the real issue:

> The formal position is clear: the BBC's decision to consult further on this important and powerful documentary arises solely from its responsibility, which must override all other considerations, to act in the public interest. Decisions on programmes involving crucial public issues are frequently taken at the highest level in the BBC. It is perfectly proper and indeed usual to make appropriate consultations; and final decisions always take full account of public policy.

Watkins pointed out that any government official would feel it his duty to advise against such a film. The Wheldon/Cawston reply was that the BBC was only seeking advice, and that the decision would be its own. Unimpressed, Watkins gave notice of resignation on September 20.

Four days later the viewing with 'government officials' took place. Phelps lists changes that the chairman and Greene had requested after the September 2 showing, but doesn't say whether they were made in time, or whether Watkins was either consulted or involved. A memo from Cawston to Wheldon on September 16 said the changes were being attended to. A caption about the bomb 'being on the open market and available to anybody' was to be deleted from the end-titles; the nationality of bishops who were quoted as saying that the bomb would be

---

confirm the BBC's anxiety not to offend the authorities. They came from the BBC's own *War Game* files, which remain closed to outside researchers. Tracey saw them by accident. A BBC official had sent Greene some *War Game* papers, and Greene passed them to Tracey, who was working on the biography, without bothering to check the contents. Greene continued to dispute Tracey's interpretation, but didn't try to stop the material being used.

'clean and of good family' and 'used with wisdom' was to be stated. The memo added that 'Watkins cannot bring himself to alter the mercy killings sequence and the public execution sequence', but suggests that 'modifications are in hand'.

Hope waned as the programme-makers picked away at the small print of a film that no one in authority was now able or willing to fight for, and Watkins continued to argue by letter, a man shouting across a widening chasm. The September 24 viewing was held in Theatre 2 of the East Tower at the Television Centre. Representing the BBC with Normanbrook were John Arkell, director of administration; Robert Lusty, the publisher; a BBC governor; and Oliver Whitley,[1] chief assistant to the director-general, a post tantamount to political adviser. Greene himself was abroad, at a conference in Africa.

The 'chairman's guests' as listed by Phelps were Sir Burke Trend; Sir Charles Cunningham, head of the Home Office; George Leitch, Ministry of Defence; an unidentified Mr McIndoe ('with male secretary'); a Brigadier Lewis; and Alan Wolstencroft, deputy director-general of the Post Office, which then had responsibility for broadcasting.

Phelps didn't know what was said at the meeting. Tracey's account said the officials thought the film as a whole would lend support to CND. At a further meeting between Normanbrook, Trend, Cunningham and Wolstencroft, the civil servants said their ministers had been told about the film, but did not wish to express an opinion. Normanbrook's note of the meeting added, 'It is clear that Whitehall will be relieved if we do not show it.'

All this shadow-play was part of the devious British way. At the heart of the ideal BBC is its independence. It serves the nation (so the story goes) without fear or favour. If it is not to transmit a film on a sensitive subject, it would be unfortunate – for a government as much as for the BBC itself – if it were thought to be bowing to pressure, or whisperings, or winks that

---

[1] Oliver Whitley, b. 1912, joined the BBC in 1935 and was a well regarded administrator. His father had been chairman of the BBC governors.

are as good as nods. The reality is that the Corporation has had to watch its step since 1923. But it is best to pretend otherwise.

Greene came back from Africa. Weeks passed and there was no decision. 'You both now appear to be utterly powerless,' Watkins wrote to Wheldon and Cawston on October 22, the day his notice expired. Cawston wrote to him in friendly terms the following month to say that 'you must have gone through Hell', adding, 'Now that we are starting on a new era, with ex-producers running most of the Television Service, it seems ironic that you should have made a film that had to be referred to levels so far removed from producers' feelings.'

The BBC announced its decision not to show *The War Game* on November 25. Wheldon and Cawston themselves knew about it just in time to telephone Watkins at home before he heard it elsewhere. Many people wondered why, if the film was judged to be so horrific, there had been any need to consult the authorities in the first place. Wheldon, according to Phelps, urged Watkins to accept the BBC's statement, that the decision had been taken 'after a great deal of thought and discussion, but *not* as a result of outside pressures of any kind.'

In his recollections, Wheldon is cavalier about details and chronology when discussing *The War Game*, but hints at wheels within wheels:

> There were troubles between the BBC and the Government, and so I knew that Hugh Greene would be more sensitive than normally . . . once he'd seen [the film], he'd know that he was in a violating situation. In the event we sent it up to Broadcasting House . . . [He] told me that it was too violent and couldn't be shown. And Hugh refused point blank to go into any kind of detail as to what was too violent. As far as he was concerned it simply couldn't be shown and that was that. And I believe he wanted really to be rid of it in a sense . . .

The BBC conceded nothing, and the *War Game* issue soon burnt itself out.[1] Wheldon had done what he had to do. The BBC lost Watkins. It was the system.

[1] Early in 1966 the film was shown to selected audiences at the National Film Theatre, and was later made available for public showing. A copy was sent around the country via Red Star rail for senior BBC staff to see in regional centres, labelled 'Bicycle Programme'. The BBC eventually transmitted *The War Game* just before the 40th anniversary of the Hiroshima and Nagasaki bombs, August 1985.

CHAPTER NINE

Rude Words

THE *WAR GAME* AFFAIR ran deep but concerned a programme that wasn't transmitted. The viewers were more interested in programmes that were. Wheldon's first year in office coincided with a period of ferment, when programmes were changing the rules about what television could and couldn't do in areas of taste and morals. In novels and stage plays, the new or newish society of the sixties could bloom and not harm anyone. On television, outspokenness and licence were guaranteed to upset some of the millions who didn't read modern novels or go to the theatre. The short-lived *TW3* and its watered-down successors had begun the process with programmes clearly labelled 'satire'. Now the breath of fresh air, or the vile stain of corruption, reached television drama. Popular perceptions of the BBC were never the same afterwards. A word here, a carnal glimpse there, have caused trouble ever since.

Wheldon was a censor with artistic leanings; or, to change the emphasis, a benevolent despot who accepted that most people have conservative tastes, and who was not prepared to risk the BBC's reputation with avant-garde experiments. His mother-in-law was still there in spirit (and still alive in the flesh), though he didn't invoke her openly as in the *Monitor* days. Nor did he make sudden moves. The BBC's freedom, he believed, came from 'deep sources within the Corporation itself', from its understanding of 'the nature of freedom to make things'. Joanna Spicer, a senior planner and manager, and one of the few BBC women whom Weldon praised unstintingly, quotes a remark of his, that 'you couldn't always be saying No, so it was important to stop people doing things that might lead to your having to say No'; to which he added that 'you couldn't stop people who lived by the imagination'.

This is an idealized view, whether hers or his: Wheldon did occasionally stop creators in their tracks. But most of the time, as Spicer suggests, the process was more subtle.

Prudery has never been far from British broadcasting. When the BBC was strait-laced it was laughed at for its pains. A guide for light entertainment producers, beseeching them not to allow double-meanings, as in the ancient pun about ladies' underwear, 'winter draw[er]s on', was still causing amusement years after it was scrapped. Cyril Connolly, writing in 1955 to a Talks producer (it was Donald Baverstock) about a programme he was to appear in, asked if words like 'Jesus' and 'homosexuality' were better avoided, and may have been joking. In January 1965 the BBC was concerned over a remark in Parliament by Lord Snow (the novelist C. P. Snow), who was certainly not joking, that two years earlier, the BBC was offering 'incest several nights of the week'. A count was made, and Lord Snow informed that six plays in three years had touched on the subject; one of them was Pirandello's *Six Characters in Search of an Author*, another was *Hamlet*.

In 1965, one drama series was offering stronger meat than people were used to. This was the Wednesday Play, devised by Sydney Newman as a showcase for contemporary work. Its first season, a year earlier, had average audiences of five million. By 1965 this had risen to more than seven million, and was attracting critical praise. Newman hung a motto on the wall of his office, 'Look back not in anger, nor forward with fear, but around with awareness.' He regards that era and the series with affection. 'If you remember the opening, it had a lovely young girl in a mini-skirt, waggling her ass. That told you it was a play for the times.'

One of the first Wednesday Plays to involve Wheldon was *Three Clear Sundays*, transmitted in April, about a gipsy street

191

trader who is wrongly accused of a minor offence, and ends being hanged for the murder of a prison officer. Debate on the death penalty was intense in 1965, and it was abolished later in the year. The play was seen by some as propaganda against capital punishment; the Conservative chief whip complained about 'the juxtaposition of the play and the standing committee on the abolition of the death penalty'. Interest had been sharpened by newspaper photographs, not supplied by the BBC, taken at rehearsal and showing the condemned man roped and hooded, about to be executed. The BBC governors were offended by this, and Greene promised he would 'suggest with the authority of the Board that the play should end before the execution itself'.

This suggestion was not followed. The play ended with six one-second shots of the hanging. The governors were furious. One of them (Sir David Milne, a former civil servant) said the whole play was false, picking on a miscarriage of justice in order to make propaganda against hanging. Kenneth Adam wrung his hands. The culprit was sought and turned out to be Wheldon, who was unrepentant. Some changes had been made in the play, in collaboration with Newman, he said, but it was essential to end with the hanging. The scene as transmitted was abrupt and impersonal, with none of the 'brooding and offensive' atmosphere of the photograph.

In his memo to Adam (April 27 1965) Wheldon seeks to 'make it clear that (i) instructions from the Board of Governors and DG are not treated lightly, and (ii) problems of this kind are not simply solved by simple cutting, and that the Board equally should not lightly dismiss what their servants carry out on their own, and the Board's, behalf'. The board's last word was that they respected his sincerity but disagreed with him.

Wheldon's phrase for them and their successors was often heard over the years: 'sodding governors'. He disliked having his judgement questioned, and took the usual BBC view, that the governors were guardians of the public interest who expressed general opinions but did not interfere in day-to-day business.

This is another ideal view. Some governors have always hankered after being editors-in-chief, and sought to interfere.

Three Clear Sundays attracted the largest and most appreciative audience to date for the series. Newman knew what he was up to, finding plays with themes hot from the newspapers that could give the drama a 'documentary' dimension. Three months later *Three Clear Sundays* was due to be repeated, and Kenneth Adam was agitated again, anxious not to 'fly in the face of board instructions'. He wanted to appease them by taking out the last six seconds of the play. For a second time Wheldon dug his heels in. He argued that a cut would be noticed and seen as censorship. The Wednesday Play script editors, who had threatened to resign once already that summer when a Dennis Potter play was taken off the air, would get to hear of it, as would the author. It would look like a nervous response to the 'Clean-up TV Campaign' – Mrs Whitehouse and friends had been campaigning for a year, and she showed no sign of going away. 'We would do ourselves a wholly disproportionate damage,' wrote Wheldon, 'by allowing the press and others to seize upon yet another occasion for attacking the Corporation as timid and susceptible to pressures that ought better to be resisted.' A day later word came down that Greene and the chairman, Normanbrook, had agreed that the play could go out uncut.

All this is as clear evidence as one is likely to find, poking about in the minutiae of the archives, that Wheldon was a champion of programme-makers. It has to be qualified by saying that the lesser good was always liable to be subordinated to the greater. One side of Wheldon supported Peter Watkins; the other abandoned him. Wheldon had no intention of giving comfort to Mary Whitehouse's lobby as such. But he could be as censorious as she was, over bad language and sexy scenes, if he felt they were unjustified, since he knew how easy it was to offend viewers. As for 'censorship', which he rightly saw as a damaging charge when levelled against the BBC, in private he knew it was part of the business of running a television service.

A Wednesday Play about mercenaries in black Africa, *For the*

West, transmitted in June 1965, found him unsympathetic, castigating everyone in sight for not having referred the play to higher authority. He found brutality, sensationalism and 'gratuitous obscenities'. All this meant was that he disliked the play and would not make allowances. In practice he often criticized producers for not referring programmes to their superiors, although in principle he deplored those who were 'babies' rather than 'men', able to decide for themselves; he liked to say that he had referred only three programmes in his career, one of them *The War Game*. Discussing *For the West* at the programme review board, Wheldon said that 'a straightforward duty of censorship lies upon departmental heads, and there is no point in being mealy-mouthed about it'.

But Wheldon knew that one didn't talk openly about 'censorship', one kept it in the family. Otherwise it spoiled the sunlit picture, the ideal BBC of many freedoms. A six-page document written by Wheldon in 1966, 'Control over the subject matter of programmes', was itself censored (or self-censored) before it appeared outside. The BBC submitted it to a parliamentary committee on theatre censorship, and later published it as a booklet. Five short passages were deleted from the typescript version, removing the word 'censorship' in five of the six places where it appeared; the sixth was probably left in by mistake. The first cut was made in the opening sentences, as indicated here in italics:

> Control over the subject matter of programmes in the BBC *very rarely culminates in an act of censorship*. It is *rather* a process in which the assumptions, opinions and experience of many of its servants are involved.

The argument is not affected by the deletions, but the tone of the statement is. 'Balance also precludes pornography and propaganda in any programme,' says a later passage, but the original sub-clause has been removed:

> *where these are part of a programme's intention or a programme*

script, then (and then only) the single and simple and violent act of censorship takes place. It is no part of the BBC's responsibility to broadcast propaganda or pornography of any nature whatsoever.

Within a few weeks of *For the West*, a Wednesday Play about politics was stopped hours before transmission because it was thought to be offensive to both the Conservative and Labour parties. This was the Dennis Potter play, an early work called *Vote, Vote, Vote for Nigel Barton*, that caused the script editors to rebel.

Once again Wheldon was angry, although this time a nervous producer had mentioned the play the day before it was to go out, so that executives were able to view it, on the day of transmission, June 23 1965, and there was time to replace it with something else and cook up a press statement to say the play was 'not yet ready'.

Wheldon reported to the governors that 'Vote, Vote, Vote' suggested 'inveterate stupidity or double-dealing or both as the hallmark of all our political parties and organizations'. The recommendation to stop the play was made on the Tuesday evening by Paul Fox,[1] then head of the current affairs group, and Newman, who were asked to view it by Wheldon. Fox's opinion concluded:

I am sure that Conservative Central Office will take offence at this portrayal of a Conservative image that is today perhaps not quite so common. Roger Pemberton is red-hot with his complaints: you should see his list of charges against 'Tonight'. I am sure the Labour Party will take offence at this portrayal of an unprincipled agent. Furthermore, on a time basis, the Tory is on for about 7 minutes – looking a buffoon – the Labour man is on for nearly 60 minutes: a bit starry-eyed, but basically the good guy.

---

[1] Paul Fox, b. 1925, a former journalist, joined the BBC in 1950 and was controller BBC 1, 1967–73. He then moved to ITV and eventually ran Yorkshire Television, before returning to the BBC as managing director, a prodigal son come home, in 1988. A paratrooper in the war, he was close to Wheldon.

> In my view, because of the documentary nature of this play and the present, near-Election atmosphere, the parties' complaints would be difficult to rebut.

Wheldon had no difficulty in deciding to stop *Vote, Vote, Vote*. As with *The War Game*, whose troubles began shortly afterwards, he took the advice of those he thought knew more about politics than he did. The internal row was contained. Newman persuaded the dissidents that the play could go out later if changes were made, and Potter agreed to make them.

One of the script editors who nearly resigned was Tony Garnett, later a producer and director. Garnett suggests that when a management makes a song and dance, and insists on changes, it usually transmits the result without bothering to look closely. He thinks the revised *Vote, Vote, Vote* was stronger than the original.

It went out on December 15. At the programme review board, Paul Fox said it was unfortunate that the play was transmitted following a party political broadcast for the Conservatives. Wheldon smiled and said it was the Conservatives who had chosen the slot.

After 1965, Wheldon introduced control systems and insisted that a stockpile of plays be kept in hand, making it possible to intervene at leisure. He claimed he could thus 'cancel the intolerable'. But shock remained part of the Wednesday Play formula. The series filled less than one hour in sixteen of all drama; *Softly, Softly* and *Dr Findlay's Casebook* were more typical of the output, as their successors are today. To make an impact and sustain a high level of interest, its producers needed to disturb and excite.

One further Wednesday Play eruption, in November, rounded off 1965, and brought Wheldon into serious conflict with the governors the following year. The play was *Up the Junction*, based on a book of that name by Nell Dunn, which in turn was based on articles she wrote for the magazine *New Statesman*. Kenneth Loach's film moved between the lives of three working-class girls in south London. Work, sex and the harsh environment were presented without the usual niceties. There was an abortion scene and a domestic quarrel. The dialogue (some of it improvised by the cast) was often hard to follow, deliberately so. The result was bold and authentic, or coarse and sordid, depending on taste.

BBC audience research showed a reaction index of fifty-eight, two below the average for television drama. The switchboard logged 464 adverse telephone calls ('Utterly disgraceful' – Heston housewife) and fifty favourable ('Courageous and useful' – Battersea clergyman). Newspaper opinion was overwhelmingly favourable. Wheldon liked the play but was mildly anxious about its effect. In the words of the programme review's minute:

> C. P. Tel said it would be unwise not to notice the need, for reasons of expediency, not to alienate the audience. This was not a question of morality, but of giving consideration to the sensitivities of the audience, particularly of family groups. He said the vigour and joy of the production had not become apparent until the chocolate factory scenes, and that the long sequence of the kiss in the derelict buildings early on should have been reduced.

The row about *Up the Junction* became entangled with a row about foul language: 'the anti-BBC hounds are baying these days even more shrilly than before,' wrote Sydney Newman. 'Whether all this is reaction to "Up the Junction", Kenneth Tynan's 4-letter word or what, the searchlight is on us.'

Tynan, then literary manager of the National Theatre, used the word in a Saturday-night programme, *BBC-3*. Mrs Whitehouse said she was writing to the Queen about it. Tynan and Mary McCarthy had been in the studio to talk live about censorship, and Robert Robinson began by asking him if he would allow a play at the National 'in which, for instance, sexual intercouse took place on stage'. 'Oh, I think so, certainly,' said Tynan. 'I mean, there are few rational people in this world to whom the word "fuck" is particularly diabolical or revolting or totally forbidden.' Wheldon, asked by newspapers to comment at home on Sunday, said the word was 'quite germane' to a 'responsible discussion'. On Monday the BBC made an official apology, regretting the use of the word. At the programme review, Wheldon said curtly that he didn't condone it but wanted it kept in perspective.

The row passed. There was no outbreak of four-letter words. Newman instructed his subordinates that 'references to sexual parts, underclothes, contraceptive devices, portrayal of near nudity, the physical handling of someone with sex in mind, couples in bed', should be 'considered carefully from every point of view before inclusion in a play'. Furthermore, 'curses like "Jesus", words like "bloody" and so on are offensive, and obscenities like "arse" etc. put people off in their hundreds of thousands'. On paper, at any rate, no organization could have striven harder to appease the offended.

As for *Up the Junction*, professionals praised it, and in February 1966 it was proposed as a summer repeat. Wheldon approved; the film was 'outstanding and unignorable', and the television service was rightly proud of it. The 'sodding governors' heard of the decision in June. They concluded that Wheldon was wrong. Greene, who attended their meeting on June 9, felt that Wheldon 'would have been wiser to seek further advice'. Normanbrook said that Mrs Whitehouse (who complained in November that the BBC appeared 'determined to do everything in its power to present promiscuity as normal') had now written to him to say a repeat would be offensive to public feeling, and he thought her point valid. The meeting had an air of cold feet. *Up the Junction* was not to be seen again.

The day after the board meeting, Greene heard that the owners of the chocolate factory where some of the scenes were filmed said they would sue if *Up the Junction* was repeated. This let everyone off the hook. The BBC announced that the play was being withdrawn because of the threat of legal action, adding that the decision had nothing to do with the Clean-up TV Campaign or any other part of the public. This didn't please at least one of the governors at their meeting on June 23. Sir

Ashley Clarke, a former diplomat, regretted that an occasion had been missed to demonstrate their authority.

But to let it be known in the BBC that the governors and the man in charge of television programmes were in conflict would never have done. Greene said it was important that the board's views were not widely known. When the governors moved on to consider a paper written by Wheldon, who was brought in to discuss it with them, the point was made in blunter language. Wheldon said he accepted the board's decision, as passed on to him by Greene. However, had he been forced to obey, he could have done so only by telling the rest of the television service what was happening. It would have been seen as an instruction from the governors. If he had not made some such statement there would have been grounds in the television service for the assumption that the leadership of the BBC and the production staff were at odds with each other.

Wheldon argued his case vigorously, defending the programme-makers, giving the board chapter and verse on the intricacies of television drama, on the director's authority and the author's rights. As on other occasions, the governors were bemused by his flow of words. Sir Richard Pim (an Ulsterman, another former civil servant) was unwise enough to say that he doubted if any of the Wednesday Plays would have succeeded in the commercial theatre. The minutes say that 'Mr Wheldon cited instances to the contrary'; the summary of his answer fills twenty-five lines. The debate faltered and was rounded off with talk of Wheldon drafting a statement about the Wednesday Play. Without the chocolate factory, things might have ended differently.[1]

When he had been controller for eight months, Wheldon held a conference for senior programme staff at Wood Norton, near

---

[1] Wheldon's Oral History account of the affair said it was the occasion of his 'one great row' with Greene. According to this, Greene passed on a 'reproof'

Evesham, where the BBC engineers have their training headquarters. For three days he and forty colleagues were shut away
from the world. The *War Game* row was going on, and *Up the
Junction* was waiting in the wings. At Evesham they talked of
larger things, of strategy and morale. The commander had
brought his staff together. At the end of it they were photographed together, like school prefects or battalion officers: the
new team, ready to knock the stuffing out of the opposition.

Wheldon had a story about Evesham and his cufflinks – 'a very
curious personal incident which I've never forgotten. It's a very odd
one and you might think it a bit high-flown. I don't know.'

His driver, George Rixon, was due to pick him up from the
house in Kew, when he discovered he had lost his cufflinks:

> and this was very marked, because I never lose my cufflinks. In
> fact I never had lost cufflinks before. Never. I lose umbrellas but
> I'm not a loser in that sense. I couldn't find these flaming
> cufflinks. I thought of getting another shirt with buttons on, but
> I'd already got this damned shirt on. I got quite desperate about it,
> and went roaring round the house and shouted for my wife, and she
> went roaring about. There it was, I'd successfully lost them.
>
> Well, then, I wondered whether I had another pair. I had, but
> they were either too big or too flashy or some damned thing.
> Eventually I remembered that when my father died – I adored
> him – when my father died, he left all sorts of odds and ends in
> old leather cases, studs and so on, and I thought there might be a
> pair. So I looked, and indeed there was a pair of cufflinks, gold
> cufflinks, with very nice little crests on them. So I bunged them
> into my shirt and off I went.

---

from the governors, which Wheldon refused to accept. Wheldon replied in
writing to say that if the reproof was not withdrawn, he would resign. He
then had meetings with Greene ('an idle kind of chap, I always thought, like
many commanders are'), and they found an acceptable formula. This is not
the story as told in the governors' minutes. No doubt Greene and Wheldon
were having private talks. But the matter can't have been settled as Wheldon
suggests. The unreliability of his account suggests he found the episode so
distasteful, his memory rewrote it.

The conference started that afternoon, all went well, the dinner was nice and the after-dinner session was agreeable, and it was perfectly clear by eleven o'clock at night we were off to a really flying start. I met Michael [Peacock] and David [Attenborough, by now controller of BBC 2] in my office afterwards, we had a cup of tea, whisky or whatever it was, and we were all agreed that we were in good form. We went over the next day's arrangements, and I prepared to go to bed. And I took those old links out of my shirt and looked at them. Really for the first time I noticed that they each had crests on them. And the crests were the red dragon of Wales in the particular style that belongs to the Royal Welch Fusiliers, and the crest of the BBC.

I gradually remembered that these links had been given to my father by Lord Reith, John Reith as he then was, when my father gave up the chairmanship of some BBC committee many years ago. And he had valued them. I had quite forgotten all this, and yet the notion of having, as it were, my father near me, and John Reith near me in this rather odd way – There is no doubt that Freud had worked in a very powerful way. He not only had arranged for me to find these, to my conscious mind quite unsuspected pair of cufflinks, but which I must have known about, but he'd also gone to the immense trouble of making sure that I lost my original ones! It was a very great feat on his part but he succeeded. And it made an immense impression on me.

As I went to bed, I can't tell you how pleased I was to think that in some way the fates appeared to be on my side. There it was. By the way, when I left the BBC I lost them again, which was odd. I don't know. Life is very very rum, it really is.

At Evesham the agenda included finance, the prospects for colour television, the autumn programme schedules that had just started, and (in Wheldon's phrase) 'the shifting moralities of our time'. It was not a conference at which people came and went, unless it was Hugh Greene, who paid a visit, and Kenneth Adam, who was not encouraged to be there at the beginning, lest anyone think it was his show and not Wheldon's.

'The idea that anyone would nip back to London was not approved of,' says Attenborough. Everything was planned, down to bedside books and pictures for the sleeping quarters, hand-picked by Roger Cary.[1] Wheldon had a picture of Bangor Cathedral, Attenborough two books about exploring.

David Attenborough was Wheldon's chief henchman and safest ally in television. He had become famous for his expeditions to film animals and people. They had been friends since the mid-1950s. When the management crisis was coming to a head early in 1965, Wheldon invited him to the house and offered him BBC 2. 'You weren't first choice,' he said. 'I offered it to Donald, but he wouldn't have it. I think he's an ass.' Management was not Attenborough's game. But he was a film-maker as well as a presenter (a low-key presenter, not in Wheldon's style), and 'it was a personal invitation from Huw to come and serve on his staff. I was very flattered. I said I'd do it for five years.'

At BBC 2 he was Wheldon's confidant, liable to be disturbed at home late in the evening by a phone call and the voice saying, 'Dai, could you come over?' Some people said Attenborough was an acolyte; he says it himself, half jokingly. But each admired the other and drew strength from the relationship. People at the Television Centre claim to have heard them laughing from the next floor.

One of Wheldon's favourite words was 'manly'. It suggested some ideal of behaviour or simply of existence. He and Attenborough had a manly relationship. There were two categories of man as far as Wheldon was concerned. You were either 'a baby' or you 'carried guns'. Attenborough liked him from the start. 'No one ever said, "I'm one of Kenneth Adam's men." But they said it of Huw.'

---

[1] Sir Roger Cary, Bt., was a *Times* leader writer, and deputy editor of the *Listener*, before becoming a BBC administrator and consultant to the director-general. His minutes of the weekly programme review, which he kept for years, are much admired. Among his sub-specialities is organizing memorial services for departed broadcasters.

The army was a touchstone. 'I am a very regimental man,' Wheldon was heard to say. He liked to tell Montgomery stories. Others still imitate him imitating the Field Marshal on the eve of D-Day – 'Bweak wanks and gather wound . . .' Few of his stories were about wartime exploits. Attenborough says he never heard Wheldon tell a story of any kind that redounded to his credit ('Occasionally they redounded to his discredit, like falling down the steps of a public lavatory in Newport and breaking his nose').

Titles, as in the armed forces, were important. Wheldon insisted that the heads of BBC 1 and BBC 2 were to be 'controllers', to show who was boss. 'Chief', the former word, was not strong enough. Baverstock, observing events from the outside, disliked the change – 'it belongs to wartime, it means controlling the energies of people and seeing they don't do any harm.' But control meant that you knew where you were. The division, the battalion, had to have its names and seniorities, and so did the Television Centre.

Some found Wheldon overbearing. He had too much to say; he was too much of a good thing. If his largeness and grandiosity upset people, there was nothing to be done. Friends and relatives still noted the lapses into insensitivity: the hurtful remark, the sudden loss of interest.

Once he came to power, the cartoon figure of a Mr Punch with great nose and inked eyebrows assembled in people's minds. At one extreme, the tales of Wheldon hurrying about the place, making his presence seem indispensable, the beating heart inside the machine, blur into caricature. David Attenborough, friendliest of witnesses, describes his oddly mincing walk, leaning against an invisible wind, visiting studios and barking 'EVERYTHING ALL RIGHT?' at the door. A woman he had known at LSE paid a courtesy call and was shown round the building. As she was going he shouted across the entrance hall, 'JO, DO YOU WANT TO GO TO THE LAVATORY?'

One of his concerns was to meet producers and talk about their trade. Evening seminars were held for twenty at a time,

5.30 to midnight, with Peacock and Attenborough in attendance. They addressed questions of style, ethics and procedure. What is the relationship of writer to producer? How should editorial control be exercised? Is BBC 1 too competitive and BBC 2 too demure?

But he saw a wider function, to tell the BBC about itself. It was 'stuffy and toffee-nosed in all sorts of ways', but there was 'no doubt of its capacity to get on with something it actually wants to get on with'. It was Machiavellian and imperfect, yet it was also civilized and strove after excellence. He was sometimes laughed at behind his back for 'excellence', since what does striving after it mean, except the commonplace that professionals do the best they can? No matter: the phrase was one of Wheldon's tonics.

His favourite means of instruction was the story, the well-turned anecdote. He admired a good tale, and said that he once lost faith in a producer when he heard him fail to tell one properly. Gilbert Harding at the opening of the Television Centre, seeing Hugh Greene and two of Greene's predecessors, William Haley and Ian Jacob, together in a corridor, was a story. 'Ah,' said Harding, 'either the Holy Trinity or Pip, Squeak and Wilfred. The latter, I fear.' So was David Attenborough, faced with a worried BBC administrator, a story. He had been filming in Peru, where, when the team needed a couple of horses while crossing a plain, they were told it was easier to buy them than to hire them, since they cost only a few pounds. At the end of the journey, the horses could be turned loose. In London the transaction showed up in the paperwork. The administrator said the horses, having been bought, were clearly the property of the BBC, and must be accounted for. What had happened to them? Attenborough thought of all the memos he would have to write. 'Madam,' he said, 'we ate them.'

The operational side of the job included supervising the programme schedules, drawn up by Peacock and Attenborough.

What goes on between a controller of programmes and the network controllers, and in turn between the three of them and the programme-makers, is of Byzantine complexity to the outsider. Wheldon had made it clear from the start that the 'output groups and departments', the baronial fiefdoms whose power had caused so many headaches in the Hood/Baverstock period, were under his control. But in practice he could rule only by consent; to be *primus inter pares* was the best he could hope for.

The three controllers circulated one another with carbons of all correspondence. They met every morning at 9.30 in Wheldon's office. 'He affected programmes,' says Attenborough, 'with, "You can't do this," or, "Don't you think this is getting a bit vacuous?" or, "Haven't we had enough of that American series?" If he said, "Go away and think about it," and you came back undeterred, he'd say, "OK".'

Composing the schedules is a compromise: interests conflict, money is limited, the time has to be filled somehow. Technicalities abound. World television is composed in twenty-five- and fifty-minute segments – half-hours and hours less commercial breaks – and that standard affects BBC planning. There is the need to make BBC 1 and BBC 2 complement one another, hopefully with programmes that start at the same time. A viewer once asked Wheldon about it on television. 'In lots of people's minds,' he said, 'including ours, before we started the thing [BBC 2], there was this notion that there was some absolutely exquisitely correct progamme to put opposite a thriller series, for example. In fact there is no exquisitely correct programme. All you can put opposite boxing is non-boxing.'

The opposition has to be contended with. As he came to be regarded as the voice of the BBC, Wheldon was forever being asked how he weighed big audiences against high ideals. The short answer might have been 'compromise', but long answers were safer. He developed a nice line in rhetoric for fending off anyone who inquired about the dilemma of choosing between giving the public what it wanted and what might be good for it. The question, he said, was irrelevant. You had to 'respond to your own needs, to the needs of the subject and to the needs of the audience in a very complex amalgam of pressures'. In other words, you compromised.

Part of the trick of competing is not the programmes themselves but their placing. Peacock made a reputation as a cold and scheming scheduler on BBC 1. When Wheldon took over, the BBC's early-evening programmes had been weak for years. *Tonight* was stale. Commercial television had *Coronation Street* (Peacock wrote of its 'preposterous hold') and *Emergency Ward 10*. Only on Thursdays, with *Top of the Pops* at 7.30, was the BBC more attractive. If the evening began badly, it was unlikely to improve. People stayed with the channel they were watching: the 'inheritance factor'.

Peacock got rid of *Tonight*, which might have been difficult had Goldie and Baverstock been in power. He used drama series like *Z Cars* and comedy shows to grab audiences. None of this could be done overnight. Wheldon's support was called for to persuade Tom Sloan, the baron of light entertainment, even to contemplate letting his situation comedies be seen at 7.30 in the evening. That was too early for stars and their agents, who might complain and threaten defection to 'the other side'. 'He had to get drunk night after night with those frightful agents,' said Wheldon, 'or write hideous letters replying to hideous letters.'

The strategy worked. Wheldon was able to report that documentaries which used to be seen by four million were now being seen by seven and a half, thanks to the inheritance factor. Then a new problem arose. Some of the comedy shows had material that caused offence so early in the evening. Wheldon called it 'a grave dilemma'. Johnny Speight's new series *Till Death Us Do Part* was criticized for bad language. 'Bloody' before 8 p.m. was still on the borderline in 1966. Unfortunately weapons like *Till Death* were too useful not to be deployed where they would do most good. Wheldon defended it at the programme review board. Compromise was the answer. A light entertainment princeling wrote to a producer in 1967, suggesting that forty-three 'bloodys' in a *Till Death* script was 'a bit much'. He added courteously, 'If we could lose the word "crap" on page 24, I myself would be grateful.'

No one could view more than a modest percentage of the output, but Wheldon did his best. Often he stayed late at the Centre, watching a closed-circuit programme. Thirsty colleagues found his office inhospitable. The Wheldon drinks cupboard contained one bottle of sherry, which lasted a year. At home, evenings revolved around more programmes. In the *Monitor* days his wife's advice was often sought. Now that he was managing programmes instead of making them, he kept his work to himself. Jay says the last occasion he consulted her was during the Baverstock crisis, when she helped draft letters and memoranda. 'It absolutely stopped, clonk, when he became controller. What I knew was *Monitor*.'

Mutual preoccupation was part of their marriage. Jay had begun to write a novel soon after 1956. Eight years (and three children) later, the typescript ran to 400,000 words, the length of four or five 'average' novels. Publishers in London and New York accepted it, but the length was daunting. When it appeared, in February 1966, as *Mrs Bratbe's August Picnic*, she had reduced it by nearly half. In one pre-publication interview she said, 'I get no encouragement to have anything to do with [my husband's] business. It is a complicated job which isn't easy to share. We go our own ways quite successfully in this respect.' In another she said, 'I haven't been in the Television Centre more than a dozen times.' *Mrs Bratbe* was well received. Its sequel, the next in what she planned as a series of connected novels, was already under way. At first there were to be three. Then there were nine. She wrote them over a decade and a half. The typescripts accumulated in her room.

Wheldon remained a family man, devoted to Jay and the children. But he was committed to the BBC, as if to a cause. Ever since some model of the good had suggested itself to him long ago, or had been suggested by the chapel-heavy air of Bangor, he had sought comfort by association. Work that suggested a higher aim attracted him. He had found it in the army, perhaps in the Arts Council. Given his ingenuity he might have found it in an advertising agency or a gas works, if there was no alternative. The thrust of his mind was towards justification. So the BBC became an ideal that was always more than the sum of its parts. He thought it a jewel of the Western world. Whether or not he was exaggerating is irrelevant as far as his role was concerned. It was necessary to be part of such an undertaking. The BBC was like his marriage, it provided a context for him to flourish in; and enabled him, in return, to give the BBC heart in the bad times that were coming.

At first, with the second channel established and colour programmes beginning, bad times were not much thought of. The job swept Wheldon along on a flood of programmes. His remarks at the programme review board are a running commentary on his tastes. A play by David Rudkin, *House of Character*, caused concern because it explored insanity. The head of religious programmes had switched over to *The Desert Song* on BBC 2 because the play 'seemed to put the clock back in terms of current coverage of mental health elsewhere in the output'. But Wheldon found it in order: 'lunacy was lunacy and "mental illness" was a euphemism'. He welcomed a play based on Henry James's *The Portrait of a Lady*, though didn't care for a scene where voices were raised: 'characters in Henry James should never shout at each other. It was a question of emphasising adverbs.'

A documentary at 9.05 p.m. called *Lord Reith Looks Back* caused dismay by attracting only three and a half million viewers, far below the usual figure for the slot. But the review board were comparing it with epic subjects, said Wheldon, and reminded them that a month earlier, a discussion about wages and policies had gone out at the same time, in a series called *Beyond the Freeze – What Then?* Taking part were a bureaucrat, a peer and a trade unionist. About three hundred thousand bothered to watch.

On the other hand, the popularity of *It's a Knockout* never ceased to grate with Wheldon. While colleagues applauded a final with Germany, he found it repellent (he called it a 'Germanic final'), containing games that 'seemed to cramp and restrict the human spirit'. When the review board discussed a piano-smashing contest in the series, those who approved said they were only old pianos anyway. Wheldon thought there was 'something brutish' about the idea of destroying a piano, whatever its condition, 'and that certainly it must at least be made clear that they were already defunct'. The following year he was insisting that his instructions about standards be adhered to: enjoyable contests with clear rules that were 'taken with total seriousness', and properly shot: 'Anything less than this led to indignity and mess'. No one suggested that indignity and mess might be the attraction for some. On one occasion Wheldon confessed why he found the series flawed: 'C.P. Tel thought the Germans in particular were responsible for the disagreeable and undignified nature of many of the games'.

Dr Who won his approval, especially if there were plenty of Daleks. When it was pointed out (in 1965) that episodes containing Daleks were expensive, and had to be interspersed with historical, non-Dalek episodes for the sake of economy, Wheldon brushed aside objections and said every effort should be made to have more of them. Two years later the head of drama serials hinted that a recent episode might have been the Dalek swan song. Wheldon protested, and 'recalled Evelyn Waugh's own view of his troubles as a writer because "he let his characters die all the time" '. The Daleks lived on.

On technical matters he had strong views. A natural history programme about insects on BBC 2, bought in from the United States, had admirable pictures but a commentary that he found 'flatulent and meretricious'. David Attenborough said that some American commentaries in the series had been replaced by an English version, but this always meant a wearisome battle with American distributors. 'C.P. Tel said, whatever the cost, these individual battles simply had to be fought, in order to avoid inflicting commentaries that were second-rate on viewers in Britain.'

Interviews came in for attention. Wheldon noted that a discussion on BBC 2, *Doubts and Certainties*, was billed as Cyril Connolly talking to Jonathan Miller, but in fact had been Miller talking to Connolly. 'CP Tel reminded the meeting of the importance of the pause in an interview: a question to an interviewee produced a standardised or forecastable answer; it was what was said next, after an uneasy pause (and one in which he was not helped), that counted. Connolly was provided with no such challenge and consequently no opportunity, by the speed and pace of Miller's long and incessant questions.' When the review board discussed coverage of the Aberfan disaster (October 1966), Wheldon mentioned a young BBC reporter who, while trying to interview a child who had escaped from the school, had asked, 'What about your friends?' He said the reporter regretted what might have been taken as callousness, adding that he himself had made similar ('though less catastrophic') mistakes through nervousness.

When the board of governors complained at the increasing use of close-ups, Wheldon agreed that the human face ('a landscape for exploration') was being done to death (someone else thought that colour was making the face more interesting; Attenborough suggested that bits of face in colour were worse than in black and white). When people bared their souls on television, Wheldon was uneasy. An edition of *Man Alive* (April 1967) about women who had been in prison made him suspect the participants' frankness. He smelt self-interest and self-pity, and thought it dangerous to programme-making. Soon after this, in a *Whicker's World* film about divorcees, the writer Robin Douglas-Home broke down and wept. Wheldon chided all the participants for letting their feelings be 'paraded in public', and wished they had 'not been so willing'. Despite Wheldon, the trend was towards more airing of private lives, not less. A controller of programmes could modify but not prevent.

Salaciousness was always with them. A comedy sketch about homosexuals (1965) stirred the review board to anger. Wheldon had missed it, but said he had 'thought for some time that the

BBC should not be afraid of being square when it came to a consideration of what constituted smut.' There had been too much smut in *TW3*. Smut, he said, wasn't worth the price to be paid. He came down on a teenage discussion in the early evening (1966) which suggested a girl was more easy to seduce after a fast drive on a motor bike. Nor was 8 p.m. late enough for an edition of the police serial *Softly, Softly* about prostitution and blackmail (1966), with 'undertones which could well be disturbing to younger teenagers'.

Nudity came up now and then. Nudes were mainly forbidden, but might be all right in special circumstances, such as Ken Russell's film about Isadora Duncan (1966), where the scene was 'highly stylised'. Something had gone wrong with an episode of *Nana* (1968), Zola's novel turned into a serial, and Wheldon was heard to ask was there not a taboo against bare breasts?

But even when issues like that arose, he would not be drawn into giving detailed guidance. 'Experienced members of the service,' he said, 'ought not to be in doubt.' He wanted his people to want to do what was right, to know intuitively what 'right' was; to be in control of things; to know in their hearts.

CHAPTER TEN

'To Hell with Them'

WHELDON'S LOYALTY TO THE BBC was unquestioned. He was too wedded to the corporation and the ideal of public service to have cut a credible figure in ITV, and it is likely that no serious temptation was ever put in his way by the commercial companies. But some of his colleagues were being tempted in 1967. The Competitor had always been richer; some feared the gap was widening. Companies had been formed to apply for a new round of ITV franchises. They were offering large salaries, cars and share options, with loans to pay for the shares. Wheldon wrote to Kenneth Adam:

> The fact is that the Television Service has to walk with increasing strain on a very narrow line between public service on the one hand and the worlds of industry, commerce and show business on the other. The anomalies are painful, constant and pressing. [Tom] Sloan earns £5,500 (or thereabouts) and his Assistant Head, brought in from Show Business, earns £7,400 plus extras. They book Val Doonican who can claim £1,500 for a fifty minute show because ABC offered him £2,000. The pressures are not negligible and differ more and more from traditional broadcasting experience.

Reporting to the board, Wheldon suggested that 'the possible prospect of £30,000 capital is unsettling not only for the man approached, but also for the man not approached ... The delicate web of relationships, friendships, functional and personal, which keeps this complex Service unified and in good morale, is under strain.'

Several managers left, among them Michael Peacock and Humphrey Burton. Peacock had been invited to join London Weekend. It won the franchise and he became its managing director. Paul Fox, who had also been approached, replaced him at BBC 1. Wheldon was understanding about Peacock's departure, seeing him as a corporation man at heart whose loyalty had kept him there so far, but who was now being offered 'the world of the tycoon'. He was more disturbed when Burton, his close aide at *Monitor* and now in charge of music and arts programmes, also joined London Weekend. Peacock had kept the BBC informed about his negotiations. Burton hadn't. 'I was a conspirator,' he says. He had grown dissatisfied with the BBC, feeling himself at one remove from Wheldon, his mentor.

Perhaps he left to escape Wheldon's shadow. People say that Wheldon banned him from the building, unable to bear what he saw as personal disloyalty. The feeling that to leave the BBC is no ordinary career-step, more to be compared with a family rift, existed before Wheldon's time, but was heightened by his sense of them all as a band of brothers. He is supposed to have sat at his desk, stunned by the news, offering colleagues Tio Pepe from a decanter when they came to commiserate with him. Daytime sherry meant it was serious.

Burton was in Bath when he resigned, a hundred miles from the wrath. Wheldon kept the telegram, handed in on June 12. 'Have accepted offer from Aidan Crawley to run drama and cultural programmes for new company. Shall tender resignation Monday morning. Deeply regret severance BBC ties above all with yourself and David but new challenge irresistible . . . with love and apologies for adding to your burden.' He was given a week to clear his desk. 'Huw,' he says, 'had some wounding phrase about the "three Cs: change, challenge and cash".' David Attenborough took the philosophic view that 'if you'd gone to Huw and told him at the start, he'd only have talked you out of it'. Time passed before they resumed their friendship.

213

The new commercial companies, obtaining their franchises on the strength of fine words, meant stiffer opposition, at least to begin with. Wheldon hammered away at the importance of keeping the BBC's share of viewers, now stabilized at half the available audience. Paul Fox emerged as an aggressive scheduler. Another baron, Aubrey Singer, heading a features group, was created to help feed Fox and Attenborough. Many series that are still to be seen, or appear now as repeats, began in the second half of the 1960s: *Omnibus*, *The World About Us*, *Dad's Army*, *Chronicle*.

A new type of cultural spectacular, Kenneth Clark's *Civilisation*, was conceived in 1966 and shown three years later: the first time that television had behaved like a literary publisher, approaching a person of authority, in this case an art historian, and offering him a large fee for a year or two of his time, in which to write and appear in the television equivalent of a book.[1] 'I fantasized this notion,' said Wheldon, 'that if Freud and Marx and Darwin had lived in the nineteen-fifties and sixties, instead of in the eighteen-fifties and sixties, we would have had an occasional television series from them as well as books.'

Although he had known Clark since the Festival of Britain, it was Attenborough, looking for means of exploiting colour on BBC 2, who thought to use him, having seen programmes he made for ITV. He mentioned it to Wheldon, who said, 'Right-ho, Dai!'

Clark comes to lunch at the Television Centre. There is no sign of Huw: this is someone else's show. Attenborough invents the title *Civilisation* as they talk. Over coffee the door is flung open, the voice bellows 'Hello!', and Clark sits blinking under the onslaught. Then, with a 'Good show!' and a 'Carry on!', the figure vanishes. Clark has decided to accept. But in Attenborough's modest account, 'Anyone could see that Huw was the generalissimo. I just happened to be in charge of that particular campaign.'

---

[1] The BBC's offer to Clark for thirteen programmes, made in October 1966, was for £10,400. He earned a lot more in the end.

It was Wheldon's type of scheme, large, striking and intellectually safe, and the thirteen programmes had the impact he envisaged. As with *Monitor*, there was some sneering at this taking of culture to a mass audience. But the series was remembered, and led to others of similar scale like *The Ascent of Man* and *America*.

Documentary programmes had been Wheldon's territory for years. He had produced dozens of them himself, hundreds if all the *Monitors* are regarded as such. Truth in television was one of his predilections. He worried – so did they all – if he thought the medium was taking liberties with the facts. The use of news film in a play had to be specially authorized. When an ITV company was found to have staged a moorland chase for a documentary, and to have presented it as cinéma vérité, the programme review board had it held up to them as a cautionary tale of 'why the BBC had to be so careful, even stick-in-the-mud, in its attitude'. After *Twenty Four Hours* had shown what purported to be Rhodesian police dealing with black Africans, it emerged that the film had been shot in South Africa. The wrong label had been put on a can. Wheldon ordered an inquiry, saying that no matter how the mistake had been made, it was intolerable – 'other errors paled by comparison'.

The old issue of 'faction', of fact and fiction used side by side, which had caused Wheldon problems with Ken Russell and Peter Watkins, arose more often. A Wednesday Play by Jeremy Sandford called *Cathy Come Home*, which caused almost as much uproar in 1966 as *Up the Junction* [1] had done a year earlier, showed a young married couple lost in the mazes of the Welfare State. The play or documentary – people called it both – was an elegy for the homeless. Its reaction index of seventy-eight was remarkable. Wheldon is said to have been proud of it because political action resulted. [2] At the review board he said that 'he

---

[1] Nell Dunn, who wrote *Up the Junction*, was Sandford's wife.
[2] Two weeks after transmission, the author, producer and director were invited to meet the Minister of Housing, Anthony Greenwood, and their

215

did not mind a play being like a documentary, or vice versa, providing the resulting programme was good'.

This was not his usual approach. There was a proposal in Wheldon's time to mount a play-based-on-fact about the Suez crisis of 1956. 'I took it for granted that this was absolute non-sense,' said Wheldon, long after, 'and that the only reason they wanted to dramatize Suez was in order to do something down.'

Unless he had a special reason to approve, any blurring of the line between factual and fictional troubled him deeply. 'I was known to be bothersome and tiresome about it,' he said. He defended the principle in a colourful row with two Left-wing film-makers. One was Tony Garnett. The other was a director, Roy Battersby. Both were from a new generation. The dispute was about a programme called *Five Women*, based on a book by Tony Parker. Parker's speciality was to tape-record people talking at length about their lives, study the transcripts and distil the essence into passages of autobiography; these combined the freshness of natural conversation with the artifice of a book. In this case his subject was recidivism: all the women (six of them in the book) had been in and out of prison.

Battersby, a director with the features group who wanted to work in drama, had known Garnett since their university days. Their proposal to make a Wednesday Play out of *Five Women* was approved by Sydney Newman, and the film was shot early in 1967. Battersby's method was to get each of the five actresses to re-enact the story in her own words, rather than learn lines from it. Tony Parker played himself. The actresses were told

---

views sought. In passing, Greenwood criticized captions at the end of the film which compared the British situation unfavourably with Germany's. In his account of the meeting the producer, who was Tony Garnett, wrote, 'Jeremy then said that turning the knife at the end particularly in the statistic about West Germany ought to be welcomed by the Minister in his fight to get more of the available Government resources for his Ministry. The Minister smiled and said we may be right and turned it into a joke by saying they had all been given hell by their wives who had seen the programme and wanted to know what was being done about the Homeless.'

whatever was necessary to help them realize the characters. 'Sometimes I'd tell them lies,' says Battersby.

The finished programme ran for seventy-five minutes. Newman referred it to Wheldon, who was agitated to see fiction used so ingeniously in the interest of truth. It was brilliant, but what about viewers who switched on in the middle? They would think these were real women who had been in prison. Before long they wouldn't know what they were watching. Why, they might end up not knowing if they could believe what they saw on the News. Battersby said, 'Don't you think that would be a good thing, Huw?'

Battersby says now that no doubt he was naïve to expect Wheldon to be converted by the argument that news bulletins are the biggest lies of all. He says that personally he liked Wheldon, who once showed him kindness and understanding during a family bereavement. But they had no common ground on *Five Women*. 'There was this wonderful moment in his office – on the wall behind his head, as I remember it, was a John Piper picture of a church. I remember saying, "Look at that picture, Huw. Is it a church or is it a picture of a church? It's a *picture* of a church, but it's more *like* a church, we see it more clearly and with more reality, than we do when we just walk past and look at a church . . ." That didn't get through at all.'

In Wheldon's Oral History account he said he was 'very bothered indeed' that viewers might be deceived. Battersby thinks the real issue was not fact versus fiction (though Garnett disagrees), but that in *Five Women,* none of the characters protests her innocence. 'They even say, "What else can you do with people like me, except what they did?" Yet by the end of it you are one hundred per cent convinced that locking people up is the worst thing you can possibly do.'

The disagreement continued into 1968. By that time Newman's BBC contract had ended and he had returned to Canada. The drama group was under new management. *Five Women* came in for criticism. One of Battersby's superiors told him it was the worst written, worst acted film he had ever seen.

If true, that would have invalidated Wheldon's argument; an unconvincing *Five Women* would have presented no threat.

Battersby campaigned for the film. He showed it illicitly to Kenneth Tynan, who wrote half a column about it in the *Observer*, in which he attacked Wheldon for banning a play that was 'too well acted to be tolerable as art', and dismissed his 'simplistic argument' about perverting reality. For this, Battersby nearly lost his job. Wheldon's recollection was of 'an enormous long piece' by Tynan, 'saying that things like this hadn't been done since the days of the early Christian church, when hideous pedantry had come down on various aspects of entertainment and so on. He was very rude and unpleasant, and wrong in my opinion, because he didn't know what he was talking about. He said this kind of thing had been solved in the theatre long ago. But the fact is that when you go to the theatre, you know perfectly well that they are actors . . . you do not know this in television.'[1]

The features group under Aubrey Singer eventually agreed to place the offending programme in one of its slots, as long as it met Wheldon's requirements. The fact that it was a documentary with actresses was spelt out. One of the five episodes was dropped altogether, so that when transmitted in 1969 it was called *Some Women*. At the programme review board, people were still grumbling that it was neither one thing nor the other. Wheldon said the programme was 'art', based on material – the original recordings – that was perhaps a hundred times as long. 'The programme had been worth doing. His only anxiety had been to make clear exactly what it was.'

Wheldon knew that to blur the lines of demarcation between one kind of truth and another was subversive. People must not be encouraged to think that the truth of a news bulletin or a current-affairs programme may be itself a contrivance. In this, as

[1] The article by Tynan said nothing about the early church or 'hideous pedantry'. Wheldon's memories, like most people's, were dramas as well as documentaries.

in most things, he adhered to corporation principles, adding his own absolute certainty that a well-controlled hierarchy was the pre-requisite of a secure life. It suited him; why should it not suit others?

In 1968, after three and a half years as controller of programmes, Wheldon tried and failed to become director-general. The job fell vacant when Hugh Greene, who had held it since 1960, decided he could stand no more of the chairman, Lord Hill, and resigned. There were five candidates, including Wheldon. Some of his friends think he was indifferent, and let his name go forward only as a formality. This is unlikely. He thought he was the right man, even if he suspected that his contempt for the governors in general and Lord Hill in particular would ruin his chances.

Hill had been chairman of the Independent Television Authority. When the BBC's chairman, Lord Normanbrook, died in office in June 1967, the Prime Minister, Harold Wilson, offered the post to Hill, allegedly telling Richard Crossman that 'Charlie Hill has already cleaned up ITV, and he'll do the same to the BBC'. The BBC regarded the new man as an interloper. Hill, the bluff-mannered 'Radio Doctor'[1] in the war, saw himself as eminently suited to come back and run the place. He brought his private secretary with him, demanded a new suite of offices (saying that the room he inherited was like a coffin), and incurred Greene's hatred by, among other things, insisting that the board should vote on every decision, instead of being steered towards a consensus by the director-general. According to Greene, Hill once insisted they vote on whether cigarettes should be provided at BBC functions.

A clever campaigner who organized his profession's opposition

---

[1] Charles Hill (MD, DPH) broadcast from 1941 in an early-morning programme, *The Kitchen Front*.

to the Health Service after the war, Hill was upset to find himself shunned. When he complained to David Attenborough about his cool reception, Attenborough replied that for the BBC it was as if the 8th Army had woken up one morning to find Rommel was their general. 'Are you suggesting Rommel wasn't a good general?' asked Hill. 'No,' said Attenborough, 'but we'd like to know he's fighting for the same things as us.' Thereafter they got on well, and Hill came to regard him as a future director-general.

Attenborough says he was surprised to find that 'Huw, who could charm anyone, didn't bother with Charlie Hill. He felt no warmth.' Hill, an ostentatiously plain man, thought that Wheldon had too much to say, too cleverly. When Tom Jackson, a trade union leader who was a governor in the 1970s, proposed a series about industrial relations, Wheldon, attending the board, 'talked and talked and talked,' said Hill, 'and we got nowhere.' Wheldon knew such programmes were death, like one about the pay freeze that attracted a third of a million viewers. The industrial-relations idea came up in other ways. Each time, said Hill, it was 'deliberately flushed by Huw'. Attenborough thinks that 'Huw was altogether too brilliant' for the chairman, not much of a basis for an understanding. 'Oh, the capacity of these exceedingly able people to win was enormous!' Hill said.

In later years Wheldon had little to say about him. They were sharply divided in 1968, in the months before Greene resigned, over a paper that the board of governors decided to sponsor, under the title 'Broadcasting and the Public Mood'. The BBC's natural idiom was arrogance, but nagging politicians and moralists had begun to unnerve it. The paper was Hill's idea. Oliver Whitley, Greene's chief assistant, wrote a draft. Hill thought the result too bland, and toughened it up.

Early in June, Hill told a meeting of senior staff in Wheldon's office that the paper would be published shortly. It was not meant as a directive, he said, but as a basis for discussion; it would not embarrass anyone, and it had 'more wisdom in it than clarity'.

Wheldon read it and was furious. He wrote to Kenneth Adam and said that on the contrary, 'it has more clarity in it than wisdom; and if I had to describe it with absolute honesty I should have to call it sectarian and philistine.' Wheldon's memo, with accompanying notes, dismissed the board's paper by implication as ignorant and moralistic, and said it would damage relations between staff and board. Of a section that read, 'There are people who are deeply hurt by the intrusion into their homes of what they believe to be the BBC's amoral or anti-moral attitude [. . .] If we do not pursue a traditional line, we should not cultivate or appear to cultivate a permissive one', Wheldon commented, 'I really think this should be cut. I do not see how to amend it. How could it not bring the chairman into disrepute?'

A passage in the paper about 'gloom' in BBC plays spoke of 'the dramatist's natural inclination to make wry comments on society'. Wheldon wrote, 'Terrible. "Wry comments!" Macbeth? Cathy Come Home?' In a general attack on the paper's philistinism, Wheldon wrote that

> the paper recognizes the BBC's duties as an energizer, a patron, but does so grudgingly, and without seeming fully to understand the central importance of this role for the BBC's own standards and future. The tone, once more, is what counts; and I cannot but see it as paying mere lipservice to some of the most important and crucial of all the BBC's achievements. If swearing, bad taste, the sordid, sexuality, 'offensive material' were truly the enemy, there never would have been any STEPTOE, or TILL DEATH, no UP THE JUNCTION, no CATHY COME HOME, no MOVING ON, no Hopkins trilogy, no Muggeridge, no Wednesday Play series, no Satire Shows. These are our glories, not our Achilles heels . . .

Wheldon was taking a kinder view of controversial material than he did at the weekly programme review. But private criticism among colleagues was one thing. He knew that for the governors to put their name to such an apologetic document, damning their own producers with faint praise, was a betrayal. If any of his anger got as far as the board, it had little effect. The paper was amended in places, and some of the uglier phrases removed or watered down, but it was published in substantially the form that Wheldon had attacked.

The following month, July, Greene announced his resignation, to take effect in March 1969. The board moved quickly to find a successor. The short-list consisted of Oliver Whitley, who at fifty-six was on the elderly side, and was interviewed as a courtesy; Kenneth Lamb, the BBC secretary; David Attenborough, who didn't want the job; Charles Curran, director of external broadcasting, who was Greene's candidate; and Huw Wheldon.

The interviews were to be at the end of July, before people went on holiday. On July 19, a Friday, Wheldon saw the chairman; probably it was Wheldon who asked for the meeting. Among the things he told Hill was that he didn't want the director-general's job 'at any cost', a remark that Hill called 'ambivalent and ambiguous'. Over that weekend, Wheldon struggled to write down what he felt he hadn't conveyed at their meeting.[1]

In the finished letter, Wheldon pleaded that in these 'mean and peevish' times, the BBC ('this great institution') must recognize its role of national leadership, grappling with art and current affairs, 'ready to meet both the challenge of its own history and the challenge of the times'. As usual, 'excellence' was the goal. Agreement about how excellence should be defined was a matter that chairman and director-general must agree on. The board must 'keep up the courage of the corporation, keep it in bad times as well as good in the knowledge that what it presides over is a matter for pride and pleasure and not only for worry and anxiety'.

---

[1] Wheldon's papers about the director-generalship consist of carbons of two letters from Wheldon to Hill, dated July 23 and August 1; and drafts and notes for the July 23 letter, both typed and handwritten, covering 79 sheets.

It was not quite vintage Wheldon. The first part of the letter was a defence of a television play, about to be transmitted, *The Year of the Sex Olympics*,[1] to whose title and resulting newspaper publicity Hill had objected at their meeting. Wheldon laboured the point, that the play was a serious work.

The weekend drafts of the letter, containing passages that Wheldon didn't send, are more revealing. He tried to say what he was thinking, and uncharacteristically, he failed. 'I was dismayed,' he writes about Hill's attitude to the *Sex Olympics* affair, but discarded the phrase. 'I do not think you trust me' was crossed out. He got rid of, 'I feel that you are impatient of my paradoxes and complexities and longwindedness and I am unable to apologize for them, for they try to deal with the actual complexities themselves.' There was a contradiction in what he was doing: he sought to be straightforward with a boss whose support he needed, but had to conceal the fact that he neither trusted nor respected him.

It is hard to believe that Wheldon thought they could work in harmony. Perhaps he hoped that with a reliable lieutenant – such as Attenborough – at the Television Centre, the two of them could hold the line. Perhaps his tactic, starting now, was to wear the chairman down with words.

Halfway through a handwritten page, Wheldon was rattling on, 'Week in, week out, there are programmes admired by those whom you and I admire; never a week without excellence, real excellence, somewhere along the line.' He stopped short; made a paragraph; said what was in his heart, more bluntly than he would put it in the final draft:

> O hell. What the bloody Board has to do is to keep its nerve, keep it in bad times as well as good, and keep it in the knowledge that what it is presiding over is a matter for pride & pleasure & not for worry or anxiety.
>
> To hell with them.

---

[1] The author was Nigel Kneale, who wrote the *Quatermass* science-fiction plays.

The governors saw candidates on July 31. Glanmor Williams, the Welsh representative on the board, says diplomatically that they all 'put up a good show, including Huw, except that he talked too much, as always'. Hill said in his autobiography that, given the support of the board, he would have favoured Wheldon – 'I should have loved working with such a man.' This takes some believing. The day after the interviews, Wheldon wrote to Hill again, saying he had done 'scant justice' to his case, and stating yet again (in three pages) his view on what BBC policy should be: in divisive times, it needed strong leadership.

A week later, it was announced that Curran had got the job. Wheldon was given second prize. He was to take over the television service at the end of the year, replacing Kenneth Adam, who was to retire. As part of a management reorganization that was already under way, Wheldon would have the title of managing director, with absolute control of the television budget.

His failure was regretted by his friends but accepted as inevitable. Aubrey Singer, a consistent admirer, says that 'the board of governors had his measure'. George Campey says that 'half of him would have made a brilliant DG'. Paul Fox wrote later that he should have been appointed, 'but the corporation was afraid of him'. David Attenborough wrote that he was the best director-general the BBC never had. Lady Wheldon denies that he ever wanted the job.

By the time he heard he didn't have it, he was spending the month of August as he did for many years, with his family on the coast of north-west Wales, at Criccieth. The little town, now lapped by holiday development, is near the Pass of Llanberis and the Snowdon range. For seventeen years or so, as the children were growing up, nowhere else was seriously considered.

In later years, a friend who lived there used to hang streamers between house and lamppost in Marine Parade, to announce their arrival. Criccieth has a larger fame as the home, for much of his life, of David Lloyd George, another association that drew Wheldon to the place. They took rooms in a guest house, facing

Cardigan Bay, and settled down to the serious business of enjoying themselves. Wheldon craved organization. Time was allocated: the bathe, the walk, the climb. He wanted maximum satisfaction for all, as though the pursuit of excellence extended into poking about in rock pools. Building sand-castles was team work. His son Wynn, aged ten in 1968, remembers them as 'solid, like the castles of Wales. Dad's manner was not childlike in this – he was capable of getting cross when a fortification seemed not up to standard.' Nor was there any nonsense about watching the castle crumble as the tide reached it. 'We worked to the last moment. We never actually *saw* the completed thing.'

Serious walking in the mountains took them up Snowdon on the south side of the Pass of Llanberis, and the Glyders on the north. Sometimes it was just father and son. They climbed the long ridge of Cnicht, optimistically known as 'the Matterhorn of Wales', and Moelwyn Mawr, above the slate mines where paintings from the National Gallery were stored in the war. They took standard equipment: Ordnance Survey map, two pork pies, two apples, large bar of Bourneville, binoculars. At the top, as they sat on a boulder and ate the pies, Wheldon always did the same thing: swept his arm at the view and said, 'Damn good.'

The first time he took his wife on to Snowdon they used the Pig track (named after Bwlch y Moch, the Pass of the Pigs), wearing, according to her, ordinary shoes and not walking boots. She once wrote to her elder daughter, Sian, describing the expedition. They reached Crib Goch, one of the ridges that radiate from the peak of Snowdon. 'It was here that I first heard the famous shout, "Body off the rock!" (which means "Stand up like a man and WALK!") *My* body, every inch, was on the rock the whole way.' Her husband was in front of her, calling 'Green fields ahead!' These turned out to be more rock and ice. After that they both had nightmares and bought climbing boots.

Jonah Jones, the sculptor, his friend from the Army Education days, lived in the area with his wife, Judith Maro, one of the Israeli instructors at Mount Carmel. Both had learned Welsh, and brought up their children to speak it. The two families went

225

for outings together. 'Organized chaos,' says Jonah Jones. 'It was a rigorous puritanical exercise, getting yourself up a mountain, Judith wouldn't come.'

Wheldon said he wanted his own children to speak the language, but he did nothing about it. The radical nationalism that began in the 1960s and has developed ever since, with powerful but law-abiding campaigns and a fringe of violence, had no appeal for him. When members of the 'Free Wales Army' were featured in *Panorama* in 1966, and the programme review board wondered if they should have been given the publicity, Wheldon thought they had 'satisfactorily emerged as musical comedy figures'. His generation took Welshness for granted. Alwyn Roberts, a former BBC governor, born 1933, suggests that 'Huw thought he knew everything about Wales, but really he didn't. He knew pre-war, middle-class Wales. He kept up connections and came back for holidays, but he was totally absorbed in the development of television in London.' Geraint Stanley Jones, a BBC colleague,[1] who was friendly with Wheldon – few prominent Welshmen were not – thinks that 'Huw was a deeply metropolitan being. His Welshness was to do with speaking Welsh in Criccieth, loudly.' Stanley Jones adds that Huw was 'deeply suspicious of the Welsh BBC. It's said that he applied for a job with the BBC in Cardiff, when he was with the Arts Council, and they turned him down.'

'Committed' Welshness has become fashionable. But Welsh-speakers are far from being politicized overall. In any case, Wheldon was too late on the scene. His Welshness remained personal and sentimental. When he was in Wales or in a Welsh mood he pretended to keep a distance between himself and the English. Michael Charlton, the broadcaster, to whom he was close in later life, remembers him saying (as they were walking on a Welsh hillside) that English was a language brimming with

---

[1] Stanley Jones, b. 1936, was controller of BBC Wales 1981–85, and is now chief executive of S4C, the Welsh-language television channel.

sibilants. 'That's why it's called "snake's tongue" in Welsh,' he added.

Criccieth in 1968, or in any particular year, is muddled up in Wheldon memories with all the other years they went there. By this time he wrote few letters that say anything about his private life, although it happens that in 1968 he replied to H., who had written an article about students – it was the year of student revolt – and sent it to him for his views. 'All is sunshine & golden splendour,' he said, excusing himself from comment until he returned to London. 'I will write further, given the Moral Fibre, the lack of which as you know is among my central qualities, when I get back. Dazzling seas outside. The porpoises wink as they roll past.' Of director-generalships and sodding governors he said nothing.

CHAPTER ELEVEN

Cash, Glory, Piety

KENNETH ADAM's unhappy reign faded away. At the last programme review board of 1968, 'C.P. Tel paid what he called a "treacherous tribute" to Kenneth Adam who had expressly asked for no tributes and no farewells.' The minute added that the retiring director of television was unable to be present, 'having a badly swollen face'. Adam hung on till the last moment (Normanbrook, the former chairman, who wanted to get rid of him, died before he could act), and he was nine months past the formal retiring age of sixty.

Wheldon had been the effective chief, but subject to the rules of a hierarchy. Now, as 'M.D. Tel', he was formally responsible for the whole service, including its finances. Until then no one was sure who controlled the money, Television Centre or the old pre-television headquarters, Broadcasting House. The change would have come in any case, Wheldon or no.[1] But being the first of a brand-new dynasty suited his style and aspirations. 'I truly did feel like an admiral with a ship,' he said.

As soon as he took over he announced that he had 'an absolute right of entry to any meeting whatsoever that took place anywhere

---

[1] 'Reorganization' was in the air, and the BBC (advised by the consultants McKinsey & Co) was moving towards new financial systems, computer-based, to make budgets more accurate and accessible. Among the innovations, each of the BBC's three arms – television, radio and external services – was given a managing director, with appropriate powers as chief executive.

in the television service'. He claimed never to have let a week go by without attending at least one meeting. His style, by and large, was benevolent, but he let everyone see who was boss.

Curran was a choleric man, but no match for Wheldon in programme matters, since he had little experience of his own. Wheldon said that Curran 'knew nothing at all about television', that they were friendly but never intimate, and that the director-general left him alone – which he respected by being considerate in setting his annual budget for the board to approve. He went further, and suggested that once the three managing-directorships were set up, they were seen as the key jobs, and the director-general became 'willy-nilly a kind of secretary-general, except in so far as political programmes are concerned'.[1] Curran made this look at least partly true.

Antony Jay suggests that Curran's remark when he was appointed, 'I am not Charles Hill's poodle', implies that he was. Hill said that Curran refused to let Wheldon have the title of 'deputy director-general' lest he, Curran, be overwhelmed. Michael Checkland, the present DG,[2] says that 'it was always rumoured that they had a deal, with Huw left free to run the television service. I don't think DGs make deals. But it is what happened. Curran concentrated on other things, like being president of the European Broadcasting Union. He was a dreadful man for knowing about frequencies.'

Wheldon as 'M.D. Tel' was a publicist from the start. He was the man who made the BBC's case. If he made his own case at the same time, it was simply that the two coincided. A day or two into 1969, just as he formally took over, BBC 2 put out *An Evening with Huw Wheldon*, recorded a year earlier. The *Evening*

---

[1] Hugh Greene, when he was director-general, opposed the 'managing directors' idea for that reason.

[2] Michael Checkland, b. 1936, was a financial administrator who was rapidly promoted (and became a friend of Wheldon) during and after the BBC reorganization. He was made director-general in 1987, the first to come from accountancy.

with ... programmes were anthologies, usually of verse and fiction. Wheldon made sure he threw in some picturesque autobiography. Between a poem by R. S. Thomas and a story by Dylan Thomas, he contrasted the gravelly speech of his paternal forbears from North Wales with the characteristic lilt of South Wales – 'the kind of sentence, "How is your wife, Mr Griffiths?" "Dead, thank you." "Oh, I am sorry, what did she die of?" "Nothing serious, thank you very much."' Between 'Naming of Parts' by Henry Reed and the inevitable 'Church Going' by Larkin he told an army story, about his initial training. A drill sergeant explained how to come to attention. '"Now," he said, "in the old days, on that word of command, the left knee would be fully bent, and the left foot slammed down next to the right foot. It has been found, however, that this is damaging to backs. So on that word of command, the left foot is simply raised from the ground, and placed next to the right foot at the angle already described. *Now*, in this regiment," he said, "we hurt backs."' It was Wheldon's usual stylish performance, and it can have done no harm for the public to be reminded of his friendly ways, now that he was running television.

The BBC's future was not as rosy as it had seemed a few years earlier. Wheldon believed that 'development is absolutely in our blood'. But the Joanna Spicers and Michael Checklands, peering into the new computer screens, foresaw the end of prosperity. Income from licences was levelling off, since most people had television sets by now. Inflation was rising.

The accounts for 1968–9 showed overspending by £900,000. There were no hidden reserves. In December 1969, Wheldon was telling his lieutenants behind closed doors that he wanted 'invisible' cuts that wouldn't harm the output. They were telling him that they already had more repeated programmes in the schedules than they thought proper. There was even speculative talk about closing down BBC 2 for the month of August 1970.

Wheldon was guarded in what he said in his pep talks to the rank and file, since he knew there would be leaks to the press, but he managed to make them sound like a frank appraisal without giving too much away. Television, he pointed out, had expanded every year since the war. He gave an annual figure of ten per cent net. 'If I did six programmes and I thought they were going to go well,' he said, 'then I took it for granted that next year I would certainly be able to do nine, and I was right.' Those days were over. They had spent twenty years building a house – sometimes it was a ship – which was now complete and had to be lived in, or sailed. 'It is,' he added, 'easier to add to a house than to live in it well.'

These morale-building talks were given early in 1970. A thousand or two people heard him, perhaps a quarter of the Television Centre staff. A talk lasted nearly two hours, with an interval in the middle. Those who paid attention would have noticed that Wheldon didn't once mention the governors or Broadcasting House. They were outside the family. Much of what he said was about traditions and principles. He told them stories. He talked about his early days directing programmes in the studio – 'I do not claim at all to have been a good studio director. If I did there are plenty of people here who could give me the lie.' But at least he had kept everyone informed – for 'who are you, if you are responsible, to treat people ignominiously?'

He told them his story about the football World Cup in 1966, as an example of how the BBC was 'in a singular position of being able to court excellence'. He conceded that although 'this always sounds, and indeed is, complacent', it was not individuals who made excellence possible, but rather the nature of the BBC itself. He described how Joanna Spicer, head of programme planning, came into his office when he was controller of programmes, saying, 'I thought you would like to see the plans for the World Cup coverage.' He studied them. Entire evenings were devoted to football. 'I said to Mrs Spicer – in a timid way, of course [laughter] – "Are we not going rather nap on the World Cup?" "Well," she said, "we are advised it is going to be a very big event, and the BBC will be expected to handle it very thoroughly." I asked whether ITV were handling it in this way,

231

and she said, "We are advised not." By this time I was getting more and more bothered. I said with the utmost hesitation, "What happens if England loses in the early rounds?" She said, "We are advised that that is most unlikely" [more laughter]. So the decision was taken. Whose decision was it? Theoretically it was mine. But it was other people's, really, the people running Outside Broadcasts, who knew what they were talking about, and were allowed to know what they were talking about.'

Was it a story about excellence, or merely about professional competence? If Wheldon could successfully pass off the one as the other, perhaps it didn't matter. He spoke about money, confiding that he had taken a quarter of a million pounds away from the controllers of BBC 1 and BBC 2, who had to make it up in better management. An experiment with a drama series had enabled the producer to save twenty-seven per cent of the film costs over six episodes. 'Some amateur arithmetician,' said Wheldon, 'immediately worked out a sum and proved to me, in a hot little note, that were this applied overall, the service would save £847,000 a year. By the same token, I am sure that the whole population of the world can stand on the Isle of Wight, could you but bring them there. I do not look forward to fatuous generalizations of that kind. On the other hand, if film shooting can be cut by twenty-seven per cent . . .'

The Wheldons were moving house. That was put to use. Moving, said Wheldon, was 'very much more complicated than running a television service. My old house is a shambles, and we are busy packing things. Some weeks ago my wife was hopping up and down buying wallpaper, and the question was, should we buy this at twenty-four shillings a length, or that at eighteen and six, or this very nice paper indeed at only twelve and six? The other night we were watching a three-minute sketch on television, and my wife suddenly said, "That wallpaper costs a hundred and five shillings a length" [laughter]. I replied, "Of course it doesn't!" She then found one of the wallpaper books, and there it was – a hundred and five shillings a roll.'

To clinch the argument about economy, Wheldon would

declare that money wasn't everything, that chains and limitations were in themselves creative: 'it is through kicking against the iron of the wall in which you imprison yourself that you get the proper relationship between form and content.' The mystery of the sonnet lay in its being a prison that made great statements possible. 'The sonnet,' cried Wheldon, getting carried away, 'was not invented by accident.' Some of his colleagues seemed to remember Wheldon the programme-maker going well over budget in his time. But the rhetoric had a life of its own.

The Wheldons' new house was at the top of Richmond Hill, as near to Richmond Park as their old house was to Kew Gardens. The distance between the houses was only a couple of miles. Like most managers in BBC television, Wheldon never lived far from the shop. The new house was bigger. It was late Georgian or early Victorian, a villa with broad steps at the front and windows facing west over a road and a terraced walk to Petersham Meadows below, and a broad reach of the Thames. The famous view from Richmond Hill was painted by Turner. Planes sank to the horizon, landing at Heathrow. There were vistas and sunsets, at a price. A large mortgage was necessary. Friends heard Wheldon joke about how he could never afford it. Tom Main, the psychiatrist, thought the jokes were too loud and went on too long.

The house had been partitioned into bed-sits, and the Wheldons lived in the basement while the builders were restoring it, which took most of 1970. 'Soon,' observes a friend with a cruel eye, 'the terrace belongs to Huw. One is taken around to see the details, the changes and the View he's created.' The same friend gave him a lift home one evening and 'saw him with the wraps off. He was the numbed husband with the boring domestic details, the broken bicycle, the bills he didn't want.'

His wife's writing was an important element in their lives. Since the success of *Mrs Bratbe* in 1966, she had been working steadily on her gargantuan novel. In May 1970, a few months after they moved to Richmond Hill, she began a 'personal journal'. She and the children had been ill; between that and the move, she had not worked on the novel for months. Only a few pages of the journal survive, or were ever written. Beginning with a disclaimer at the idea of keeping a journal at all ('how to overcome the pomposity of the undertaking?'), she asks how one finds the time: 'Any time which could be used for writing – which means quietness, isolation, no one about – a room, a place of your own, your head to yourself, no possibility of an interruption – the ghastly sickness of being dragged up from a deep place, like being skinned – all that time was, I thought, not for journals or notes, but for writing my fiction or else being eaten with anxiety about it.'

Unable to write, for the moment, she turned to books: Kafka's journals, Malcolm Lowry's letters, *Howard's End* by E. M. Forster, *The Wide Sargasso Sea* by Jean Rhys. 'So I have been reading, and I have been learning,' she wrote. 'But there is no one to talk to. Huw is, in many ways, wonderfully fresh & loving for a man so driven by ["anxieties" crossed out and "problems" substituted] that they take from him sometimes preoccupation which it would be better for him to be able to place elsewhere among us, his family, or to his own pleasures in which he is very abstemious.'

Underlying all are the demands of fiction. Stoicism has 'given me an appearance to my neighbours & friends of one who "writes a little" when in fact, behind the talkative, sometimes not talkative me, when "passing the time", there is an obsessed & red-eyed fiend – holding every one of my wasted moments against them. Not only does one carry the burden of a work of art not going well – but also of a life not going well. Oh, it'll do. But it is not brilliant for the children & Huw who, despite my "appearances," do not do well in competition with my obsessions.'

Looking back, twenty years later, Lady Wheldon regards that middle period of their marriage, when her writing consumed so much, with resignation. 'Those bloody books,' she says. She was restless, unpunctual, missing meals, a night bird, at her desk at all hours. 'Once Huw was managing director, every day there was something. He was busy, and I was sort of absent.' She has memories of him in a chair, reading BBC papers, and her on a sofa with a book. Occasionally he waved.

Wheldon laid down an everyday pattern for the family. His energy and laughter saved everyone. 'Life is large,' he used to say: large, but in his case well organized. When a joint walk with the Murphys was planned for Richmond Park, participants had the option of the long 'A' walk around the perimeter or the babies' 'B' walk in the middle, a mere two or three miles. Sian says that even television viewing was planned: choose the programme (by discussion if necessary), arrange the chairs, and make sure people saw what they were going to see from start to finish, not wandering in and out. Megan remembers 'committees' to discuss their mother's birthday. There were always jokes.

Only now and then is there a minor reservation. Wynn says his certainty could be oppressive.

David Attenborough had moved into Wheldon's old job, except that he was called 'director' and not 'controller' of programmes. Hill asked him to do it (Attenborough says 'told' him), with an eye on higher things. If Wheldon suspected that his friend was being got ready for the crown that had eluded him, he must have had a shrewd idea that Attenborough, who had already spent four years in management, would eventually find animals more seductive than power.

'What was there for me to do as director of programmes?' says Attenborough. 'The answer was, all the boring bits – politicians, unions, finance, systems.' The programmes themselves were not boring. But Wheldon, although he was at one remove from them – and now left it to Attenborough to chair the weekly programme review – was never far away. Attenborough says he accepted against his better judgement. Colleagues remember them as a powerful duopoly. Checkland saw Wheldon in action during

Attenborough's time and after it, and has no doubt that the managing director was at his best when the two were together. Paul Fox was still controller of BBC 1, another trusted friend. They had all grown up together in the family firm.

Wheldon's term of office was fixed by his age. He wanted to stay on as long as possible, but there was little hope beyond May 1976, when he would be sixty. That gave him seven years to leave his mark on television. He had first to show he was an effective chief executive. Friars, his old school in Bangor, wrote to solicit a contribution for the magazine about his life and 'present position'. He wrote (May 19 1971) that his job was

> a kind of ragbag. A lot of time is taken up with finance and appointments, a lot with various programme policies: could we do more of this or less of that – spend less here, more there? And more time than you would think in knocking people's heads together. There are . . . writers, engineers, designers, accountants, producers, carpenters, librarians, cameramen; all sorts. It is sometimes rather like sitting on top of a volcano. It is also very enjoyable.

How best to manage the BBC's resources as times grew harder was a problem that never went away after the late 1960s. The BBC had to develop sophisticated systems for planning and budgeting. Wheldon leaned on the advice of a television accountant; from 1971 this was Checkland. He and a senior engineer made up a committee run by Joanna Spicer, who now had the title of assistant controller (development). This triumvirate never-endingly drafted and refined future budgets. Spicer and Checkland, said Wheldon, were among his four most valuable aides (the others were Attenborough and Fox).

The more the managers could do, the freer Wheldon was to deal with larger issues. Defending television was becoming a full-time job. Wheldon sent a friendly letter to Michael Peacock, after each had written newspaper articles disagreeing with the other, to say it was true that the BBC was vulnerable, 'but I see that condition as meaning that it badly needs friends. The same is true of democracy, another highly vulnerable concept . . .'

The politicians suspected television. Whether of Left or Right, they itched to supervise it. The BBC's arrogance, the corollary of Wheldon's 'excellence', didn't help. A backbench committee of Conservatives set itself up to look into 'complaints of Left-wing bias' in January 1971, as the programme review board noted uneasily. Within months BBC television was being attacked from the Left it was supposed to be biased towards, when Harold Wilson and the Labour opposition thought they were being lampooned in a film called *Yesterday's Men*. Wheldon was involved in the row, but not crucially – news and current affairs were the direct responsibility of the director-general's office, especially an issue like this. His later accounts to friends, and his speech to a Royal Television Society dinner, make the affair into an entertainment; one wouldn't guess from it that the episode had deep political undertones, damaging to the BBC.[1]

The film was one of a pair to be transmitted on consecutive evenings in the *Twenty Four Hours* slot, the first about Harold Wilson's opposition, the second about Edward Heath's government. The row began when Wilson objected to questions about his earnings from his memoirs, put by David Dimbleby in a pre-recorded interview. Then Labour MPs, several of whom had been interviewed, realized that the tone of the programme was not going to be as respectful as they would have liked.

Wheldon's story ('in six chapters', when he was giving the full version), began at the Television Centre, the evening before transmission, where he and Curran were hosts at a dinner, from which they were called to the telephone to speak to Harold Wilson and a succession of Labour politicians. Later that night they had difficulty finding the flat of Lord Goodman, Wilson's solicitor, who, when located, spoke of injunctions. By now the BBC's legal department had advised that although none of the participants had signed their contracts – which they assumed put them in a strong position – they were unable to rescind their

---

[1] Curran's chief assistant and political trouble-shooter, then John Crawley, concluded that the affair 'did us great harm'.

verbal agreement and refuse to let the interviews be used. (It seems not to have occurred to anyone at the BBC how infuriating that would be to the politicians.)

In private Wheldon saw grounds for objecting to the title, *Yesterday's Men*, especially since Wilson and the rest had thought the programme was to be called *Her Majesty's Opposition*. Paul Fox said it was like doctors, expecting to appear in a programme called *Group Practice*, discovering the title was *Quack Quack*. ('I instantly purloined the joke,' said Wheldon, 'and used it on all sides.') The film also featured a satirical song commissioned from a group, and Wheldon didn't like that either. Otherwise he thought the film in order. Title and music were no more than a lapse of good manners. 'Manners,' he declared in his account later, 'are frequently more important than morals.' There was no hint that he thought the BBC's attitude might have been seen as high-handed.

Some governors saw the film, formally or informally – no one was ever sure – and Curran made the decision to transmit. Wheldon's account took in the BBC box at Royal Ascot, on the day the film went out, with Wheldon presiding, and Lord Goodman, invited long before, turning up and eating bowls of strawberries. It extended to the week after, when the governors met formally to consider what had happened, and debated the terms of a press statement to be issued next day. Wheldon was present. One paragraph couldn't be agreed, and Wheldon took it home, promising to telephone it to the chairman by 10 a.m.

The story became a domestic farce. Jay had taken their younger daughter, Megan, to hospital – a false alarm, it turned out – leaving Wheldon to get the other children's breakfast and see them off to school next morning. At 8.50 a.m. he sat down to write the paragraph. Suddenly Sian returned to say the cat had been run over and killed. A taxi was summoned to take her to school, weeping. Wheldon sucked his pencil. Mewing came from the basement. The dead cat's kittens, two days old, were hungry. The vet was telephoned and said they would soon be dead unless a fountain pen and special milk were procured.

In the end George Rixon, his driver, came, and took charge of the kitten problem. By this time Lord Hill was on the phone, complaining it was after 10 o'clock. Wheldon hadn't written a word. In despair, he dictated the paragraph out of his head. When he had finished, the secretary said, 'What was the word after "strong"?' Wheldon had no idea. The only word he could think of was 'reason'. Hill was listening on another phone. 'Don't think it was "reason",' he said. 'Wasn't it "element"?' 'I do so beg your pardon,' said Wheldon, 'I can't read my own writing. Yes, "element".'

Wheldon's tale of *Yesterday's Men* exists in more than one version, all of them comic and unreliable.[1] It was a good laugh about politicians on TV. But the affair had been bungled. When Labour was next in power, in 1974, it was quick to revive an idea from its previous term of office, an official inquiry into broadcasting chaired by Lord Annan, and the outcome was not favourable to the BBC. Wheldon was inclined to wash his hands of *Yesterday's Men*. But the episode lies uneasily alongside the self-congratulatory rhetoric.

Moralists were as busy as ever. The ranks of Mary Whitehouse and friends had thickened. 'Violence on television' was much discussed inside the BBC. Wheldon, raising it at the weekly programme review (March 25 1970), played his favourite game of running through a list of quality programmes – *Steptoes*, *Man Alives*, a Chekhov, a George Eliot – before attacking the peevish, as he called them: 'M.D. Tel said that the political and press situation made it only too easy for the BBC to be a whipping-boy, because it was the easy demagogic line to blame any elements of violence in society on television.' The following month he said they hoped they could get away with doing

---

[1] The longest version is in Wheldon's speech – which consists of little else – at the last dinner he attended as president of the Royal Television Society, in December 1985. He dwelt on 'Chapter 6' of the tale, about his children and the kittens; perhaps unconsciously stressing the 'home' side of his life, which for so long had suffered in the cause of television.

nothing, but by July a bone was flung to complainants in the shape of a 'research advisory group'. There was talk of a 'broadcasting council', even a 'morality council'. In 1971, in the wake of the *Yesterday's Men* affair, the governors approved a meek body called the programmes complaints commission. Wheldon noted at his managing-director meeting that newspapers had been 'on the whole sardonic' about the thing, which was hardly surprising.

The more specific a complaint, the more Wheldon enjoyed rebutting it. He was not much of a man for dialectic. Plain answers sufficed. He was rarely evasive. One of his godchildren, Clare Burton, daughter of Humphrey, sent him a postcard asking for *The Partridge Family* to be brought back, adding that 'BBC's Childrens tv is detereorating drasticly.' This called for a rebuke. Her comment was 'one of those hollow sentences that sounds as if it had been picked up from a newspaper. As a matter of fact Children's Television is rather good at the moment.'

With the public he sounded more honest than most spokesmen, packaging what he said in the best possible way, but not dodging the issue. Appearing on BBC 1 in *A Chance to Meet . . . Huw Wheldon* (November 21 1971) he told a woman who asked if his children were allowed to watch anything on television that her question was an invasion of their privacy, adding that, yes, they could watch and read anything in the house. To a professor who said, 'It's not all good, surely?' he replied, 'I would prefer there were more good programmes. We don't make bad programmes on purpose. The programmes that are made are supposed to be good, quite frequently they fail, and I am sorry that they fail. I am sorry that the thing isn't better.' He agreed that a reporter who interviewed a politician 'went over the top' and took 'a slightly hectoring tone' – defending him as a reporter, but regretting the lapse. Answering a question about religion, he didn't fail to bring the answer round to Larkin's 'Church Going'. The presenter, Cliff Michelmore, saw what was coming, and said, 'We must move on,' but the managing director murmured 'I can be quick' and threw them a stanza before the next question.

240

To a woman who mentioned Reith and his vision of broadcasting, Wheldon replied:

> I live at a different time, I live in divided days, where there are many discordant voices in the country, when one of the jobs of the BBC is to allow these voices to speak their part, in order that between us we can grope our way, which is a painful way, to new forms of belief and behaviour, and that, in a way, is a kind of vision of broadcasting. Our job is to make good programmes, which themselves speak for different voices.

He was as concerned with programmes as ever. His style was still demonstrated in endless dialogues. When there was a move in 1970 to drop the expensive Met Office weather forecasts and replace them with cheap news-agency material, Wheldon intervened to keep things as they were. Harman Grisewood, formerly of the BBC, wrote to him privately on New Year's Day 1971 about Ned Sherrin's *Quiz of the Year* programme, and a joke about the Last Supper that he didn't find amusing, Wheldon replied to say that he agreed, and so did a meeting that he called of senior programme people, 'in consequence of which this programme and this cast and this format will not in fact reappear.' When a play about Lloyd George in a series called *The Edwardians* was put out in 1973, and praised by the review board, Wheldon complained that it showed him as deceitful. He had known Lloyd George; he was 'adorable and not dismissible as a trickster.' There were complaints from the family. These were treated more sympathetically than complaints from Labour politicians over *Yesterday's Men*. The following year the series was repeated: all except the Lloyd George play.

Discussing an adaptation of a Sartre novel, Wheldon said the violent language used by soldiers was justified: 'bad language need not be corrupting, neither was the vision of a woman's body.' He found a 'Paul Temple' play 'a touch kinky', and said he was embarrassed to be watching it with his children. When two men kissed in another play, he found it 'shattering', a taboo broken, and hated it. He said that television's four great

241

achievements were Daleks, Quatermass, the Maigret series and Gilbert Harding; perhaps he was serious.

Much of Wheldon's time was taken up with 'co-production', the new business of finding overseas partners to put money into BBC programmes. Co-production became a necessary evil. Kenneth Clark's *Civilisation*, financed by the BBC and first seen in Britain in 1969, caught the eye of American sponsors, and Xerox paid $450,000 for a single film compiled out of the series and shown on NBC (when the book of the series was published in America it was on the *New York Times* best-seller list for months, overtaking *Everything You Always Wanted to Know about Sex*). The success of *Civilisation* helped the BBC effect a co-production deal with the Time-Life organization. Wheldon would explain to anyone who listened that the purity of their editorial control was untouched; no dollars could sully it. 'The BBC's general line is straightforward,' he reminded the governors in his 1971 report. '"We make them, you help pay for them; we share the glory."'

In practice there were problems. What happened when a contract gave 'artistic and editorial control' to the BBC, but obliged it to consult its partner over 'form and content'? When the first episode of *America*, a thirteen-part blockbuster with Alastair Cooke, was shown to Time-Life in 1972, the Americans asked for three amendments. A BBC memo at the time suggested that two of them (which included removing shots of the severed head of a moose after a moose-hunt) came within the terms of the agreement. The third called for a new opening to the film, a two- or three-minute 'shirt-tail' before the first Xerox commercial, as a trailer for the series, which would mean cutting the rest of the film by a similar amount. The memo said that this would mean acting 'even if at one remove [at] the behest of a commercial organization', and would set 'an unfortunate precedent'. Nevertheless it recommended doing what Time-Life wanted, on the grounds that 'if we do not do so, the Americans will certainly do it themselves and make a botched job of it.' No wonder Wheldon told his managing-director meeting (1973) that 'co-productions are a potentially dangerous area'.

Attenborough says that Wheldon grew impatient with American buyers. 'He'd say, "I'm fed up with these buggers coming over, wanting to do Shakespeare on television. It lasts about three weeks, they'll do this and commission that, and *it's all bullshit!*"' The uneasy balancing act went on throughout Wheldon's time. Time-Life kept wanting to tailor programmes for the American market. In 1974 Wheldon told the board that the BBC's refusal of the latest demands meant half a million pounds less in co-production money. 'So be it,' he wrote. 'We cannot possibly make programmes to their tune.'

Wheldon was not an innovator. He was tradition personified, the BBC with knobs on. He was also old enough to be the father of producers and directors now entering the BBC. The authoritarian manner he embodied was not always welcome. Curran told a meeting that the BBC was not a democracy, that although it depended on consent, in the last resort it 'must work by authority' (January 1971). Wheldon concurred. Later that year his weekly meeting discussed 'Unofficial Staff Literature' that was circulating – scurrilous publications with titles like *Shit, Urinal, Burial* and *Gangster Gazette*. These were thought to originate with malcontents at Kensington House, a satellite building where the features group lived. Wheldon said the problem was one of confidence in leaders. 'M.D. Tel added that it was difficult for some members of staff to accept that the BBC was not a democracy, but that it was essential to make a stand on this point.'

The Kensington House brigade was of little consequence, but Wheldon was aware of radical currents that he may not have sympathized with, yet knew he must take note of. In retirement he spoke of newcomers in the sixties and seventies who were 'keen on a certain kind of independence, quite frequently a rather sour independence. And sometimes a very Left-wing and sour independence.' He qualified this by citing Tony Garnett, the producer with whom he had disagreed over the *Five Women* film. Garnett's productions were in the category guaranteed to incense the political Right and worry the BBC, although to its credit it went on supporting them.[1] Garnett's other programmes included *Cathy Come Home* (1966), *The Big Flame* (1969) and the *Days of Hope* cycle beginning in 1974. 'Life becomes complicated,' said Wheldon in the Oral History. 'I rather admired Tony Garnett, you see, and he certainly wasn't set on deceit. He made no pretence of where he was. It was quite clear that if he was making a programme, it did have this kind of slant, and he was absolutely clear about it. And I admired this clarity of stated intention as well as operation, so that I was accustomed to the notion that there were now coming into the television service, people who were more difficult to deal with in terms of ordinary BBC tradition.'

Garnett on Wheldon is also unexpected. 'Now and then he'd give me a call and say, "Lunch", and we'd meet at the Savile. In a sense I was the black that liberals invite to a party, I was conscious of playing that role. Huw wanted to know what was in the air. I had radical ideas about reorganizing the BBC – not that they ever did anything about them.' Garnett talked with him about 'cross-fertilization' between departments. 'Huw and the sixth floor welcomed this until I said, "Why not let me edit *Panorama* for a quarter?" Then they said, "Ah, perhaps it's not such a good idea." '

Garnett didn't join the permanent staff for fear of being 'institutionalized or taken for granted'. He was in and out of the place, on two-year contracts. Wheldon kept in touch. 'Huw and I were chalk and cheese. He was Welsh, I'm from Birmingham. He was cheery and extravert and effusive. Politically we were miles apart. He was in the tradition of Tory patronage, feeling a

---

[1] The BBC estimated in 1975 that during the previous two years it televised about 150 new single plays, of which a dozen could be called 'political', and 'several hundred episodes of series and serials which project a less controversial picture of the world.' The figures come from a paper on 'committed' drama requested by the governors because, in the words of the BBC's chief secretary, Colin Shaw, they feared that 'the BBC might be being taken for a ride, its liberal impulses exploited by those who had only contempt for liberal values.'

deep sense of culture, aware of the needs of the underprivileged. By the time I went to the BBC his conservative instincts were paramount. That's not necessarily bad. He wanted to disseminate things through television. He saw the BBC as a culture with a destiny. He told me over lunch, "These things are not immutable. Unless we're vigilant and lucky, we'll have advertising on BBC 1." He said with passion that the BBC was one of the great achievements of Western civilization. More than anyone I think Huw took over the Reithian moral sense of the BBC's importance and reinterpreted it for permissive times. Or at least that was his view of himself.'

Reflecting on *Five Women*, alias *Some Women*, Garnett says that 'my main fact/fiction argument with Huw was that I thought the most accomplished piece of fiction the BBC put out every night was the News, that Current Affairs dealt in fact, and told lies, whereas I dealt in fiction, and told truth – not *the* truth but *a* truth.' Garnett and Wheldon had their disagreements, but 'I was fond of him, and for one reason. He was vulnerable. There was a lot of suspicion of him, and dislike, because he was such a facile performer, gifted with words. Huw could be hurt, and save us from those who can't be hurt. I think he was hurt every day. The confidence and the necessity to perform disguised a vulnerability.'

If there was a watershed in Wheldon's seven years, a point beyond which the atmosphere changed and the winds blew colder, it came in 1973. Attenborough went; Fox went; financial troubles multiplied. David Attenborough had decided by 1972 that enough was enough. He left at the end of the year to become a programme-maker and a traveller again. Wheldon said his strength was that he was a polymath, his weakness that he liked to be liked. He had no taste for sacking people. Nor did he much enjoy 'the process of meetings and manoeuvre ... The odd thing for so cheerful and sociable a man is that he does not at all mind being by himself.' In this judgement, is there an acknowledgement of Wheldon's own need for a perpetual audience?

Attenborough's replacement was Alasdair Milne, who left in the row of 1965, then returned two years later as controller of BBC Scotland. Wheldon offered him the London job in the garden at Richmond Hill. The new relationship was cordial, but no substitute for the old. Fox, who would have been the alternative to replace Attenborough, didn't want to be director of programmes. A 'mighty figure', in Wheldon's phrase, he was not expected to leave, and Wheldon was upset when he did: another breach of loyalty. He went off to Yorkshire Television to be the programme director there, and later managing director.

Fox came from London's East End and began as a sports journalist. In the Oral History, Wheldon saw him as brought up to respect 'the world of the sporting ring, the world of cigar-smoking tycoons, just as for me, professors and so on seemed in my youth to be Mr Big.' So 'when the chance of becoming a panjandrum at Yorkshire Television with a slice of the equity and God knows what came his way, it was irresistible, and so he went to Yorkshire, and I'm extremely sorry that he did.'

Fox says that when he left, Wheldon snapped, 'You're leaving? Push off!' It was 'all of four weeks before he was ringing me up again.' But Wheldon was angry enough at the time to make a statement for the BBC press office to issue, to the effect that the managing director regretted Mr Fox's departure exceedingly, and Mr Fox would live to regret it. He was persuaded to withdraw this as being unnecessarily heartless. Explaining to the programme review board the following week, Wheldon said stubbornly that it expressed what he felt then, and what he felt now.

Money, the third and largest cause of anxiety, was a creeping problem. Wheldon was cheerful about finance. He made sure he was given good advice. 'I aided and abetted him to get more money,' says Checkland. Some of the anecdotes present Wheldon as the man with programmes in his blood, unable to show any enthusiasm for a balance sheet. No doubt he was better at spending than encouraging. He wore half-moon spectacles at meetings and gave an impersonation of the good housekeeper. Paul Hughes, who preceded Checkland as television accountant, and went on to be the BBC's director of finance, says that 'Huw paid lip service to being cross when people were overspent. Programme costing was a subject on which I invariably failed to totally engage his attention.' Hughes describes a meeting in Wheldon's office where he had some vital matter to discuss, and 'Huw, who was sitting sprawled in an armchair, suddenly said, "You know, you should grow your hair a bit, have sideburns, get rid of that stuffy accountant's image."' That was Wheldon the card, seen through auditor's eyes.

But Wheldon had to present the annual budget to the governors, and Wheldon saw inflation at work, threatening the service. A shiver ran through the place early in 1973 when 'The Plan', the pattern of six thousand productions for the coming year, assembled after rounds of 'offers meetings' the previous autumn, was found to be overspent. 'Steam has been hissing out of the joints,' Wheldon told the governors, 'and what happened this year was that the lid finally blew off.' The matter was kept quiet. Wheldon said that the gathering crisis had been obscured by earnings from co-productions and improved efficiency. Now they were having to repeat more programmes than they wanted to, and abandon projects, especially in children's programmes and drama. As Wheldon pointed out, in the old days things were more casual, and hiccups in the Plan could be accommodated. 'Actual inefficiency, be it only the inefficiency of simple humanity without computers, did provide a margin.'

A year later Wheldon was giving the governors chapter and verse about how he had had to 'water the wine'. At the end of the 1960s, both channels were repeating a total of five hours a week between 7.30 and 10.30 in the evening. By 1974 it was more than nine hours. 'Adding insult to injury,' said Wheldon, 'some were second repeats.' This was because daytime television, not permitted before 1972, had to be filled with something. ITV could afford to repeat old plays in the afternoon. The BBC

247

couldn't, so it was driven to use cheaper programmes, some of which had already been repeated in the evenings, like *Horizon* and *The World About Us.* 'The arithmetic,' said Wheldon, filling pages with figures, 'is brutal.' Appendices, methodical in the BBC way, told the governors all about it, down to the cost of a false moustache for an actor, £2.50 in 1970, £4.60 in 1974.

The mainstream of programming continued; few of those who watched the programmes may have been aware of crisis; but from now on, straitened circumstances began to humble the BBC, making it dependent on regular increases in the licence fee, and thus the goodwill of governments. By the end of 1974, Wheldon's weekly meeting was discussing the need for 'visible sacrifices', presumably to impress politicians and journalists. Wheldon said he had already given the lead. His lunches now had two courses instead of three, with sherry and wine to start, and wine or beer with the meal, but no spirits. He rather spoiled the effect of this heroic gesture by adding that there would be occasions when 'more generous entertainment, including spirits' was called for. Still, it was no laughing matter. 'Modified plans' for Christmas programmes saved more than £150,000, by taking some new productions out of the schedules, and replacing them with ancient films and more repeats.

Economies stretched away into the future. After so many years of expansion, they were hard to come to terms with. Wimbledon coverage that summer, 1975, had no slow-motion replays in the first week. The programme review board was told that £30,000 had had to be taken out of the Wimbledon budget. Fewer replays saved some of it.

The same meeting heard about the battle the Outside Broadcast unit had been fighting at Wimbledon over advertising. They insisted that bottles of Robinson's Barley Water be turned around, so the label couldn't be seen. Coca-Cola had supplied an ice-box. When it first appeared, six cans of Coca-Cola were standing on it, part of the arrangement for which the company paid a fee to be the 'official carbonated drinks supplier'. The BBC men said six cans were far too many. So what about a doubles match? There was more argument. In the end they agreed on three cans of Coke for singles, four for doubles. To the BBC it was serious stuff – the need to appear unsullied by that other world of commercialism and carbonated drinks suppliers that Wheldon and his colleagues, in good times or in bad, would have died rather than embrace.

One of Wheldon's persistent themes, as he talked his way towards the end of his career, was The Story itself, 'an invention of huge significance . . . it is through stories that we learn how to live with ourselves . . . television is overwhelmingly a story-telling medium.' The BBC was presented as a haven for talent, and especially the talent of writers, whether they told their stories in the form of drama or situation comedy or even documentary. He enthused about the mystery of stories (*Dr Who* was about 'something archetypal . . . the path into the unknown forest', *Dr Findlay's Casebook* perhaps about 'the relationship between father and son'). He talked about *Elgar*, and how the real story of Elgar's life was in the music.

He had a bottomless bag of stories about programmes. How *The Forsyte Saga* was so popular when shown in Yugoslavia that it became a national obsession, and led to the Yugoslav army being made available ('quite cheap, of course') when the BBC came to film *War and Peace*. How a drama series about *The Six Wives of Henry VIII* was thought to be worth doing because a BBC director remembered seeing the silver codpiece that had come loose from Henry's armour at the Tower of London, 'and the reason it became loose is because generations of Cockney women have given it a bit of a rub on their way past, as a kind of fertility symbol.'

There was a story about how his mother was under the impression that her favourite programme was *Panorama*, although really it was the *Harry Worth Show*. 'She will, in the last resort, miss *Panorama*,' he said, 'but she will never miss Harry Worth, and why should she not like Harry Worth best? There is no reason in the world, but she does not like saying so. As a matter of fact the great British public do not like saying so, and they include me. I was proud of *Monitor*, I was pleased to have made it. And yet pressed to it, if I had to choose between being remembered for having invented and made *Monitor* or having invented and made *Hancock's Half Hour*, I would certainly be very hard put. It would be a very nice decision. I think actually, in the end' – smiling at the dilemma – 'I'm not sure.'

Wheldon had no trouble finding platforms. Banquets, dinners, ceremonies of all sorts appealed to him. He was a governor of this and a fellow of that. Invitations flowed in. His son Wynn says that when refusing them, he sometimes said, 'I'm terribly sorry, I'm visiting a submarine.' Wynn adds, 'He had a simple set of criteria for accepting invitations: cash, glory or piety. One of these three had to be fulfilled. The American Bar Association – cash. The Dimbleby Lecture – glory. The American School in Richmond – piety.'

There is an instructive letter to an officer of the London Welsh Golfing Society, who had written to ask for £3. 10s. for a dinner Wheldon had eaten. 'The invitation to the Dinner in fact came from you,' replied Wheldon, 'and it so happened that I had to cancel or decline two further invitations, both of which I would have liked to have accepted.' He had felt bound by his promise: why then should he have to pay for his dinner as well?

The more dressing-up there was, the better. At a University of London degree-giving ceremony he wore a gaudy cloak and musical-comedy hat, and was heard to claim that by rights they should be seen only on a doctor of music at the University of Lausanne. His wife says he attended a niece's wedding wearing a rust-coloured morning suit and top hat, nineteenth-century vintage, borrowed from the BBC costume department; he made a point of telling everyone where they came from.

One of the invitations he accepted for piety was to preach a university sermon at St Giles's Cathedral, Edinburgh. This was the other Wheldon in action, who might have followed his grandfather, and thundered weekly in a pulpit; except that thundering was a dying art by Huw Wheldon's time. His theme was the spiritual illiteracy of the age, his text the evergreen 'Church Going', in which a modern man, religionless, cycling through a suburb, stops to look in a church, and finds that the 'frowsty barn' is somehow 'a serious house on serious earth'. He – and Wheldon, identifying himself with the poet – catches an echo of mortality and the last things from

> this ground
> Which, he once heard, was proper to grow wise in,
> If only that so many dead lie round.

In the poem Wheldon detected 'the authentic tone of the Old Testament: God is not mocked.' His sermon made two 'adjurations' to the congregation. One, that the modern consciousness is revealed 'not so much in the works of sociology and actual books about modern consciousness, as in the poems and plays and the novels and the serials written out of that consciousness.' Two, that this reading of modern man 'needs to be done in the context of greater stories and greater texts'; above all, the Bible, 'the original script'.

Wheldon preached at Edinburgh in April 1973, shortly before his fifty-seventh birthday. His hair had greyed but he was as lively as ever. The previous autumn he had been taken ill while travelling to the Labour Party conference. He wrote to an ex-army friend, Colonel Joe Harper:

> The whole thing was preposterous and sensational. I got on to a train in Euston hale and hearty and got off at Blackpool with a temperature of 150°. I laid about in my hotel like a Rear Admiral. I ordered doctors; demanded aspirins; made (in my delirium) adjurations about the nature of life, and so on. I was terrific. I was eventually got back to London and eventually recovered. I have rarely enjoyed something so much in my whole life. People tip-toed around my bed. It was bliss. When I recovered I was so shocked not having been able to breathe properly for ten minutes that despite myself, I gave up smoking.

251

My body insisted. It had nothing to do with my mind, still less with my will which, as you know, is a Broken Reed. I can only conclude that something of this kind happens to most people. In my case I am certainly fitter than I was before being ill . . .

He took to healthy jogs in Richmond Park before breakfast, returning to a half-awake Jay with a detailed account of squirrels, rabbits and other fauna he had observed, together with notes on his favourite trees. Then his driver would be there.

Wheldon's seven years were like an evangelical mission to convert the heathen. No one must be allowed to doubt the virtues of public-service broadcasting or underestimate the hardships. 'There have been many good people,' he said, musing on figures like McGivern and Goldie, 'but I am doubtful about golden ages. There are always difficulties. There always were.' He believed that the easy life was contemptible, or thought it prudent to act as if it was. Keep busy, was the motto. 'Institutions have to be defended in order to persist. I believe there is nothing wrong with being an organization man. If you walk along the pavement and there are no cracks in it, it's because somebody has taken pavements sufficiently seriously to care about the damned things.'

There were trips to Antipodes and Americas, putting on a show for strangers. He liked to imply how different it all was at the BBC. The agony of the licence fee was not mentioned. Interviewed (in a London pub) for public television in New York, he was asked if the BBC gave people what was good for them. He registered shock and surprise. 'Oh, no, no, my dear chap, oh, no. I mean, you must – oh, no! There is a question, the answer to which, in broadcasting in this country, is taboo, and it's not less than taboo. It's much more taboo than incest. And the question is this. Do you give them what they want or do you give them what they ought to have? That's a taboo question because there is no answer to it.' Shakespeare, said Wheldon, wouldn't have acknowledged such a question. When he started on *Twelfth Night*, all he cared about was writing as good a play as possible, to make a living and enable him to write the next one.

This shaky parallel between a writer and a broadcasting organization was often heard. Wheldon sometimes talked too much, and repeated himself, and dressed up platitudes as insights. Donald Baverstock, whose mistake was not to play the organization's game of nods and winks, sees Wheldon as 'a frontispiece, a kind of public orator', making speeches in a special language of his own, 'full of flannel'. His manner was personal and compelling. Where his detractors say he overdid things, his admirers drew warmth or courage or were simply entertained. Aubrey Singer found him 'the greatest of men, I suppose in the way that Lloyd George was.' Colin Shaw contrasts him with Grace Wyndham Goldie: 'Some of the people Grace cast her wand over ended up sadly. With Huw, they didn't. Grace took things out of people. Huw put them in.'

His way of dealing with people and affairs involved the whole business of being Wheldon. He always committed himself. No doubt he needed the experience to make him feel secure in the affections of those he stoked up with his comedy and pathos. Michael Charlton, eleven years his junior, found him intuitive, an 'animalistic observer' of those around him. He would know if someone liked him or not, 'in the way that an animal's fur might bristle'. Sometimes he knew before they met.

The BBC demanded more of his time than ever. Strikes were more frequent. Inflation grew worse. But he kept to large themes. It was impossible for broadcasters to be loved by everyone in divisive times like the present, he would say, quoting a phrase of Oliver Whitley's, 'The nation divided puts the BBC on the rack.' Another borrowed phrase was 'slums of the mind', which he got from Goldie, a warning that mediocre television creates mental slums that future generations will abhor, just as today we abhor the physical slums that the Victorians, for all their ideals, were so ready to tolerate. Why, cried Wheldon, should we accept 'cardboard as against art', even if the alternative was 'third-rate art as against first-rate cardboard'?

Wheldon's rhetoric carried him into extreme positions like that, which he could never have justified, programme by programme. BBC schedules had their fair share of cardboard. But the reality was in the act of aspiring. He was a propagandist for the good, even if it was the unreal good of perfectibility. It was a flag to wave for the troops; like his remark during a 1969 union dispute, when expensive 'over-runs' of studio timetables were under attack, and Wheldon refused to ban them, arguing with bombastic sincerity that 'the BBC must continue to allow itself to search for perfection in programmes as part of its concept of public-service broadcasting.' Antony Jay sees him as 'the principal instrument through which the BBC preserved its belief in itself. He provided the language in which the BBC made its case.' It is a large claim; Wheldon was a large man. Without his endless reiteration of the virtues of the place, morale might well have crumbled earlier than it has done. The absence of anyone of his stature to speak for, and to, the organization was evident when the enemy finally reached the gates late in the 1980s.

One side of Wheldon knew quite well that perfection was a chimera. Lady Wheldon says that 'he used to say to me all the time, "The perfect is the enemy of the good." It wasn't until after he died that I thought, "Well, if that applied to anyone, it was he who needed reminding." Because he never stinted on trying to make things better, on the one hand, and on the other hand believing that he would never be able to do so.'

In December 1974, Curran confirmed to Wheldon that his term of office would end the following December, five months before he was sixty. Ian Trethowan, a former political commentator, who had been managing director of BBC radio since 1969, was being prepared for promotion. He was to be Wheldon's successor, and the governors wanted him to take over at the start of 1976; by 1977 he would be director-general. To sweeten Wheldon's early departure – he would have stayed at least until his birthday if he had had any choice – the governors agreed that for a year after he left television, Wheldon would be retained on full salary (by then about £20,000) as an adviser to Curran, with the courtesy title of deputy director-general.

He had other prospects. A royal series to end all series had been conceived, with Wheldon as presenter (his motives presumably glory and cash, or cash and glory). The London School of Economics, having appointed a chairman of its court of governors who dropped dead after six weeks, turned to Wheldon, who accepted (no cash, some glory, perhaps a measure of piety), and was installed in June 1975.

One of the last major events of Wheldon's tenure at the Television Centre was the 'inquiry into broadcasting' under Lord Annan that the newly elected Labour Government revived in 1974. By the time Annan reported, in 1977, Wheldon was off the premises. But in 1975 he was busy with discussion groups, exhorting staff yet again to marathons of talk about the future. He helped draft the BBC's written submission, and gave oral evidence when, in September, the committee spent two days with the television service. Those who were there say he didn't shine. For the Annan Committee, an air of complacency hung over the BBC. If Wheldon sensed hostility, he would have bristled. In later years he referred to the committee as 'lightweight' and said he 'didn't quite trust it'. Even the hospitality went astray. A meal laid on by Wheldon for the committee was thought to be over-lavish, given the state of BBC finances. Colin Shaw says there were 'things in aspic that people referred to afterwards'.

But Annan remained unfinished business for Wheldon. A week before Christmas 1975, at his last programme review board, he recalled his first, at Alexandra Palace, when he was television publicity officer. He ended a brief speech with one of his lists of praiseworthy programmes to come, in the light of which 'it was hysteria to think of the BBC being in real trouble'. His last comment on a programme under review concerned *Love's Labour's Lost* which he commended, except that it had gone out too late in the evening. 'There is something scandalous,' he concluded, 'about an important play by Shakespeare ending after midnight.'

His new headquarters, where he was to produce a report on the BBC regions – a subject that interested him not at all – would be Broadcasting House, in central London. The television service gave him a dinner and he cleared his desk. Colin Shaw remembered him there, one Saturday morning when a strike was in progress, and they were both on duty. 'You and I are the palace guard,' said Wheldon, striking an attitude. 'However corrupt the emperor is, we shall stay.' He was always a figure in one of his own stories.

CHAPTER TWELVE

Sir Huw

When Huw Wheldon was still managing director, Freda Lingstrom, who had launched him on his career with the conker programme, wrote to ask if she could be put on producers' lists of people to employ. She was nearly eighty then, and bored with a decade and a half of retirement. 'Are there any [lists]?' replied Wheldon, holding out little hope. He went on:

> The BBC is a very ruthless place it seems to me when it comes to those who have left its service. I shall have to leave myself in two or three years' time and do not look forward to that particular side of things. Perhaps 'ruthless' is the wrong word. It is more as if what matters is today and tomorrow; and everybody is so busy looking after those two categories of time that there is nothing left over for yesterday.

The prospect of being poor when he retired had haunted Wheldon for years; his children were still being educated. As it turned out, the old firm did him well. He had his salaried year to report on the regions, in effect a sinecure, and a large contract for the royal series. This began as seven programmes, for each of which he would receive £1,800, but became ten. With subsidiary fees, repeats and sales overseas, the income for each programme was doubled or trebled.

In the early months of 1976, his engagement diaries show it was the royal films he was busy with, not the future of the regions. The BBC had a long history of wanting to make programmes about the royal family but being unable to find an acceptable formula. In about 1950, when Prince Charles was a year or two old, a BBC cameraman followed a car containing the infant to some open space – Richmond Park, perhaps, or at Windsor – and there filmed the heir playing on the grass with his nanny. The film was edited for use in *Newsreel*, but no one dared authorize transmission without first asking Buckingham Palace. The palace refused permission and ordered that the negatives be burnt. The nitrate film had to be taken there by the miscreants and ignited in the grounds. One of those watching the blaze was Richard Cawston, the editor who had cut the film.

Nearly twenty years later, when he was head of documentaries, Cawston made *Royal Family* for a BBC–ITV consortium, letting them be seen and heard in comparative informality for the first time. Almost half the population watched it. Delicate problems arose over the use of microphones, which might have picked up royal indiscretions. The Duke of Edinburgh was promised that the sound tapes would be kept by the producer, and Duke and Queen could decide what was heard. All the film shot was held in a vault and labelled 'Religious Programmes'. *Royal Family* was first shown in June 1969. A condition of its being made was that the Queen kept the copyright.

The latest venture, ultimately called *Royal Heritage*, began with a suggestion from the unit in Bristol that made the *Antiques Roadshow* programmes. Arthur Negus would admire royal furniture and talk about it. When the idea was put to the palace, the Duke of Edinburgh suggested something grander, a series about the royal collections. Although the BBC elaborated his original idea, he was the real initiator. It took two years for the project to be approved on all sides. The office of the Lord Chamberlain, Lord Maclean, granted the BBC a licence to make the films, for a large fee and on terms that gave the Queen sixty per cent of all 'royalties and profits' from the series. But the exact nature of the programmes had not been decided. The palace team – Duke, Lord Chamberlain and the royal keepers and custodians – thought it was going to be about things: castles, paintings, jewels. The BBC had other ideas.

Cawston was in overall charge, but the series producer was Michael Gill, who had made *Civilisation* and *America*. At first Gill was lukewarm about the idea, fearing it might become 'a monstrous plug for royalty'. He changed his mind, he told Cawston,

> after attending one of Huw's Annan Committee evenings. In a divisive time it would seem a Good Thing for the BBC, among other duties, to reinforce those elements that unite the country: I don't mean by pap or by looking back with nostalgia.

Gill argued for a series that used the concept of kingship as a way of looking at British history, while making the most of the visual material – the castles, paintings, jewels and the rest. It was his ideas that the BBC adopted, on the principle that the individual producer must have the power. 'But if I had offended the royals,' he says, 'I would have been out of the programmes very quickly.'

It was late in 1974 when the two-year negotiations with the palace ended, and Gill and his associate producer, Ann Turner, began work. The choice of 'anchorman' was crucial. Among his attributes must be an 'ironic eye for human foibles, yet able to write up to the level of great events'. Gill had two candidates, Robert Kee for a 'cool' image, Wheldon for a 'hot'. Wheldon was chosen; he still had a year to go as managing director, and he was already filming before he left. Sir John Plumb, the Cambridge historian, was hired as adviser, and wrote the original text from which the scripts derived.

The palace heard about Wheldon at the first meeting of the Duke of Edinburgh's committee, which had been set up to agree the programmes in detail. This was held in the Lord Chamberlain's office just before Christmas 1974, with half a dozen palace representatives and three from the BBC: Alasdair Milne, as director of programmes, Cawston and Gill. The Duke was in the chair. Gill's approach was not much liked. The palace wanted royal history to be incidental to royal collections, not the other way round. This led to disputes over the next couple of years as royal keepers and custodians tried to concentrate the film-makers' attention on their choice of the beautiful, and the film-makers, while only too happy to fill the screen with ornate images, looked for the human element as well. The news that Wheldon would present the series was warmly received. By the following spring a doubt had crossed the palace's mind. At a meeting at Windsor Castle in April, the Duke of Edinburgh made it clear that they didn't want Mr Wheldon giving his views, or Professor Plumb's for that matter, and trying to sound like Kenneth Clark in *Civilisation*.

Some animosity developed later towards Wheldon, the non-expert brought in to popularize. The scripts that he and Gill eventually prepared on the basis of Plumb's treatments were not over-awed by their subject. When he was told that a funny story in his script of Programme 7, *Victoria and Albert*, couldn't be used because no historical evidence for it existed, he inserted the words, 'I know that historians would not agree with me.'

By January 1976, Wheldon was free of deskwork at the BBC, apart from the tiresome regional business. He was also 'Sir Huw', having been knighted in the New Year Honours, an occasion for letters and memories. A woman wrote from North Wales to say that the last time she saw him, 'except on the Box', was at his christening, the wettest day she had ever known. 'Thank you very much for one of the nicest letters I have had during this last week,' replied Wheldon. 'I am sorry it rained.' His congratulators were a cross-section of his life: television and Wales, the army and public life. John Schlesinger wrote from California; Sydney Newman from Canada; Donald Baverstock from Manchester; General Horrocks from Somerset; the Leepers from Surrey; heads of departments from Whitehall; an ex prime minister or two; the Duke of Edinburgh; Lord Snowdon, who made a film for *Monitor* once; captains of industry; some diplomats; masters of colleges; sundry MPs; golfers. Someone suggested that he was one of the few knights who would look right in armour, with a sword.

'TV will miss you,' wrote Nancy Thomas, his *Monitor* colleague, 'I shall miss you and the strengths your belief in public service and the BBC brought to us working in programmes. I rather fear it is a dying creed and more's the pity.' A letter came from Gerald Beadle, the one-time director of television who wasn't keen on watching programmes. He said he had watched more of them since he retired.

Many of Wheldon's replies stressed how busy he was, having to turn things down, now he had left television. Idleness had to be held at bay. 'Jay is busy writing books,' he told a friend, 'and has a collection of eight separate books, all of which are to be published at the same time because they in fact constitute one simply gigantic novel.'

Those who wrote to say 'Whel don!' were told that their pun had only been made a thousand times before. He made no secret of how much he was going to enjoy being a knight. 'I always have liked people who are not afraid of using words like "joy",' he told one correspondent.

A woman who had been a junior BBC secretary when Wheldon was publicity officer confessed it was she who had put a single red rose on his desk; she signed her name but gave no address. Celia sent a note, headed only 'Switzerland'. It had a whiff of Thunderbolt: 'I remember that you said you would never be the man your father was: perhaps you are not but you seem to have made the grade in this imperfect present-day world and I am sure he would have been thrilled. I am not much of a believer in knighthoods myself but I cannot help feeling immensely pleased that you have one!'

For the first six months of 1976 he was involved in planning and writing scripts, and filming more of his narratives to camera on royal premises. He saw little or nothing of the palace people or the royal family – deliberately so, according to Gill, who thought integrity better preserved if there was no contact between scriptwriter and royals: 'the words he had to speak might not be the words they would have chosen'.

Some of the royal family were drawn in as participants. Filming planned or in progress included the Duke sailing a yacht and driving a four in hand, the Queen describing the state crown, the Queen Mother giving a conducted tour of the gardens at her private castle, Prince Charles rowing in a loch and talking about Balmoral and Princess Anne riding a horse. Princess Margaret declined to be filmed coming and going from her apartment at Kensington Palace. Meanwhile disagreements went on about the scripts. Why, demanded the advisers, were there so many references to Charles II's mistresses? Why was time that could be better used perusing great works being wasted on close-ups of the royal family in their box at Ascot? Why was there so much about Victoria's reign, a time when the royal taste in art was unfortunate?

Gill and the BBC rode out the little storms and remained on good terms without seriously damaging their intention, to make films that went beyond the palace's concept of *Royal Builders and Collectors*, the Duke of Edinburgh's choice of title. There was much discussion at the BBC about what to call it. The Duke was anxious not to give anti-royalists a chance to jeer. Gill favoured *Inheritance*, but there were fears that the palace wouldn't have it. In the end he took a departmental vote on all the proposals, which included *Golden Sovereigns* and *This Sceptred Isle*. *Royal Heritage* got thirty-four votes, *Inheritance*, the runner-up, thirteen. With *The Story of Britain's Royal Builders and Collectors* as a sub-title, which no one would notice anyway, the palace approved.

Wheldon's mother had been ill for some time. One of the letters about his knighthood was from a Welshwoman who asked after her. He replied that she was in a nursing home at Carmarthen, near Mair and Richard Rees, her elder daughter and son-in-law. She could no longer recognize anyone, he wrote, and 'there are not the laughs that were'. She died in July 1975.

A month later there was less expected news. Wheldon, briefly unwell, saw a consultant in August. Bowel cancer was diagnosed. He was admitted to the private King Edward VII Hospital for

Officers almost at once and a colostomy performed. The night before the operation, Jay wrote him a courageous love letter, with characteristic touches: 'Darling Huw – what did I ever do to deserve to marry the *one* man I truly fell in love with? (And if you *dare* even to suggest that the answer is "Wait about outside his club to waylay him" I shall know you are feeling good again & rejoice, rejoice!) . . .'

After several weeks in hospital, and a stay at its convalescent home – Osborne, appropriately enough, Queen Victoria's residence on the Isle of Wight – Wheldon made a full recovery. For a while *Royal Heritage* had been in jeopardy. No one knew when, or whether, he would be able to go on filming. The production was half completed. In four of the episodes, Wheldon had done all the 'sync' filming, those parts of the commentary where his lips could be seen moving. It would have been impossible to write him out of the programme. But he was in action again by early the next year, performing as if nothing had happened.

He wrote to George Campey, who had also retired from the BBC, in January 1977:

The illness was very nasty, & least said soonest mended is the only line. All is now set for a return to normal, d.v. as they used to say and they were right! D.V. it is indeed. Whether or not being driven into the ground by a programme series now very seriously behind schedule is a help or not is difficult to say. It is, I need hardly mention, A Dog's Dinner (not a bad title) almost by definition – an uneasy meal between Royalty, Art, History, Guided Tours, & a Poshed Up Open University Introductory series. My absence has put things back, coupled with the fact that in pure desperation they shot off film here there & everywhere so that we now have 9 programmes at 60 minutes each to finish by April 26 instead of 6, no 7. I hop skip & jump from a Palace to a Cutting Room & from another Cutting Room to another Palace avoiding at all costs Royalty and (if possible) film editors. I start a consultancy with NBC in April (d.v., as they

263

say, and they are right . . .). God knows what I shall suggest to them. Any ideas? I am desperate for them. How to support or help or stimulate a great American network is the challenge – yours, I mean. Please give it thought.

Wheldon, of course, was writing casually to a friend, not delivering a statement about the making of a television programme. He wrote similarly to Celia, who had asked him to sign a copy of the book that accompanied the series. As he explained, it was not really his book but Plumb's. Wheldon's name was there to link it with the series and sell more copies, although that didn't prevent a long wrangle between the two, via their solicitors, about how the royalties were to be split. Sixty per cent was demanded by Wheldon, twenty-five per cent was offered by Plumb. Eventually they agreed on sixty/forty, in Plumb's favour.

The letter to Celia, who was still living abroad, was dated July 23 1977, and was the last Wheldon wrote to her:

Dear Celia,

I did not know what to write in that book. It was either Love, Huw or With Compliments, Huw Wheldon. I settled for Love, Huw Wheldon, thereby getting, I suppose, the worst of all possible worlds,

The book is Plumb's really, not mine. My name is there to help sell it. The pattern was that Plumb, I, & the Producing people went round & round the subject, & settled on a shape. Plumb then wrote an Essay, on that basic structure. I digested the essay, added or modified it according to my own thoughts, & made it into a Camera script. This went back to Plumb. He said this was inaccurate or that over-emphasized. I amended accordingly. Everything was then changed by filming conditions, & then by work in the cutting room. The essay, in Plumb's hands, affected by my modifications, became The Book, & the essay, in my hands, became The Series. The Series is, and feels, much more like me. The Book seems, & and feels, much more like Plumb. The two are parallel, mutually influenced & complementary, & neither could have existed without the other. I hope you do see the series somewhere. It was very difficult, and I feared it would be a Dog's Dinner. There was so much – too much – to draw upon, what with places & kings & lives & art & history & everything else. I think it matriculated, in the event, into a Dog's Breakfast, more or less, & I was content.

Love, Huw

Neither Plumb nor Gill is very happy with this light-hearted account. Plumb says Wheldon had nothing at all to do with the book. He points out that his film treatments (what Wheldon calls 'essays') were in fact reshaped during long sessions with Wheldon, Ann Turner, Michael Gill and himself, where Gill contributed at least as much as Wheldon. What Plumb admired most was Wheldon's work in front of the cameras, especially after his illness.

Gill says that the film was structured by its directors, and Wheldon steered through the writing of a complicated script. 'To strike the proper tone and to put vitality without gush or Mandarin sensibility into descriptions of eighteenth-century furniture and Sèvres china was not an easy task,' says Gill, who thinks it was 'probably the most difficult writing that Huw had ever engaged in. He brought it off triumphantly – I can't think of anyone else who could have done it so well. However, that doesn't gainsay the fact that he has grossly exaggerated his role in the team in the letter you quote' – the one he sent Celia.

According to Gill there were subtleties in Plumb's treatments that eluded Wheldon. What Wheldon wanted, for example, was more the familiar caricature of George IV, a fat man picking his teeth. What Plumb offered was a psychological study of a complex character who had more taste than most British monarchs. Since George IV was the subject of the pilot film – the first to be made, though it was not used till late in the series – differences of approach between Plumb and Wheldon emerged early. They met over lunch to discuss Wheldon's 'rhinoceros-like' approach to the 'feline delicacy' of Plumb's George IV essay – the descriptions are Gill's. He says he was afraid that

Plumb might leave the lunch. No doubt the programmes were a 'team effort', and one has to leave it at that. Wheldon had the knack of attracting attention to his part in anything, irritating to those who are overlooked.

Royal Heritage began as planned in April with episode one, *The Medieval Kings*. The series was much praised and did good business around the world. Wheldon's performances were the best he ever gave for television, lucid and flexible, changing the mood to suit the occasion. An article in the *New York Times* (January 1978) said that:

> The eccentric who fronts the programmes takes the amiable form of Sir Huw Wheldon (who used to run the BBC) in loose clubland suits. Every few minutes after the camera has finished doting on a masterpiece by Rubens or a Fabergé egg, he looms into view with an excursion among the ironies of British history or a potted biography of a painter [. . .] or an affectionate dig at a king's foibles [. . .] A wily humorist, Sir Huw avoids pomp in every circumstance. He never reduces royal persons; rather does he magnify them to size.

Wheldon kept busy. The work for NBC, the American television network, which he mentioned to Campey, was one of various commissions. He became a well-paid television consultant, and travelled widely, making new friends and seeing more of old ones, like the Podhoretzes in New York. He wrote and presented occasional public-relations films for companies. He did after-dinner speaking for a fee. The 'public-service' side of his life was catered for by his being, among other things, a trustee of the National Portrait Gallery, a council member of the Royal College of Art, a vice-president (eventually president) of the Royal Television Society, a governor of the National Film School and a member of the Honourable Society of Cymmrodorion. Institutions continued to offer him honours, which he accepted with alacrity, whenever possible dressing up for the occasion. He collected D.Litt.s from the Universities of Wales and Ulster, an LL D from Oxford, a doctorate from the Open University. On the latter occasion he recalled an earlier Open University event at Alexandra Palace, which he attended as a BBC executive:

I did not much want to go. I had much disliked prize giving ceremonies at school. I never won anything, and I grew weary of watching my precocious or even my superior friends getting awards. I particularly disliked seeing them being photographed afterwards, smirking by their proud parents.

But duty called. I went. I was impressed and moved. After the ceremony we had tea on the Alexandra Palace terraces overlooking London. The sun was shining. And I saw – this completed my conversion – I saw children taking photographs of their parents.

The Royal Television Society, a body he respected, awarded him its silver medal for his work on *Royal Heritage* in 1978. He liked honours. Yet part of him despised them, or himself for liking them. Writing to H., with whom he still kept up a spasmodic correspondence, he said:

[the family] are not impressed with these Honours; which is indeed just as well. My own danger is falling for my own vainglory. Mercifully (from that point of view) we have such trouble on other fronts, including Jay's mother [who was ill] & various other things, that PERSPECTIVE of some kind seems forced upon me. Trumpery remains trumpery. The Royal Television Society is certainly trumpery. However, I am not complaining. Difficulties (as mentioned above) apart I have had a marvellous year. You do things, apart from necessity & pure Pleasure, for Cash, Piety or Glory. I have been able to combine all three which is unusual, & undeserved. 1978/9 however brings, unhappily, a very mediocre programme about The Library of Congress which the Critics will fall upon with glee; brings some difficulties with an American outfit I get paid by; & will bring in, & I cannot conceive on what scale, demands from The Revenue. I look back with longing to Pay as You Earn, & look forward with horror, to 1979. Smellie [Professor Smellie, Professor Emeritus of Political Science at the London School of Economics], making a most touching & amusing response to the Toast of the Honorary Fellows (very nice occasion) claimed he could say with Conrad, 'I have lived, obscure, among the terrors and wonders of my

267

time'. Marvellous line. Could Joseph Conrad have said it? Was he so obscure? Was, is Smellie? If so, their obscurity is preferable to most glory, & certainly to mine. I think, incidentally, that TV professionals see themselves, always, as makers (good, bad or indifferent) of programmes & no more as Sorcerers or Priests or New Scientists than you do. They (& I suppose you) may be wrong. I doubt it.

To the London School of Economics, where he was chairman of the governors till a few months before his death, Wheldon brought the zeal of a late vocation in life. It was a piece of 'service' he could get his teeth into. When the call came in 1975, the LSE was unsettled, having lost a strong chairman, the ageing Lord Robbins, by retirement, and the replacement who died soon after he was installed. A strong director, Ralf Dahrendorf, a German academic and writer, had just been appointed to succeed a weak one.

Wheldon's name was proposed by a Welshman on the appointments committee. Some of the academic staff were distressed at the idea of having a broadcaster. Nor was Wheldon seen as having the fund-raising potential of a Robbins, who brought in millions. Politics played little part in Wheldon's election. He was not viewed as a radical, which was just as well. Despite the Left-wing reputation of its students, the LSE is a conservative institution, anxious for a quiet life. According to Dahrendorf, there was a touch of compromise about choosing him. Wheldon hesitated before accepting. He told H. (July 1975) that he had been 'truly apprehensive. It was really that I "did not like to say No", like Meg eating gooseberry tart at her Aunt's house, although it is well known she dislikes it. I did not like to say No. It seemed churlish, and worse; so I said yes, and am now correspondingly nervous. The White City [Television Centre] Hot Seat only looks hot from the outside. To me, it seems warm and comfortable. LSE seems chilling and frightening.' The LSE, as he saw it in his youth, had been the first of Wheldon's ideal institutions, a place with some inner coherence that enabled him to make sense of the world and himself from within its framework. The army, perhaps, was the second, the BBC undeniably the most significant. Now he came back to the school, on his own terms but no doubt hearing echoes of himself and his uncertainties when young.

From the start he got on well with Dahrendorf, who found him supportive but not interfering. One of the chairman's duties is to take the standing committee of the court of governors at its monthly meeting. At this he was not a great success, according to Dahrendorf, who thinks he was not at ease, and uses the word 'shambolic' – too strong for others who saw Wheldon in action. John Pike, financial secretary, says Wheldon was sometimes out of his depth. None of this seems to connect with the BBC's Wheldon. Perhaps the detail bored him; perhaps old misgivings came to light in the presence of academics who knew more than he did. Dahrendorf found him 'a little in awe' of the place, inclined to be nervous. He also talked too much at full meetings of the court of governors.

Where he was at his best and most characteristic was on public occasions, perhaps a dozen times a year. Then, says Dahrendorf, the charm and wit flowed, and he was able to perform his trick of making people feel better, about themselves and about others. In a crisis, too, such as a student sit-in,[1] he was reliable; 'totally on top of it,' says Dahrendorf. But there are several versions of a story about a woman student on the standing committee who made some remark that Wheldon deplored, to which he responded with, 'My dear, you're a very pretty girl. How can you say such things?' The student was too astonished to reply. Wheldon's candour could be unsettling. As a

---

[1] A letter from Wheldon to a BBC producer in Cardiff, about a programme they had been making, was written while his office at LSE was occupied by students. The Social Democrats had won the students' union election, but the Trotskyists were challenging it 'on the grounds that being a Secret Ballot it was undemocratic! A democratic ballot, according to them, is one in which you stoutly stand up to be counted ("not to say shot," I hear you murmur). Orwell, thou shouldst be living at this hour!'

fund-raiser he was an enthusiastic supporter of Dahrendorf's schemes. In New York once, they visited the chairman of a large company. After a minute or two of pleasantries, Wheldon said, 'Let's be frank about this. What we've come here for is MONEY!' But did it work? 'Yes,' says Dahrendorf.

After his operation in 1976, Wheldon insisted on talking to Dahrendorf about the prospects that they might lose another chairman by the end of the year. He said the doctors had told him he might have six months, or then again it might be ten years. 'He wasn't terribly afraid,' says Dahrendorf. 'He faced things. We sat there and made alternative plans.' An odder side of Wheldon's candour presented itself when he learned that Dahrendorf's partner was not his wife, and declined to invite the two of them socially until, in due course, they were married. Such prudery doesn't sound like Wheldon at sixty something. Perhaps it was the LSE again, raising ghosts of himself at twenty something.

Publishers asked him more than once to write his memoirs, but he never fancied it. He told Jay he was going to be the one ex-BBC man who didn't write a book. Sometimes he joked to her about being idle. He had planned to be a dilettante once he retired; now he found he hadn't the knack. Often away, he always returned to Richmond with pleasure. Hugh Burnett, who lived in the town, bumped into him one Saturday morning outside Dickins & Jones. He was standing on the pavement, holding a pair of braces he had bought, wondering whether to buy his wife one nightdress or two. Burnett asked how much, and was told thirty pounds. In that case, wasn't one enough?

'Come on,' said Wheldon, and took Burnett in the car, away from the shops and up Richmond Hill – 'into the desk, out with the money, and sweeping back to the Green. "Where do we park?" inquires Wheldon, accidentally outside Richard Attenborough's house [the film producer, David's brother]. "Not here," I say, explaining where we are. "Right," says Huw. "You stay in the car. If a warden appears, Sir Huw is visiting Sir Richard." And off he goes to Dickins & Jones. He returns with

270

two nightdresses, and we're on our way to Richmond golf club. Then we sit surveying *his* club, each with a beer, me listening to a long story about foxes on the greens . . .'

On another occasion in Richmond, Burnett met David Attenborough, who said he hadn't seen Sir Huge for some time.

Michael Charlton, who got to know him well only after the operation, says he was sobered and more inclined to examine his past. He regretted his 'indolent youth', and said it was the war that rescued him. His lack of interest in politics, too, was something he debated with himself. He and Jay had become regular visitors to Aspen, Colorado,[1] where he led seminars and (he told Charlton) realized how easily he might have developed political interests. The two men played golf together, a game that Wheldon 'adored for the humour it involved. He liked the obliquity of it.' Charlton glimpsed a ferocity in Wheldon's nature. 'I never saw him happier than in scenes I utterly deplored, playing golf in a bloody awful downpour. He loved it. He looked like Lear, striding over those ghastly dunes, the wind slashing him. "I love it," he said. That's very unEnglish. There's an almost Wagnerian element.'

Perhaps it was acceptance rather than ferocity. 'There it is!' was a phrase he used continually in letters and conversation to close a subject – as though to say, Nothing can be changed. Jay remembers him coming back from a morning's golf at Criccieth when it rained and blew, and balls got lost in the murk. 'We had a wonderful time,' he shouted. 'We've seen a hare and a bull.'

Jay had her own problems. The novel in its many parts had become fixed in her life, immobilized. After her mother's death in 1978 she barely touched it. In 1984, when Huw was sixty-eight, he became tired and depressed. Jay thought he might be worried about money. She told him what a marvellous life they had had – 'a very *intellectual* life, full of good things, with a

---

[1] The Aspen Institute for Humanistic Studies, built in the mountains in a former mining town that is now a ski centre, brings together the inquiring and the talkative to consider 'major issues in contemporary society'.

lovely family. If necessary we could live in a flat.' But it was not depression; or it was not just depression.

They remained close, understanding one another, even if, at times, he surprised her with an idea or an interest: 'He was what you might call a free man. You couldn't be sure what his answer would be to anything.'

He had never been a man for giving things away. Without the letters to Celia and Jay, the evidence for his drive to master his nature – a drive that helped to shape him – would lack a focus. In later life he wrote few letters and made no confessions. One may guess that if he dwelt on his past, he enjoyed not having been defeated by it. But he never expected too much. His wife knew that beneath the cheeribee, he was 'a pessimist to the bone', that he had a sense of not living up to his best lights. 'God will not be mocked': the phrase creeps in all the time.

By 1985 they knew he had cancer again: this time of the lung. 'He was very angry at being cut down,' says Roger Cary. Until the end of the year he kept himself going. When he spoke at the Royal Television Society's dinner in December, and told them the *Yesterday's Men* story ('in six chapters'), he was almost as sparkling as ever. But he had had to prepare himself for the effort, as he prepared himself soon after for the annual Christmas party at 120 Richmond Hill that he refused to cancel.

Not long before he died, he told Jay what a magnificent day he had just had. His son had bought him a book about Poulenc, and he had been listening to Poulenc's music on Radio 3. Many friends visited him in the last weeks. He made jokes about the chair lift that had been installed on the stairs. When Paul Wright was there, he insisted on getting out of bed, saying 'I want to watch you go down in that fucking chair.' Wright knew it was the last time he would see him. He knew that Wheldon knew, too.

He died on March 14 1986. Paul Fox wrote that he was unlike any other BBC executive; Melvyn Bragg that he served 'not himself but the Programme, the Story'; David Attenborough that 'he was called many things – Huge Welshman, the founding father of arts television, the last of the great actor-managers, the best director-general the BBC never had. He was a great man.' At the memorial service in Westminster Abbey, the royal family, media, arts and learning were represented. Somewhere in the congregation was Celia.

His ashes are in Kew Gardens, his grave at Nant Peris, in the shadow of Snowdon. By coincidence, a letter in the *Guardian* a week after his death, headed 'School Hero', about his association with the LSE, appeared next to a 'Country Diary' column that began, 'NANT PERIS: Ice flowers bloomed across all the rocks as earlier this month I traversed the Crib Goch knife-edge.'

Wheldon's headstone calls him 'Soldier, Broadcaster, Administrator'. The graves of his father, mother, brother and forbears back to the eighteenth century are adjacent. The little church of St Peris seems to have no distinction except that of antiquity, and, in winter, loneliness. Larkin's agnostic on a bicycle might drop by any minute, casting an eye over

> this ground
> Which, he once heard, was proper to grow wise in,
> If only that so many dead lie round.

Notes

Abbreviations

HWP, Huw Wheldon Papers: this covers everything in the possession of Lady Wheldon. It includes engagement diaries from the 1940s to the 1980s; several hundred letters from Wheldon to his father and other relatives; letters to and from his wife; files of his personal correspondence when he was managing director of BBC television; typescripts and printed versions of speeches; television scripts and other material about programmes; some BBC memos, correspondence and other documents; letters and notes about family history; papers relating to his father's career; letters from his father, between the 1930s and 1960s. Apart from the BBC material, which was mostly in labelled files and boxes, and some of his father's documents, the papers were largely unsorted.

OH: material from the BBC's Oral History archive – Wheldon's contribution, unless otherwise stated. The Wheldon material is in two parts, the second indicated by 'II'.

Cav: the BBC's written archive centre at Caversham, Reading.

PRB: minutes of the television programme review board (also known as the weekly programme review), at Caversham.

PRO: Public Record Office, Kew.

MDTel: Minutes of managing director, television's, weekly meeting, at Caversham.

'Interviewed' means interviewed by the author. All subsequent quotation of the person concerned is from the same interview, unless otherwise stated.

Chapter One: WELSHMAN

2. *McGivern's memo*: Cav, Wheldon's file, 1952–8.

2. *Wheldon's Oral History*: the verbatim record has been tidied up throughout, to remove repetitions and obscurities, and some passages have been condensed. The conker story: OH, p. 14.

4. *T. J. Wheldon's biography*: D. D. Williams, *Cofiant T. J. Wheldon*, Caernarfon, 1925. A work of piety.

4. *Useful with his fists*: Wheldon lecturing at University College of North Wales, Bangor, about 'The challenge of youth today', September 1961. Text, HWP.

5. *Mortgaging the will*: Wheldon interviewed by Penelope Maslin in the *Western Mail*, 16.2.68.

7. *Figures in Wheldon's childhood*: unpublished monograph, 'Sir HW, a public man', by Pom Hoare. HWP.

7. *Wynn's 'misbehaviour'*: D. D. Williams, op. cit.

7–8. *Appointing the principal*: letters and other documents in HWP.

8–9. *Wheldon at school, and looking for girls in Bangor*: his 'Challenge of Youth' lecture, op. cit.

9. *Wheldon assessed*: the institute's report is in HWP.

10. *Mythical Wales*: Wheldon to Allan Tyrer, 12.10.76, 'I intensely dislike The Mabinogion [Welsh medieval romances], although patriotic feelings tell me that I should treasure them.' Copy in HWP.

10–12. *Wheldon to H. W. Griffith*: undated, headed 'private'. In Griffith's possession, as are all Wheldon's letters to him.

12. *Wheldon to Griffith*: undated letter.

13. *Wheldon to Mair*: 11.5.34. HWP.

13. *Wheldon to Griffith*: on Hitler and British morality, 4.7.34; on girls, undated and 4.7.34.

13. *T. J. Wheldon to Wynn Wheldon*: undated. HWP.

13. *Wynn Wheldon advises Huw*: e.g., 'You can't be involved in everything & then expect to succeed', 8.1.35; 'your last letter contained too many complaints', 20.5.35. Most of the early letters from father to son are in Welsh. HWP.

13. *Letting his father down*: Wheldon to Griffith, 3.7.35.

14. *A good background*: Wheldon to Griffith, undated.

14. *'Unspeakable nonsense'*: letter written about 12.1.46. HWP.

14. *'Best on the market'*: undated, probably November 1935.

14. *'Malicious' Laski*: quoted in Pom Hoare, op. cit.

275

14. *'Wonderful time'*: quoted in an unidentifiable magazine article, about 1956.

15. *Holding the fort*: letter dated 8.3.36.

15. *'Short, sharp steps'*: Desmond Leeper, interviewed January 1989.

15. *Infuriating pacifists*: letter dated 5.12.35.

15. *The Welsh arsonists*: letters of 9.9.36 and 25.10.36. Wheldon also wrote, 'Good old Saunders Lewis & Co! Best thing the Blaid [the nationalist party] has done yet, I think. Shows guts, the more so coming from cultured men.'

16. *'Third class brain'*: letter postmarked 15.11.37.

17. *'Experientia docet'*: letter addressed from 'Oakwood Park Hotel, Conway, Monday', to 'Dear People'. HWP.

17–18. *Wheldon to Leeper*: undated. In the possession of Mr and Mrs Leeper, as are all his letters to them.

18. *'Money for dirt'*: letter written from Glasgow, 15.12.38.

19. *'Without nepotism'*: letter dated 31.1.39.

19. *The woman who helped appoint Wheldon*: Miss Ida Groves, in 1939 careers guidance officer with Kent education authority. She is adamant that neither she nor her director knew who Wheldon was when they appointed him. Telephone conversation, 9.12.89.

Chapter Two: SOLDIER

20 ff. Celia was traced through a forwarding address at a London bank, which was in a diary Wheldon kept in the early 1950s. Her testimony is from a long interview at her flat and subsequent phone conversations, May 1989; and correspondence.

20. *Wheldon at work*: Ida Groves (see note to p. 19) says he may not have taken to the office routine but he was good with people. She remembers him after fifty years as 'light-hearted Huw'.

20. *'Luvvely' women*: Wheldon to Griffith, undated.

21. *Murphy to Wheldon*: 25.2.45. HWP.

22. *Letter from Australia*: HWP.

22–3. *H.'s story*: in an interview, June 1988, and subsequent phone conversations.

23–4. *Wheldon to his father*: undated, probably September 1942, from Ilfracombe. HWP.

24. *In pulpit mood*: letter postmarked 21.5.40.

24. *Bedside books*: to the Leepers, 21.1.40.

25. *Naziism, liberalism, Deal under snow*: to the Leepers, undated.

25. *'Evil Hitlerism'*: to Desmond Leeper, undated.

25–6. *Wheldon at the training barracks*: culled from letters to his parents and the Leepers.

26. *Attractive Communism*: letter to his father, undated, 'I must say that Communism attracts one's sympathies. The army doesn't make one delight in the Old British Methods.' HWP. Letter to Desmond Leeper, 3.10.40, 'Red-hot revolutionaries all.'

27. *To his father*: from Colwyn House, Barmouth, undated. HWP.

28. *The shepherd story*: letter dated 9.1.41. HWP.

28. *Wynn Wheldon letter*: to General Minshull-Ford, 22.11.40. HWP.

28. *At Wrexham*: two undated letters to his father. HWP.

28–29. *At Whitby*: letters to (Mrs) Ben Leeper, 5.3.41, and his father, undated.

29. *At Bellerby*: letters to Desmond Leeper, 4.10.41, and his father, 30.10.41.

29. *The film interview*: Wheldon's account of near-death by drowning was for a BBC series, *The Commanding Sea*. But he was unable to make the story short enough, despite several takes, and it was never used.

29–30. *To Richard Rees*: undated, probably 1960s. In the recipient's possession.

30. *Tom Main*: interviewed April 1989.

30. *Wheldon changes his mind*: Wynn Wheldon to his wife, 28.5.42. 'I felt quite sure that he wd decide this way after our talk at Bournemouth on Monday night.' In the possession of Mair Rees.

30. *To Desmond Leeper*: letter headed 'Bellerby Camp, Friday'.

31. *'A little cross and a trumpet call'*: Wheldon's 'Challenge of Youth' lecture, op. cit.

31. *Amateur film*: the Royal Ulster Rifles regimental museum in Belfast has a copy on video cassette.

31. *Brigadier John Drummond*: interviewed March 1989.

32. *The mock wedding*: Sandy Smith, interviewed February 1989.

32. *'A battlefield one day'*: letter dated 8.11.42.

32. *Envying the English*: to his father/mother, 3.5.43. HWP.

32–3. *Prestatyn letter*: 30.3.43.

33. *'Teeming with trout'*: 1.5.44. HWP.

33. *To Ben Leeper*: undated, May 1944.

33. *The church parade*: 13.5.44. HWP.

34. *To Tomos*: 3.6.44. Letters to Tomos are in the possession of his widow, Mrs Nerys Vaughan.

34. *To H.*: 4.6.44. Letters to H. are in her possession.

35. *Communal relief*: Wheldon told the anecdote in a booklet, *Red Berets into Normandy* (1982), and more racily in conversation.

36. *On Hill 30*: information from John Drummond; Bob Sheridan, interviewed February 1989; battalion circular letter, 24.6.44.

36–7. *To his father*: 29.8.44. HWP.

37. *Leeper to his wife*: extracts from this and similar letters were supplied by the Leepers.

38. *Wheldon in Normandy, 1944*: to Ben Leeper, July 15; to Desmond Leeper, July 22; to his father/mother, July 25 and 29, August 2 and 29.

Chapter Three: SUITOR

47–8. *The Cambridge letter*: letter-card, headed 'Baker St P.O. En route for Bloody B. Thursday.'

49 fn. *T. Mervyn Jones*: interviewed November 1988 and January 1989. A former chairman of the Wales Gas Board, he was a friend and confidant of Wheldon. He died February 1989.

52–3. *The gloves*: Lady Wheldon still has them.

53. *Letter about 'Gloves II'*: 5.2.45.

53–4. *Letter about concert*: 16.1.45.

55. *Murphy to Wheldon*: 23.2.45. 'Gethogh' was Murphy's rendering of an Irish word, 'ciotog'; it means 'awkward with women' as well as 'left-handed'.

56. *To Ben Leeper*: 4.4.45.

57. *Celia and the Burma story*: letter to the author, 18.7.89.

Chapter Four: CANDIDATE

62. *Teacher-training job*: Wynn Wheldon to Huw, 10.7.39. HWP.

63. *To Ben Leeper*: 1.10.45. A letter on the same day to his father says that the stevedores 'are, it seems to me, entirely without sense of social duty and are very close to hooliganism'. HWP.

63. *Celia 'finished'*: letter dated 10.12.45.

64. *'Bomb-throwing fools'*: to his father/mother, 22.11.45. HWP.

65. *To his father*: undated, about 12.1.46. HWP.

65. *To Desmond Leeper*: 11.1.46.

65. *Alan Champion*: interviewed (by phone) June 1989, and correspondence.

66. *Leeper on Wheldon*: letter to his wife, April 1945.

66. *Jonah Jones and Judith Maro*: interviewed March 1989, and correspondence.

67. *Wheldon to Leeper*: 8.11.42. His father would have seen the Beveridge Report before it was published.

67. *Huw to Wynn Wheldon about politics*: 23.1.45. HWP.

67–8. *Huw to Wynn about Socialism*: 7.3.46. HWP.

68. *Wynn to Huw about lecturing*: 24.1.46. HWP.

68. *Wynn to Huw about Coleg Harlech*: 22.12.45. HWP.

68. *Wynn to Huw about W. E. Williams*: 24.2.46. HWP.

69. *Wynn to Huw about the Arts Council job*: 3.3.46. HWP.

70. *Wynn to Huw*: 31.3.46. HWP.

70. *Huw to Wynn, 'frightened'*: 21.4.46. HWP.

71. *Wynn Wheldon resigns*: letter from Mary Glasgow to the Arts Council office in Cardiff, 4.6.46, 'I am very sorry to have to ask you to take Sir Wynn's name off the list of Welsh Committee members. I am sending the Committee a note about Huw Wheldon's appointment and his father's resignation.' PRO, EL 3/66.

71–2. *Ruth*: interviewed (by phone), June and July 1989.

72. *Wheldon to his wife*: 29.9.59.

73. *Arts Council stationery*: T. Mervyn Jones.

73–4. *Wheldon and Welsh culture*: his views are set out in 'A memorandum on Arts Council policy in Wales', 19.2.47, PRO, EL 3/67. A confidential appendix is missing. The Public Record Office also has some of the early Arts Council correspondence dealing with Cardiff. The Welsh Arts Council (as it now is) has kept none of its early papers, apart from the minutes.

74. *Mary Glasgow to Huw Wheldon*: 'Don't think me very rude, but I think some of your wording should be a little more formal! I jib a bit at phrases like "up to" and "by and large". The rejection of the Council's offer on page 3 sounds a bit bald! Was that all there was to it?' PRO, EL 3/67.

74–5. *Wheldon to Eric White*: 1947, month illegible, PRO, EL 3/67.

75–6. *No towels*: letter dated 10.2.48, PRO, EL 3/68.

76. *Wheldon's appointment*: he was first approached on 14.1.49. On February 3 he heard he had got the job, at £900 a year plus expenses. This soon became a salary of £1,000 with annual expenses of £100. HWP.

76. *£400,000 to spend*: actual Arts Council spending was £343,000. Festival of Britain White Paper, Cmnd 8872.

76–7. *Paul Wright*: interviewed April 1989.

79. *Cliff Tucker*: interviewed (by phone) May 1989.

79. *The Doctor*: interviewed (by phone) May 1989.

80. *Welsh reference*: B. Ifor Evans, then provost of University College, London, 9.10.51. HWP.

80. *'Glamorous' BBC and buying a TV set*: OH, p. 2.

80–1. *Gladstone Murray*: Wheldon described him picturesquely in a letter to his wife, 'Old Gladstone Murray was the man slated to succeed Reith as DG but who was incurably alcoholic (head wound in the Royal Flying Corps) and who blotted his copy book to put it mildly by suffering indescribable five day jags during which it was his whim and uncontrollable wish to use the BBC's incomparable telephone & communications system to ring up and insult the great. So poor Haile Selassie, Greta Garbo, Baldwin, Gandhi, not to mention the Pope & the Emperor of Japan, were the much-to-be-envied recipients of his extraordinary communications. However, it would hardly do for the BBC. There are limits. And he was sacked.' 9.9.59. HWP.

81. *Wheldon on joining the BBC*: interviewed (by Adam Hopkins) on BBC Radio Wales, about 1980. The text has been condensed.

82. *'Rather humiliating'*: OH, p. 3.

Chapter Five: DAYS OF INNOCENCE

83. *Keeping TV payments low*: private information.

83. *Haley's dinner party*: Grace Wyndham Goldie, OH, in conversation with Huw Wheldon, 1978, p. 11.

84. *Thought on television*: Goldie, OH, p. 12.

84. *Wheldon on Barnes etc.*: OH, pp. 4 and 8.

84–5. *Publicity memo*: 5.1.53. Cav, R13/331/2.

85. *'That maniac McGivern'*: OH, p. 8.

85. *Memo of 4.12.52*: Cecil Madden to Cecil McGivern. Cav, T23/35/2.

85. *McGivern's drinking*: Wheldon, OH, p. 36; and various interviews.

85–6. *The Lourdes conversation*: Donald Baverstock, interviewed March 1989.

86. *McGivern's admonitory memos*: HWP.

87. *Wheldon retaliates*: Peter Black, interviewed April 1989, and his book *The Biggest Aspidistra in the World*.

87. *Hired as Conker King*: OH, p. 14; Freda Lingstrom, interviewed May 1988. Miss Lingstrom died April 1989.

87–8. *Avoiding precocity*: OH, p. 18.

88. *The harpsichord: Monitor* 6.4.58. BBC film library.

88. *Sandwiches and cake*: memo dated 22.10.53. Cav, T2/5, TV children's programmes file.

88. *The bird-watchers*: ibid.

88. *Michael Gill*: interviewed May 1989.

88–9. *George Campey*: interviewed April 1989.

90. *Knocking papers on the floor*: Hugh Burnett, interviewed April 1989.

90. *Wheldon on Goldie*: OH, p. 115.

90–1. *'Facts & Figures' memo*: 21.2.55, Cav, T32/150/3.

91. *Peacock on Wheldon*: interviewed April 1989.

91. *Ian Jacob's opposition*: a note from a Miss Singer says the DG is doubtful about the Churchill broadcast, being 'so afraid that it will be too much like an obituary'. Cav, 32/110/1, Churchill Birthday Programme, File 1A. Confirmed by Sir Ian in a letter, December 1989.

91. *Three endings*: Goldie, *Facing the Nation*, p. 170.

91–3. *Wheldon's Churchill story*: OH, p. 48.

94. *Ken Russell on Wheldon and Welles*: interviewed July 1989.

94–5. *Wheldon's Welles story*: David Jones, interviewed January 1989.

95. *Melvyn Bragg*: in an interview recorded for an *Omnibus* television obituary, *Huw Wheldon by his friends*, broadcast 11.4.86.

95. Harding Finds Out: Cav, that programme's file.

95. *Wheldon on the Harding programmes*: OH, p. 47.

95–6. *McGivern memo*: 25.2.55, Cav, *Harding Finds Out* programme file.

96. *Miall on autumn programmes*: January 1955, Cav, *Is This Your Problem?* File 1, general.

96. *An experimental programme*: television programme board, 26.10.55, Cav, T16/436, which also has the Religious Broadcasting comments.

97. *Artificial insemination*: memo of complaint from the assistant head of television broadcasting, 17.10.52, Cav, 16/162/1, TV policy, standards of taste file.

97. *Dancers in tights*: memo dated 17.3.54, Cav, ibid.

97–8. *Wynn Wheldon's letter quoted*: Cav, *Is This Your Problem?* file.

98. *The warden's letter*: Cliff Tucker.

101. *Henry Dicks*: his obituary in the *British Medical Journal*, 30.7.77, notes that 'among his many publications, *Marital Tensions*, published in 1967, is still widely read'.

101. *G.'s story*: in an interview, April 1989, and telephone conversations.

101ff. *Lady Wheldon*: in eight interviews and many conversations between May 1988 and August 1989.

106. *In Cornwall*: Diana Rose (sister of the first Mrs Murphy), interviewed March 1989.

108. *Saying yes to Horrocks*: McGivern to Horrocks, 9.12.55: 'We would very much like to follow up your suggestion for a series of short talks on the anniversaries of some of the famous battles of the 1939–45 war.' The letter adds that a Talks producer will discuss details with him, 'I think an excellent person for this will be Huw Wheldon,' whose wartime career is described. Cav, Horrocks file.

108. *Wheldon's Horrocks story*: OH, p. 10.

108. *Horrocks enthralled*: Horrocks to Donald Wilson, drama department. Cav, Horrocks file.

108–9. *Wheldon to Jay*: two letters, both undated, one postmarked 25.10.56.

110. *BBC in shock*: Grace Wyndham Goldie said that commercial television 'shook me to the core . . . [the BBC] was like a grandfather in a patriarchal household, you could gird against it and you couldn't harm it. These tuppenny-halfpenny little chaps who were interested in advertising, they couldn't possibly do things the BBC could do . . . and we didn't really believe it would have any effect whatsoever. And of course it was better.' Goldie, OH, p. 52.

110. *Jacob and the programme board*: Cav, T16/436.

110. *Women announcers*: McGivern's memos, 11.5.55, 21.3.56, Cav, T16/147/2.

110. *Barnes and leadership*: private information.

111–12. *Wheldon and Macmillan*: memos in Cav, T16/509; Cav also has Goldie's papers, see S135/27, part 3. OH, p. 51.

112. *Wheldon on* Tonight: OH, p. 26.

113. *Adam to Miall*: 19.3.57, Cav, *Monitor* general file, 1957–8, RMC location 001925.

113–14. *Letters to Jay*: one dated 3.12.57, two postmarked December 3 and December 5. HWP.

Chapter Six: LETTERS FROM AMERICA

115. *Draft paper*: 1957, but undated. Cav, T16/310/2.

116. *Catherine Freeman/Dove*: interviewed May 1988, with subsequent correspondence.

116. *Fifty names*: Cav, *Monitor* general file, 1957–8, op. cit.

116–17. *Leonard Miall*: interviewed February 1988.

117. *'Gigantic row'*: OH, p. 21.

117. *Goldie's ruling*: Cav, memo of 2.12.57, *Monitor* 1957–8 file, op. cit.

118. *'Little faith' in arts programme*: OH, p. 21.

118. *Discussing the title*: Cav, *Monitor* 1957–8 file, op. cit.

118. *Sharing a bed*: Cav, *Brains Trust* file, memo of 5.8.58.

119. *Groans about expenses*: Cav, *Monitor* 1957–8 file, op. cit.

121. *Baverstock and Newington*: in an interview with Newington, June 1989.

121. *The weeping girl*: Ann Turner interviewed January 1989.

121. *Wheldon's authority*: OH, p. 22.

121. *Wheldon on provincial theatres*: memo of 13.2.58, Cav, *Monitor* 1957–8 file, op. cit.

122. *Wheldon on gossip*: letter to Mr R. Swickart, 30.3.60, Cav, *Monitor* file for programme of 9.10.60.

123. *'Emphatic no'*: Ursula Vaughan Williams, 14.2.58, Cav, *Monitor* 1957–8 file, op. cit.

124. *'Rare birds'*: from a 26-page typescript draft on blue paper, headed 'Programme Possibilities Associated with Monitor', and beginning 'Mr Birkinshaw, ladies and gentlemen'. Heavily corrected in Wheldon's hand, perhaps for publication. The text has been condensed. HWP.

124. *Wheldon to his wife*: 29.12.58. HWP.

124. *Simenon's rituals*: 'blue typescript', op. cit.

125. *The public relations job*: OH, p. 32.

125. *Hole to Wheldon*: 15.1.59. HWP.

125. *Wheldon to Hole*: typescript draft, 17.1.59. HWP.

125–6. *Wheldon to Goldie*: 8.3.59. HWP.

125–6. *Wheldon's job application*: dated 25.2.59. His biographical sketch begins, 'I was born & bred to the idea of public service, and have had a good deal of experience of representing public bodies and carrying out their work in circumstances of some complexity.' HWP.

128. *The reporter*: in the *Western Mail*, 16.2.68.

129. *Meeting Richard Burton*: 8.10.59. HWP, as are all the American letters.

129. *Knocking them cold*: 23.9.59.

129. Variety: 30.9.59. 'Speaking extemporaneously . . . BBC producer Huw Wheldon cracked, "The public service battle was won in England ages ago. Nobody in England could ask if public service has a place. The English public's no better educated, no more literate than the American. If the English can take it, God knows the Americans can."'

129. *Radio interview*: 2.9.59.

129–30. *Bangor, Wis.*: Wheldon's family letter dated September 17 was circulated by his father.

130. *Faded glories*: 13.10.59.

130. *Meeting Mrs Faulkner*: 14.10.59.

130. *Red shoes*: 11.9.59.

130. *'I like a laugh'*: 11.9.59.

130. *To his father*: 9.9.59.

130. *In Plainview*: 9.10.59.

136. *Jay to Wheldon*: 23.10.59.

136. *'You are rare'*: 22.10.59.

136–7. *Counting the hours*: 30.10.59.

137. *Talks Dept report*: Cav, T16/310/3.

137. *New York, with Humphrey Burton*: undated letter on 'Metropolitan Opera' paper, headed 'Desperate snatched moment. Friday 7 p.m.'.

137. *Wheldon on women*: London *Evening Standard*, about 18.8.60.

139. *Dropping Wheldon*: letter dated 14.12.60. HWP.

139. *Supporting* Lady Chatterley: Cav, *Monitor* 1960 general file, Wheldon to Goldie, 2.9.60, with a copy of his letter of the same date to the solicitors Rubinstein, Nash & Co, to say he would be 'very glad' to go on their list of names, but that he must seek BBC permission. Goldie's memo in reply is 8.9.60. Both memos are marked 'Confidential'.

Chapter Seven: ARTS AND CRAFTS

140. *Explaining Tolstoy and Milhaud*: Wheldon's blue typescript, op. cit.

140–1. *Mrs Stroud*: blue typescript, op. cit.

141. *Pinter interview on* Monitor: 5.6.60.

141. *Colin Davis interview on* Monitor: 8.11.60.

141–2. *The collage story*: in an interview.

142. *West Indian novelists*: broadcast 11.9.60.

143. *'Guild of Mastersingers'*: Humphrey Burton, interviewed April 1989.

143. *The Duchamp item*: Nancy Thomas, interviewed February 1989.

143. *The Duchamp review*: *Church of England Newspaper*, 29.6.62.

143. *Ann James*: interviewed March 1989.

144. *The journalist*: Susan Barnes in the pre-Murdoch *Sun*, 13.12.65.

145. *Durrell interview on* Monitor: 14.2.60.

145. *Allan Tyrer*: interviewed January 1989.

145–6. Monitor *review*: *Daily Telegraph*, 11.1.63, 'Interviews with artists' by David Holloway.

145–6. *Mary McCarthy interview on* Monitor: 28.2.60.

146. *Orson Welles interview on* Monitor: 13.3.60.

146. *'I talk away my ideas'*: blue typescript, op. cit.

146–7. *Joan Murphy*: interviewed November 1988.

147. *Emlyn Williams's 'childhood' film*: *The Private World of George Williams*, Monitor, 8.10.61.

147–8. *'I am doubtful' etc.*: blue typescript, op. cit.

148. *Recruiting Ken Russell*: Wheldon, OH, p. 41.

148. *In Edwardian clothes*: Ken Russell's autobiography, *A British Picture*.

149. *Prokofiev film*: the Baxter and Russell books, op. cit.; interview with Russell, July 1989. The film was *Portrait of a Soviet Composer*, 18.6.61.

149. *In the dubbing theatre*: Russell, recorded for the 1986 *Omnibus* obituary programme, op. cit.

149. The Miners' Picnic: broadcast 3.7.60.

149. *Russell's postcard*: Cav, *Monitor* file, programme of 3.7.60.

150. The Light Fantastic: broadcast 18.12.60. Relevant BBC memos, Cav, *Monitor* 1960 general file.

150–1. *Wheldon on the dancing film*: blue typescript, op. cit., text condensed.

152–3. The Preservation Man: Russell in his interview; also Bruce Lacey, interviewed (by phone) December 1989.

154. *Talks department paper*: draft summary of third-quarter output report, 1961, Cav, T16/310/4.

154. *'Culture snobs'*: Tynan quoted in the Dublin *Sunday Independent*, 1.10.61.

155–8. *The* Birdcage *episode*: John Bowen to the author, 19.7.88, and papers from his files; Faber & Faber archives; HWP.

158. *Bliss's proposal*: letter dated 4.7.58, suggesting 'a short film', Cav, Elgar programme file, RMC 001934, which is the source of other Elgar material.

159 ff. *Russell's treatment*: seven pages of typescript, headed 'SIR EDWARD ELGAR, a film treatment by Ken Russell'. It is undated but a note at the end says, 'Elgar died 25 years ago this year', which places the treatment in 1959. Also in the file (RMC 001934, op. cit.) is a memo of 2.6.59 from Music Productions belittling the treatment, with a sentence that says, 'I am convinced that there is not much value in shots of Elgar firing his catapult at cats in the yard or trying to drive a stubborn mule. After all, the aim of "Monitor", surely, is to concentrate on art and its relation to the public, not to indulge in gossip-column stuff.' Russell's treatment has nothing about cats or catapults. Presumably there was more than one version.

159. *'Good afternoon, Mr Chopin'*: Wheldon, OH, p. 43.

159. *Dialogue not part of the plan*: Baxter, op. cit., p. 114.

161. *Melvyn Bragg*: interviewed October 1989.

163. *'Après Huw'*: *Radio Times*, 1964.

163. *Miller on Wheldon*: recorded for the 1986 *Omnibus* obituary programme, op. cit.

Chapter Eight: WAR GAMES

165. *The 'Black Book' inquiry*: Hugh Greene, OH, interviewed 1977 by Frank Gillard, p. 8.

165. *Muggeridge banned*: Greene, OH, p. 6, confirmed by Jacob in 1989. Greene added, 'After I became director-general he was perhaps on the air too much.'

165–6. *The Big Ben lobby*: Greene, OH, p. 13.

166–7. *John Read*: interviewed April 1989.

167–8. *John Drummond*: interviewed December 1989.

168. *Antony Jay*: interviewed May 1989.

168. *David Attenborough*: interviewed March 1989.

169. *One of Wheldon's vanities*: OH, p. 57.

169 ff. *Peter Watkins*: much of the information about Watkins and his films, in particular the controversial *War Game*, is from a dossier about the making of that film (see p. 182). A copy of this is in HWP. Joseph Gómez's book *Peter Watkins* has also been used.

169. *Watkins joins the BBC*: HWP.

170. *Proposed programmes*: HWP

170. *Costing* Culloden, *and Equity*: Cav, that programme's file; HWP.

170–1. *Wheldon on the filming*: OH, p. 59.

171. *Keeping the rushes from Wheldon*: HWP.

171. *Trip wires and the BBC retraction*: Gómez, p. 55.

171. *Programme review board*: 16.12.64.

172. *Sloan on the new comedy*: interviewed by the author (for an article) January 1963.

173. *Newman recruited*: interview with Newman, February 1989.

173. *Resolving the 'single-plays' row*: Adam to Baverstock and Newman, 13.7.64, Cav, T16/62/3.

173. *'Donald's dead'*: Tony Garnett, interviewed April 1989.

174. *Stuart Hood's departure*: interview with Hood, January 1989.

174. *'Inscrutable monk'*: PRB, 24.11.71.

174. *Keeping an eye on Adam*: Charles Curran, OH, p. 137.

175. *The senior secretary*: interviewed April 1989.

175. *'Absolute control' memo*: Wheldon to Adam. HWP.

176. *'£500 more' memo*: Wheldon to Adam. 'I am concerned that this should be so, not so much in order that those below me should be aware of it, but in order that my employers and seniors should be in no doubt about the command position.' HWP.

176. *The 1962 conversation*: in an undated 'Brief for DG from Kenneth Adam and Huw Wheldon'. HWP.

177. *Baverstock to Adam*: 'The reorganization of the leadership of television programmes', 12.1.65. In Baverstock's possession.

177. *Memo of February 23*: HWP.

178. *Bernard Levin*: Daily Mail, 25.2.65, 'Bernard Levin tells the inside story of a TV revolution'.

180. *Watkins on 'strong subjects'*: memo to Wheldon, 9.10.64. HWP.

180–1. *Wheldon to Adam, 31.12.64*: HWP.

180–1. *Goldie's view*: quoted by Wheldon in 31.12.64, above.

181. *Security aspects*: there is no later indication of whether lawyers were consulted, or what they advised. This part of the affair is probably one reason for the BBC's extreme sensitivity about the matter, after a quarter of a century.

181. *Greene's attitude*: HWP.

181–2. *Baverstock accepts* The War Game: planning memo, confirming the decision, 22.1.65. HWP.

182. *Wheldon appoints Cawston*: Cawston, OH, interviewed by Leonard Miall, 1980, p. 68.

182. *Cawston on Watkins*: OH, p. 83.

182. *Watkins's research*: HWP.

182–3. *February 22 memo*: HWP.

183. *Greene and Normanbrook opposed*: HWP.

183ff. *Wheldon's reactions to the film at different stages*: HWP; Gómez, p. 51ff.

185. *Greene's letter*: to the *Listener*, 27.11.86.

185 fn. *Tracey on the papers*: in a telephone conversation, December 1989.

186. *Wheldon tries to dissuade Watkins*: memo, headed 'YOUR FUTURE', 15.9.65. HWP.

186. *Watkins on government officials*: HWP.

186–7. *Cawston to Wheldon*: HWP.

187. *Sept. 24 viewing*: HWP.

188. *Cawston to Watkins*: 15.11.65. HWP.

188. *Wheldon's recollection*: OH, p. 64.

188 fn. The War Game *in 1985*: The *Times* reviewer, Nicholas Shakespeare, wrote of the film as a 'triumph' for Watkins. 'The enduring images were the simplest. A bucket of wedding rings, and a finger turning the record of "Silent Night".' 1.8.85.

Chapter Nine: RUDE WORDS

190. *Wheldon on the BBC's freedom*: OH, p. 24.

190–1. *Not saying no*: Joanna Spicer, interviewed February 1988.

191. *Connolly to Baverstock*: undated, probably May 1955, Cav, T32/287/7.

191. *Snow on incest*: Cav, programme management board, 28.1.65.

191–2. Three Clear Sundays: broadcast 7.4.65. Written by Jimmy O'Connor, produced by James MacTaggart, directed by Kenneth Loach.

192. *Greene's suggestion*: Cav, board of governors minutes, 18.3.65.

192. *Governors furious*: Cav, board of governors minutes, 14.4.65.

192. *Wheldon to Adam, 27.4.65*: Cav, T16/62/4.

192. *Respecting Wheldon's sincerity*: Cav, board of governors minutes, 29.4.65.

193. *Audience for* Three Clear Sundays: board of governors, ibid. 'DG said that the play had had the biggest audience of the whole Wednesday Play series and had achieved the very high Reaction Index of 68. There had been no public reaction to the [hanging] scene as shown.' It was a 'very high' figure for a single play, not necessarily for more popular programmes.

193. *Adam agitated*: memo to Wheldon, 13.7.65. 'The trouble I feared is already emerging with the board . . .' Also Wheldon to Adam, 12.7.65, warning of timidity. Cav, T16/62/4.

193–4. For the West: transmitted 26.5.65. Written by Michael Hastings, produced by James MacTaggart, directed by Toby Robertson.

194. *Wheldon castigates the play*: PRB, 2.6.65.

194. *Only three programmes referred*: OH, p. 64.

194. *Censorship committee*: Joint Committee on Censorship of the Theatre, 1967, H.L. 255, H.C. 503.

194–5. *The censored typescript*: Cav, T16/543. '28.9.66' has been added by hand on page 1.

195. Vote, Vote, Vote for Nigel Barton: producer James MacTaggart, director Gareth Davies.

195. *Wheldon to the governors*: quoted in memo from Wheldon to Adam, 25.6.65. Cav, T16/62/4.

195–6. *Fox's memo*: Cav, *Nigel Barton* file.

196. *Fox at programme review board*: 22.12.65.

196. *Cancelling the intolerable*: 'The Wednesday Play', a Wheldon paper for the governors, 17.6.66. Cav, G.60/66.

197. Up the Junction *at programme review board*: 10.11.65.

197. *'The hounds are baying'*: memo from Newman on 'Violence, sexual relations and blasphemy in drama', to producers, directors and story editors, 22.11.65. Cav, T16/594.

198. *Newman on sexual references*: ibid.

199. *Wheldon at board of governors*: the paper under discussion was about the Wednesday Play, G.60/66, above.

199–200. *The Evesham conference*: Wheldon's report to the governors, Cav, in G.9/66.

200. *The cufflinks*: OH, p. 77.

202. *Cary on Evesham*: interviewed January 1989.

203. *The 'lavatory' remark*: telephone conversation with 'Jo', June 1989.

203–4. *Wheldon's seminars*: described in Wheldon's report for the governors, Cav, G.18/67.

204. *'Stuffy and toffee-nosed'*: blue typescript, op. cit. HWP.

204. *Gilbert Harding story*: in Wheldon's talk to senior staff, 4.2.70, but often told. HWP.

204. *Eating the horses*: as told by David Attenborough. Wheldon's version in OH, p. 35.

205. *Wheldon talks about BBC 2*: Talkback, BBC 1, 25.2.68.

205–6. *Wheldon on what to give the public*: Bakewell and Garnham, *The new priesthood. British television today* (1970), p. 223.

206. *Early-evening strategy*: Cav, T16/310/7.

206. *Wheldon on Sloan*: OH, p. 85.

206. *Larger audience, grave dilemma*: Wheldon's report for the governors, 'The problem of 7.30 p.m.', Cav, G.18/67, 15.2.67.

206. *Forty-three 'bloodys'*: Cav, *Till death* programme file, 24.11.67.

207. *Jay in 1966 interviews*: (1) 'Ruth Martin meets Jacqueline Wheldon', *Trade News*, 5.2.66. (2) 'Enter the girl with a nose for disaster' by Marshall Pugh, *Daily Mail*, 9.2.66.

208–11. *Programme review board quotes*: Rudkin play, 17.1.68. Henry James, 24.1.68. Reith, 6.12.67. *It's a Knockout*, 17.5.67, 13.9.67, 15.5.68, 11.9.68. Daleks, 26.5.65, 31.5.67. Insects, 20.3.68. Connolly and Miller, 19.10.66. Aberfan, 26.10.66. Faces, 31.1.68. *Man Alive*, 19.4.67. *Whicker's World*, 26.4.67. Homosexuals, 10.3.65. Seduction, 9.2.66. *Softly, Softly*, 6.4.66. Russell film, 25.10.67. Zola, 11.9.68. 'Experienced members . . .' 25.10.67.

Chapter Ten: 'TO HELL WITH THEM'

212. *Wheldon to Adam*: 5.3.67. HWP.

212–13. *HW to board of governors*: Cav, G.40/67, 26.4.67.

213. *Burton's telegram*: HWP.

214. *Wheldon invents cultural spectaculars*: OH, p. 81.

214fn. *Clark's payment*: Cav, his file.

215. *Review board*: 23.11.66.

215–16 fn. *Meeting the Minister*: memo dated 1.12.66, Cav, *Cathy Come Home* file.

216. *Suez play*: OH, p. 95.

216. *'Bothersome'*: OH, p. 96.

216–17. *Roy Battersby*: in an interview, March 1989.

218. *Tynan article*: 9.6.68.

218. *Wheldon on Tynan*: OH, p. 95.

218. *Review board on* Some Women: 3.9.69.

219. *Hill's office*: Hill, OH, p. 16.

219. *Greene on voting*: Greene, OH, p. 40.

220. *The Rommel story*: Attenborough; Hill in OH, p. 16.

220. *Wheldon and Tom Jackson*: Hill, OH, p. 25.

221. *Wheldon to Adam*: 8.9.68. HWP, which also have a draft of the paper dated 5.6.68, and three pages of Wheldon's notes attacking it.

222. *July 19*: Wheldon's diary has the appointment; his remarks to Hill are referred to in his letter of July 23.

224. *Glanmor Williams*: interviewed April 1989.

224. *Aubrey Singer*: interviewed January 1989.

226. *Free Wales Army*: PRB, 14.9.66.

226. *Alwyn Roberts*: interviewed March 1989.

226. *Geraint Stanley Jones*: interviewed April 1989.

226–7. *Michael Charlton*: interviewed June 1989.

Chapter Eleven: CASH, GLORY, PIETY

228. *Normanbrook and Adam*: Charles Curran, OH, p. 137.

228. *The admiral*: OH-II, p. 28.

228–9. *Right of entry*: OH-II, p. 29.

229. *Wheldon on Curran*: OH-II, p. 8; on DG as secretary-general, OH-II, p. 43.

229. *Hill on Curran*: Hill's OH, p. 33.

229. *Michael Checkland*: interviewed June 1989.

230. *Overspending and the consequences*: MDTel, 3.6.69, 8.2.69, 2.12.69.

230–3. *Wheldon's pep talks*: HWP have typescripts of three, all variants on the same theme. (1) was to senior staff, 4.1.70; (2) to staff at BBC rehearsal rooms in North Acton, 14.4.70; (3) again at North Acton, 17.4.70. (1) occupies 21 pages and is more explicit than (2) and (3), which occupy 43 pages each. Quotations in pp. 292–5 are from the talks.

236. *Bangor letter:* HWP.

236. *The four best aides*: OH-II, p. 47. Wheldon added that Aubrey Singer and Humphrey Burton were 'just underneath them, so to speak'.

236. *Wheldon to Peacock*: 8.12.70.

237. *Backbench Conservatives*: PRB, 27.1.71.

237. *Wheldon's account*: OH-II, p. 18, 'a quite preposterous story'; Royal Television Society dinner 10.12.85.

237. *'In six chapters'*: this was how Wheldon introduced the story at the RTS dinner.

239–40. *Hoping to get away with it*: MDTel, 14.4.70.

240. *A bone for complainants*: MDTel, 22.7.70.

240. *Morality council*: MDTel, 27.10.70.

240. *Sardonic newspapers*: MDTel, 12.10.71.

240. *Clare's postcard*: HWP.

241. *Weather forecasts*: MDTel, 28.7.70.

241. *Wheldon to Grisewood*: 8.1.71, copy in HWP.

241. The Edwardians: PRB, 10.1.73.

241–2. *Dates of PRBs*: Sartre, 9.12.70; men kissing, 21.1.73; four achievements, 23.6.71.

242. *What Xerox paid*: PRB, 6.5.70.

242. Civilisation *book*: PRB, 27.1.71.

242. *Report to governors*: G.60/71, 12.5.71. HWP.

242. America *memo*: 13.9.72, headed 'Confidential', in the programme's general file. Cav.

242. *'Potentially dangerous'*: MDTel, 27.3.73.

243. *Half a million pounds less*: Wheldon, report to the governors, 30.5.74, G.72/74. HWP.

243. *Curran on democracy*: quoted by Wheldon, 'from memory', 'I am aware that what I am about to say may seem to be autocratic, but I think that nevertheless it has to be said. The BBC is not a democracy. You would not believe me if I were to try to argue that it was. The BBC is an operation which is carried out under executive command . . . In the last resort, despite [an] element of consent among the participants, the BBC must work by authority.' MDTel, 5.1.71.

243. *'Unofficial literature'*: MDTel, 14.12.71.

243. *'A sour independence'*: OH-II, p. 26.

243–4. *Wheldon on Garnett*: OH-II, p. 27.

244 fn. *'Polemical or "committed" drama and documentary'*: 17.10.75, Cav, G.215/75. *'Taken for a ride'*: Shaw to Wheldon, 29.12.75, Cav, 'Drama – programmes policy', management registry file B170–1.

245. *Wheldon on Attenborough*: OH-II, p. 45.

246. *In the garden*: Alasdair Milne, *DG: The Memoirs of a British Broadcaster*.

246. *Wheldon on Fox*: OH-II, p. 47.

246. *Paul Fox on his resignation*: in an interview, January 1989.

246. *Wheldon's press statement*: PRB, 4.7.73.

247. *Paul Hughes*: interviewed January 1989.

247. *The lid blows off*: Wheldon, report to the governors, 11.5.73, G.68/73. HWP.

247. *Watering the wine*: Wheldon, report to the governors, 30.5.74, G.72/74. HWP.

248. *'Visible sacrifices'*: MDTel, 26.11.74.

248. *Saving £150,000*: Wheldon at PRB, 4.12.74.

248–9. *Wimbledon*: PRB, 2.7.75.

249. *'A story-telling medium'*: 'British traditions in a worldwide medium', speech 'at the invitation of Standard Telephones and Cables Ltd', Dorchester Hotel, London, 12.4.73.

249. *The mystery of stories*: 'Perspectives on Television', speech to the Institution of Engineers and Shipbuilders in Scotland, 28.3.68.

249. *Yugoslav army*: 'A conversation with Bill Moyers', television interview with Wheldon for WNET/13, New York, 13.3.75, recorded in London; also broadcast by the BBC.

249. *Henry VIII's armour*: ibid.

249–50. *Lady Wheldon and Harry Worth*: 'Perspectives on Television', op. cit.

250. *London Welsh golfers*: letter dated 30.11.70. Copy in HWP.

250–1. *The sermon*: preached 29.4.73. Wheldon's sermon and notes are with the order of service. HWP.

251–2. *The pneumonia letter*: 12.6.75. Copy in HWP.

252. *Golden ages*: Wheldon, 'The achievement of television', 1975.

252. *Organization man*: OH-II, p. 320.

252–3. *Interview in a pub*: by Bill Moyers, op. cit.

253. *Colin Shaw*: interviewed January 1989.

253. *'Slums of the mind'*: Wheldon talking to Goldie in her OH, p. 94.

253. *Art v. cardboard*: 'Creativity and collaboration in television programmes', Frank Nelson Doubleday Lecture at the Smithsonian Institution, Washington, 7.3.70.

254. 'Over-runs': PRB, 30.7.69.

254–5. *Curran to Wheldon*: 4.12.74. HWP. The plan outlined in Curran's letter was for Wheldon to take charge of submitting evidence about BBC television to the Annan Committee, after he ceased to be managing director. This didn't happen. He inquired into the BBC regions instead.

255. *Wheldon on Annan*: OH-II, p. 14.

255. *Wheldon's last programme review board*: 17.12.75.

Chapter Twelve: SIR HUW

257. *Wheldon to Lingstrom*: 13.11.73. Copy in HWP.

258. *The cameraman and Prince Charles*: Cawston, OH, p. 91.

258. Royal Family: Cawston, OH, p. 98.

258. *Queen's copyright*: PRB, 25.6.69. Wheldon commended the film's lack of sycophancy.

258. *Genesis of* Royal Heritage: Cawston, OH, p. 183.

258. *The BBC's licence*: Cav, *Royal Heritage* files 1 and 2, RMC 4/01427.

259. *Gill to Cawston*: 5.11.74, ibid.

259–60. *Duke of Edinburgh's committee*: ibid.

260. *The Programme 7 script*: PRB, 8.6.77.

260–1. *Knighthood letters*: HWP.

262. *Disagreements about scripts*: *Royal Heritage* files, op. cit.

262. *Duke, programme title and anti-royalists*: memo in HWP.

263. *Jay Wheldon's letter*: HWP.

263. *Unfinished films*: Gill to Cawston, 1.9.76, *Royal Heritage* files, op. cit.

263–4. *Wheldon to Campey*: 15.1.77. In Campey's possession.

266. New York Times: 22.1.76, 'A regal package of art from Britain' by David Hughes.

268–9. *Ralf Dahrendorf*: interviewed September 1989.

269. *John Pike*: interviewed September 1989.

269 fn. *Letter from Wheldon*: to Selwyn Roderick, 8.3.81. BBC Wales record centre.

BIBLIOGRAPHY

Abse, Joan (ed.), *My LSE*, which includes an essay by Jacqueline Wheldon (Robson, 1977).

Addison, Paul, *Now the War is Over* (BBC/Cape, 1985).

Bakewell, Joan and Nicholas Garnham, *The New Priesthood. British Television Today* (Allen Lane the Penguin Press, 1970).

Baxter, John, *An Appalling Talent. Ken Russell* (Michael Joseph, 1973).

Black, Peter, *The Biggest Aspidistra in the World* (BBC, 1972).

Bowen, John, *The Birdcage* (Faber, 1962).

Briggs, Asa, *Governing the BBC* (BBC, 1979).

Briggs, Asa, *Sound and Vision*, volume IV of his 'History of Broadcasting in the United Kingdom' (OUP, 1979).

Briggs, Asa, *The BBC. The First Fifty Years* (OUP, 1985).

Briggs, Asa and Anne Macartney, *Toynbee Hall. The First Hundred Years* (Routledge & Kegan Paul, 1984).

Burns, Tom, *The BBC. Public Institution and Private World* (Macmillan, 1977).

Clark, Kenneth, *The Other Half. A Self-Portrait* (John Murray, 1977).

Cockerell, Michael, *Live from Number 10. The Inside Story of Prime Ministers and Television* (Faber, 1988).

Goldie, Grace Wyndham, *Facing the Nation. Television and Politics 1936–1976* (Bodley Head, 1977).

Gómez, Joseph, *Peter Watkins* (Twayne, Boston, 1979).

Greene, Hugh, *The Third Floor Front. A View of Broadcasting in the Sixties* (Bodley Head, 1969).

Hill, Charles, *Behind the Screen. The Broadcasting Memoirs of Lord Hill of Luton* (Sidgwick & Jackson).

Hood, Stuart, *A Survey of Television* (Heinemann, 1967).

Jones, Jonah, *The Gallipoli Diary* (Seren Press, Bridgend, 1989).

Jones, T. Merfyn, *Going Public* (Brown & Sons, Cowbridge, 1987).

295

Leapman, Michael, *The Last Days of the Beeb* (Allen & Unwin, 1986).

Milne, Alasdair, *DG. The Memoirs of a British Broadcaster* (Hodder & Stoughton, 1988).

Norton, G. G., *The Red Devils. The Story of the British Airborne Forces* (Leo Cooper, 1971).

Quis Separabit, the magazine of the Royal Ulster Rifles. Vol. XI No. 1, Nov. 1944; Vol. XII No. 1, May 1945.

Russell, Ken, *A British Picture* (Heinemann, 1989).

Sherrin, Ned, *A Small Thing – Like an Earthquake. Memoirs by Ned Sherrin* (Weidenfeld, 1983).

Shulman, Milton, *The Least Worst Television in the World* (Barrie & Jenkins, 1973).

Tracey, Michael, *A Variety of Lives. A Biography of Sir Hugh Greene* (Bodley Head, 1983).

Warner, Philip, *Horrocks. The General Who Led from the Front* (Hamish Hamilton, 1984).

Wheldon, Huw (ed.), *Monitor. An Anthology* (Macdonald, 1962).

Wheldon, Huw, *Red Berets into Normandy* (Jarrolds, 1982).

White, Eric W., *The Arts Council of Great Britain* (Davis-Poynter, 1975).

Williams, D. D., *Cofiant D. J. Wheldon* (Caernarfon, 1925).

Wright, Paul, *A Brittle Glory. An Autobiography* (Weidenfeld, 1986).

INDEX

Adam, Kenneth, 115, 157, 173, 201, 202, 212, 219, 221; appointed programme controller, 111; approves arts magazine, 113; director of television, 165 fn.; drink problem, 174; negotiates programmes-controller post with Wheldon, 175–6; and *The War Game*, 180 ff.; and *Three Clear Sundays*, 192–3; retirement, 224, 228

Air-landing Brigade, 1st, 30

Air-landing Brigade, 6th, and 6th Airborne Division, 31 fn.; D-Day landing, 35; in Normandy, 38 ff.; returns to UK, 39; in the Ardennes, 48 ff.; at the Rhine crossing, 55; advances to the Baltic, 57–8; plans for Singapore, 58; goes to Middle East, 61; and the Palestine problem, 63 ff.

Allegri string quartet, 143

All Your Own, 31, 91, 116, 119, 164; originally *It's All Yours*, 87; Wheldon as presenter, 87–8, and dropped from programme, 139

Alwyn, William, appears on *Monitor*, 123

America, 215, 259; amended for American market, 242–3

American Bar Association, The, 250

American School in Richmond, The, 250

Amis, Kingsley, in first *Monitor*, 118, 119

Anderson, Lindsay, 116

Annan inquiry and report, 239, 255, 259

Antiques Roadshow, 258

Arkell, John, BBC administrator, 187

Army Bureau of Current Affairs (ABCA), 62–3, 68

Arts Council (formerly CEMA), 1, 141, 208, 279; origins, 69; Wheldon told of post in Wales, 69; other candidates, 70; Wheldon appointed, 71, and in Cardiff, 73 ff.; Wheldon represents on Festival of Britain committee, 76 ff.; Wheldon leaves, 82

Ascent of Man, The, 215

Asian Club, Wheldon produces, 91

Aspen Institute for Humanistic Studies, The, 271 fn.

Attenborough, Sir David, 168, 201, 204, 209, 210, 213, 223, 224, 270, 271, 272; and *Zoo Quest*, 89; and Anthony Eden, 111; accepts BBC 2, 202; Wheldon's man, 202, 203; invents title of *Civilisation*, 214; likens Lord Hill to Rommel, 220; shortlisted for director-general, 222; director of programmes, 235; and co-productions, 243; returns to programme-making, 245

Attenborough, Sir Richard, 270

Ayrton, Michael, appears on *Monitor*, 123

Barnes, Sir George, 89; biog., 81 fn.; advises Wheldon to accept BBC publicity post, 82; contempt for television, 84; resigns, 110

Barry, Sir Gerald, 76 fn.

Battersby, Roy, and *Five Women*, 216 ff.

Baxter, John, 148, 151

Baverstock, Donald, 91, 119, 170, 181, 191, 202, 203, 205, 253, 260; biog., 90 fn.; plans *Tonight*, 111; launches it, 112; Wheldon's rival, 121; rising star, chief of BBC 1, 164–5; his critical nature, 166; backs *TW3*, 172; differences with S. Newman, 173–4; out of favour, 175; rejects job offers, 176–7, and resigns, 178; 'a very constitutional man', 178; his BBC career destroyed, 178 fn.

BBC (British Broadcasting Corporation), Welsh Orchestra, 74; 'upstart' television, 83; early days of programme

297